# KEYS TO THE HIDDEN MYSTERIES

## JOHN HENDERSON AND
## LILLIAN EDDLEMAN

This picture was taken June 17th 1946 just three days before their wedding. They had just been discharged from the U.S. Navy. She was a Lt. (JG) in the Navy Nurse Corps and he was a C.P.O. They were standing on a snow bank high above Crater Lake in Oregon.

# KEYS TO THE

# HIDDEN MYSTERIES

BY

JOHN AND LILLI HENDERSON

MILLENNIUM 500 PUBLISHING COMPANY
P.O. Box 771
Albany, Oregon 97321
© 1992 by John and Lilli Henderson
All rights reserved
Printed in the United States of America
First Edition, First Printing
ISBN 0-9632472-0-4
Library of Congress Catalog Card Number 92-093332

Cover design by Kate Phillips
Book design and layout by DIMI PRESS, Salem, Oregon

# TABLE OF CONTENTS

## TABLE OF CONTENTS (CONTINUED)

# LIST OF ILLUSTRATIONS

## ACKNOWLEDGEMENTS:

For editorial assistance:

Georgia A. Blickenstaff
Jerry L. Blickenstaff
Doris M. Bowen
Charles A. Eddleman
B. Estelle Henderson
Thomas A. Henderson
The participants in our many classes and retreats

We wish to thank each of these for their invaluable assistance and critical suggestions. Each has had a beneficial impact on this work.

# PREFACE

This book had to be written. We can relate to the hordes of people who stumble through life, not because they are derelicts, but who, despite education and success, never found the eternal purpose of mortal life. To them life offers only short term goals bringing only temporary satisfaction, so they reach for another and another, only to find each as empty as the first.

We felt there must be more to life than the empty feeling we had when we left church on Sundays, but unable to discover a true purpose in life we drifted from church to church and finally joined in the search for "success" which seemed the most reasonable alternative. Eventually we discovered there are "Keys" to the hidden mysteries of the kingdom of God.

The story of how we sought these keys and finally discovered them are outside the scope of this page. But having once received them we clearly saw that God is beneficially moving in the lives of all people who will respond. We discovered that mortal life is not by happenstance. It is a planned process with eternal objectives. We could not rest with the secret of this knowledge until it was shared with others. But there proved to be no point at which we could say it is shared, because there are always more who have not discerned God's outreach to them.

We first began writing studies for small groups, and were pleasantly amazed at the lives that were turned around by the studies. They seemed suddenly rejuvenated with a burst of fresh energy as the true purpose of mortal life was unfolded to them. We prepared special retreats and through them again saw lives given new meaning, hope and exuberance.

We would like to continue to teach on a personal level as in the past, but age is making us aware that at some point our work will end. In an attempt to perpetuate it to touch more people, we have committed it to this book.

This has been a work of dedication, and love. It has been a non-profit work done at our own expense, yet we have been richly rewarded by having the privilege of participating with God in people's lives and seeing hopeless people who were in despair transformed into joyful beings who had caught the vision of God's kingdom and were lifted to the path leading to the gate of the kingdom.

Through the years the clear and simple gospel has been severely twisted and distorted and vital parts have been omitted, until it has become difficult to understand and nearly impossible to apply it to life. The dilemma of an individual, who is trying to pick a route to the kingdom, is a path that leaves his mind shot through with questions of Why? And How? "Why did God do this?"

"How can I avoid Hell?" "How can I have the assurance I will attain the Celestial Kingdom?" and "How can I know I am acceptable to God?"

Uncertainties and confusion foster fear and a dread of the future. Fear of death places a dampening cloak over the freedom and joy of life. This is a needless burden, because the intent of God's plan is to bring freedom and happiness to us in this life while also fulfilling God's eternal purposes in us.

The Ancient Keys message regains the clear, easily understandable message originally intended.

The following are a few of the hidden mysteries opened by the keys we discovered.

1. Why was man not created perfect in the beginning and placed directly into the heavenly kingdom without the trauma and trials of mortal life?

2. Why was earth created separate from God's Kingdom as a home for men and women?

3. Why were Adam and Eve deliberately "Set Up" to fall?

4. God has hidden a process in mortal life. How do we use it to maximum advantage?

5. Does God speak with men and women today? If so, how do I contact him?

6. Apostle Paul speaks of the Third Heaven? How many are there?

7. How can fasting bring me spiritual insight and power? The scriptures name a number of ways by which we are "saved," we are, however, judged and rewarded by "works," but they are works which we cannot do.

# INTRODUCTION TO OUR STUDY GROUP

"If there really are keys to the hidden mysteries of God's Kingdom, I'd sure like to get my hands on them." Art said jokingly but still serious "I'd open things up and look around inside."

Don added, "Jim Boca promised that this study would change our lives; his wife suggested we probably need the change."

"She was just joking," Sandy replied, "but I'm sure we do. Somehow the gospel never really makes much sense to me.

"I've even tried to read the Bible but by the time I finish Exodus I'm so confused I quit."

Lilli assured Sandy, "You will find it will make sense and those confusing things that bothered you will come into focus so you can see that the scriptures are not a lot of separate little doctrines scattered about, but it is one large mural and everything fits neatly into its place to make a beautiful picture. There is a silver thread of continuity woven through everything binding it together."

"Tell me." Sandy asked, "What are the hidden mysteries?"

"Perhaps we will find out soon" Jan called from the dining room. "John and Lilli want us seated around the dining table and I have it cleared now"

"Oh, I see there's more than one way to be fed at this table," Sandy joked.

# THE KEYS

"Things will begin falling into place as we move along" John said, as everyone was finding a place around the table. "In fact, I think we will do just as Art suggested, we will use the keys to open some doors and see what is inside."

When everyone was seated, John added, "I think Lilli and I are the only ones here who know each of you, so before we begin I'll ask Lilli to introduce you."

"I'll just go around the table from my right." Next to me is Jan. "I met her when she was a model—"

"That was before I married Bob and began eating at his restaurant." Jan interrupted, "I suddenly had to change careers, I'm a real estate broker now."

"Next to Jan is Bob," Lilli continued. "You have seen his restaurant, that plush Lakeshore Restaurant on Lakeshore drive. John and I have eaten there so I understand Jan's problem. The food is excellent."

Bob nodded and took the hand Don extended to him.

"Next to Bob is Art. He is an electronics technician. He speaks electronics fluently but nobody understands him, except another technician.

14

"Art is the reason it took six weeks for us to get together," John said. "He couldn't get off the bowling team until the end of league play."

"They couldn't find anyone with a handicap high enough to match mine," Art joked.

Lilli continued, "Next is Art's wife Fran. Fran is a Spanish teacher at Central High School. We had to drag her away from her homework tonight."

Fran laughed. "For the last three years I've been saying 'Next year I'm only going to teach conversational Spanish,' so I don't have all that homework."

"That leaves Don and Sandy," Lilli continued, "He is a chemist at that big plant you pass on the way to town, and Sandy is an executive secretary there. It wasn't easy to get Don here either. He has been working overtime nearly every night for weeks," Lilli added.

"I have an uneasy feeling that my wife exerted influence at a high level to get me off the overtime," Don said.

"Okay," John announced, "now that we know each other we have a few ground rules. They are very simple. We are informal. Anytime any of you has a question, or a comment, you are invited to interrupt the reader and we will discuss it. If you disagree with anything we read, or say, you are free to state your own beliefs. In all the time we have led classes like this we have never had an argument. People are free to express what they believe."

"I have a question." Jan interrupted. "What are the keys?"

"That question bothered me for a long time." John responded. "There is a book, *DOCTRINE AND COVENANTS* which states, 'This greater priesthood administereth the gospel and holdeth the key of the mysteries of the kingdom, even the key of the knowledge of God.' After reading that I worried about what the keys were and prayed about it for more than a year.

I suddenly became aware they are certain vital scriptures, and understandings which are keys to understanding the work and plans of God; when I understood these, they opened other scriptures to my understanding. Do you see what I mean. Just like using a key in a door to open it and look beyond."

"Yes," Jan nodded, "I had never thought of such a thing though."

"As we move along I believe it will be apparent what these key scriptures are that open the meaning of other scriptures and reveal God's purposes to an understanding far beyond where we have been" John said.

"To me," Lilli explained, "it was like I was lost in a dark forest of scriptures, doctrines, and preachers' interpretations until I didn't know which way to go. Then pointing to the papers John had distributed, she added, "I think of these keys as handholds that let me climb out of the valley so I could look back from the mountain top. Now I get an overview of God's whole plan for our lives. I not only see the overall plan now but I can see that it is beautiful."

"Let's get started so everyone can share the view Lilli sees," John placed his hand on Lilli's shoulder, and asked "would you begin our reading at the beginning of the 'Creation story' in the study material?"

# CHAPTER 1

## CREATION STORY

### KEY NUMBER 1: THE MASTER KEY
### GOD'S PLAN FOR MAN'S ETERNAL LIFE

We make a mistake when we assume God created for six days and rested on the seventh day because he had made man, in his image and likeness and his work was completed. Then we are further misled by assuming that we are the completed polished product of God's creativity.

When looking at ourselves and God's work from this perspective, we have already taken the wrong track in trying to understand God's eternal plan. What he intended to achieve by our creation is so obscured that we cannot see what purpose our mortal lives accomplish by our being here. We are trying to solve the problems and equations of life by the wrong formulas. Continuing to struggle with the multitude of notions about life, we finally come to the basic questions: "Why didn't God, who is all powerful and wise create man perfect and place him in celestial glory in the beginning without all the heartaches and trauma of mortal life?" and "What is the purpose of this life?"

"Oh, I've wondered about that," Fran commented "Why didn't he put us in heaven as soon as he created us before we got our lives mixed up with the sin he tells us not to get into?"

"Perhaps he needed to try us out first." Lilli laughed, "or maybe he has some more work to do on us."

# START OVER

There must be something we have missed. We need to back up and switch to another track. This time listening carefully to what God has told us. No more dead ends.

Whenever we set out to build something, for example a house, we have some idea of why we are building it. There must be some reason, an ultimate objective. We also have a concept, either a written or a mental picture of how it is to be done, and the procedure to be followed. The work has a point of beginning, a place where it started. These are only minimum rational requirements for any sort of project we undertake. However, when it comes to the most vital concern of our lives, preparing for eternity we often become hazy without study, planning, or preparation. We don't even have a firm mental image of what it is all about, how it occurs, or the result we should expect.

"Hey, I've seen some houses that didn't look like the builder had any idea what he wanted to build. They look like the rooms were just shaken up and dumped out like a set of dice—a real mess." Art said.

"I'm sure you've seen some lives that way too," Sandy added.

Lilli continued reading: God has not been hazy about his plans for us. He has a definite objective for our lives, and a procedure. The whole plan has been written for us, and it is of

18

the most urgent importance that we understand both the objective and the procedure. In Gen.1:27 God spoke to Christ who was with him from the beginning and said, "Let us make man in our image, after our likeness." This was the intent and it has never been changed. It is also the purpose of mortal life. It was restated when "Moses was caught up to an exceeding high mountain." (D.C. 22-23b) "...for this is my work and my glory, to bring to pass the immortality and eternal life of man." These are two of the most important statements in all scripture. They reveal to us what God is working to accomplish, what his objective is. John urged the group, "These two statements become our master key in opening the scriptures and should be memorized, because we will come back to them through all of our studies. They reveal that God made it his personal project to make us into his image and likeness. Throughout history his actions have been directed toward the accomplishment of that great objective."

"Are we to understand that these two scriptures can open all the Bible?" Bob questioned.

"They do seem like small keys to open such large doors, don't they" John said. "Let's continue reading I think it will explain how they can be so effective.."

Jan begins reading.

# IMPORTANCE OF KNOWING THE OBJECTIVE

To illustrate the value of the information shared with us in the keys above, consider watching a man pile building materials beside a river to begin construction. It may perplex us if we don't know what he is planning to build. The materials he stored may not seem right for a house. The foundation he is laying is not right for a barn, and the location is wrong for a business. However when he informs us he is building a bridge over the river, everything fits together in an understandable way.

Knowing that God's plan and his actions, are designed to construct a bridge to move all mankind from this life to immortality and eternal life, we can see clearly how everything is leading us toward the celestial kingdom. The pieces fall into place. He has the right blueprint and building materials to build us into kingdom people.

"Okay, but how do we use the key?" Don joined in as the interest built around the table.

"Hey, look at the next paragraph," Art suggested.

## HOW TO USE THE MASTER KEY

The master key is used to unlock complex problems. Whenever we have disturbing questions about God's commandments to us, or his actions, we use the master key to unlock the answer. We do this simply by asking ourselves, "How will this commandment, (or action) lead me to immortality and eternal life?" It is one of the great discoveries of life to learn this key opens virtually every secret of God's great plan to our understanding. As we experience using the key we discover every phase of God's plan for us, his every action has been to the end that mankind should become inheritors of the celestial kingdom.

Looking up from her paper Jan said, "That seems too simple."

"I thought so too until I tried it," Lilli said. "It was like playing Jeopardy on TV, the game where they give you the answers and you ask the questions. These keys give us the answer. This is my work and my glory to bring to pass the immortality and eternal life of man. and Let us make man, in our image and after our likeness. I ask the questions, 'Why does he tell us to be baptized?' or 'Why does he tell us to love each other?' And I've asked negative questions, like, 'Why does he tell us not to lie or steal?' And more complex questions like, 'Why did he allow Israel to be destroyed and scattered?' Since I know the answer the reasons become obvious"

"Yes," John said, "it really works." We must remember that God has made it his personal work to bring to pass our immortality and eternal life, so he will make it as simple as he can for us.

"That sounds reasonable," Bob remarked. "But I always understood it the other way around. I thought God was trying to make it so difficult that only selected people would achieve it."

"Many people have felt just as you have, and it makes it difficult for them to fulfill their purpose in this life because it reverses their understanding of what God is trying to accomplish in us and how we should respond to him" John replied. "The actual scriptural story is simple, compared to some of the ideas people have. I suspect that as the story unfolds, we will find a lot of surprises."

Jan continues reading.

# THE LIKENESS OF GOD

Man's physical body is only a vehicle for his spiritual being. It was not enough for God to jump-start the body and get it functioning. What needed to be created and molded was the inner being of spirit. Look at Gen. 1:27 quoted above. Consider what is the "image and likeness of God" that we are to be forged into. What does God envision for us? There is no question that man's physical image is not the image of God.

"You know, I thought it said right in the first part of Genesis that God created us in his image, so we must be like him," Don asserted.

"Because 'created' is written in the past tense it leads to some confusion here, " John responded, "but that will clear up as we continue. However, when we remember that Moses had to be translated before he could look upon God, and God can be everywhere at the same time, and he seems to pass through what we consider to be solid material, I think there is much we do not understand about God's physical being. I also believe we will find it is our spiritual being which is in the image of God. Okay?"

"Sounds reasonable" Bob answered as he took over the reading.

Our question therefore must be "What is the image and likeness of God?" The physical attributes of God are outside of our experience and understanding, but many facets of his nature (his likeness) are made known to us, such as:

- He is all powerful
- He is all wise
- He is absolutely honest and true
- He is creative and imaginative
- He is loving and the source of all love
- He is compassionate in concern for his creations
- He creates and appreciates beauty
- He is impartial
- He is not a respecter of persons
- He is free to choose and act, restrained only by truth, love and justice

We could add more, but it is already apparent we are not yet created in the likeness of God. This is not a mistake. God is not a haphazard worker, nor does he fail, so a deeper, more significant revelation must illuminate our understanding. Consider other possible reasons that even though we are God's creation we are still imperfect.

God's stated purpose of creating us in his image and likeness, and bringing to pass our immortality and eternal life has not been completed, so we conclude that he is still at work on the task. This means he is working on it right now. So the purpose of mortal life is to accomplish the creation of man in God's likeness. Therefore, every day of our lives is a day in our creation. Obviously, our creation is not to be accomplished at a snap of God's fingers, but by a process of molding and building his attributes into us.

This process requires us to be put through many and various situations. In mortal life we will make thousands of decisions in all kinds of situations and, through the results of these decisions, our lives are formed and will finally be judged.

At this point it is well for us to clearly see mortal life as a process that we are being put through as surely as the process a block of marble is put through by the sculptor in creating a beautiful statue. The marble would likely cry out in pain as the sculptor chisels, and grinds, hammers and polishes on it if it could feel and speak. God, as our sculptor has a clear concept of the image we are to be made into. During all of our lives he will be processing us into that image. There will be times we will be hurting and want to cry out as he chips, hammers and grinds on us, but it will be more bearable if we know of the magnificent finished eternal creature he is forming.

Bob exclaimed, "You are coming from the premise that we were not created like God at birth, but he is just now creating us. That's a totally new concept to me but it explains a lot of things."

"Tell me, honey," Jan asked, "what does it explain?"

"For one thing it explains the question of why God didn't create us perfect and put us in heaven to start with."

"Sure" Fran said, "and it explains why so many disastrous things happen to good people. Right?"

"You know, " Don began, "that may tell us a lot about how our lives should be conducted while we are here."

Lilli putting her hand on Fran's added, "Isn't it wonderful to see how God is working?"

Art, looking around the circle, said, "Hey, I don't see why everyone is getting so excited all at once."

"This is a sharp group," John said, "we are usually farther along before the class gets into this much and sees how God is working.

"We have a play coming up in a few minutes that will explain this even better and get Art as excited as the rest of us.

"Let's continue reading."

# THE COMPLETED PLAN

Writers of the old testament often gave the impression that God had no plan, but created mankind and then began herding people like a band of sheep, reacting whenever and however the occasion required to keep the band moving in a chosen way, plotting the course as they travel. But this is not true. See Isa. 46:9–10: "I am God, and there is none else; I am God, and there is none like me, declaring the end from the beginning, and from ancient times the things that are not yet done, saying, my counsel shall stand, and I will do my pleasure." Every detail of God's plan for each person who would live in all time was worked out in minute detail to the end of time before Adam was created and put in motion as a physical being.

The major emphasis of this book is a study of that process. The better we understand it the better we can cooperate with God in our own creation.

# A DRAMA

Sometimes vicariously living an experience through a play can release greater understanding of events that took place. So we present the following drama of creation.

To best bring out the message of the drama it is suggested that different parts be assigned to different individuals of your study group, and the role of each character be played.

# CHAPTER 2

# CREATION DRAMA

## THE SETTING:

The setting is a large room with a drafting table in the center. On the table lie drawings, specifications, blueprints, estimates, etc., as used by engineers in planning a project.

Standing at the table studying the materials are three engineers. They are God, Christ, and Holy Spirit.

Circulating about the room supposedly as an aide, but actually eavesdropping is Lucifer, the chief of the servants.

Planning for the creation of man has run into a difficult problem. Since man is to be created in the likeness of God he must have the attributes of God. This means he too will be creative. He too will have intelligence and can think and reason and he too will have agency by which he can make choices. It is this last part which is the problem, because if man has the potential to be as God, even able to choose for himself, he can choose not to follow God and become a god unto himself. He can turn his abilities into the means of his own misery and destruction. On the other hand if he is not given agency he will be like God's other creations, such as a pansy, beautiful and nice, but not at all like God.

## HELPFUL TERMINOLOGY:

Engineers: God, Christ, and Holy Spirit
Servants: The angels and Lucifer
Laboratory: Mortal life
Agency: Freedom of Choice
Capacity for Scheming: Intelligence

# THE CREATION

GOD:  I have a magnificent project in mind. Let us make man in our image after our likeness.

CHRIST:  That would be virtually impossible, even for you.

HOLY SPIRIT: I know you can do anything and no one can stop you. You created the universe and worlds without number. Your power is greater than lightning, but nothing we have done would be as difficult as what you propose.

GOD:  Yes, there are some real problems to overcome on a project like this.

HOLY SPIRIT: A project like this will give us more difficulties than anything we have ever worked on. It has one problem that seems absolutely insurmountable. If man is created in your likeness, he will have to be a free agent, as we are, capable of thought and independent action. He will have freedom of choice which means he will be capable of scheming.

CHRIST:  It seems that way. In all our experience, we've never known of anything with more difficult problems to overcome than creating man in your image and likeness. It really does seem insurmountable. If man is created in your likeness, perfect and fit for the kingdom, he has to have the experience of living as a God himself. It is the only way he can understand the righteous living of the kingdom.

GOD: It is true that creating man with the right of agency will bring problems we have never had to deal with in other creations, but if he does not have choice, he will not be at all like us. To fulfill our purpose in creating him, he must have the freedom to act . . . still, I think we can do it. How do you think we can best start on this?

HOLY SPIRIT: If we make him free, he will become rebellious, contaminated and filthy. He will be completely unfit for the kingdom. He will have to be cast off forever and utterly destroyed.

GOD: Yes, go on.

CHRIST: Besides power, to be in your likeness, he must have all your attributes such as infinite wisdom, creativity, love, intelligence, appreciation of beauty and, of course, he will have to have freedom to act. The minute we give him free agency, it will be like letting him light the fuse to a bomb; he can blowup the whole package.

GOD: Despite all the difficulties, there must be a way.

HOLY SPIRIT: All our projections indicate that if we give man power and creativity like yours, then give him freedom to use it however he chooses, he will become a god to himself without principle, or compassion or love. We certainly couldn't turn a monster like that loose in the celestial kingdom.

CHRIST: Let's review this from the beginning and see what we are up against. First, suppose we do give man great power and creativity, and intelligence. He will have to go through a process of using his intelligence over a period of time so he can gain experience he will need to build his wisdom. It is unfortunate we cannot give him a fully developed wisdom but that comes through experience in the use of intelligence, and we cannot just hand him experience. To get it, he has to be put into operation. It is a vicious circle. He has to have wisdom, but to get it he has to have experience; and if he gets experience without wisdom, he will become too corrupt to get wisdom.

GOD: Every approach to this seems to bring us right back to the problems created by giving man agency.

LUCIFER: (Seeing his great moment, speaks smoothly) If I might make a suggestion, I think I can offer a solution to this.

GOD: What do you suggest?

LUCIFER: You go right ahead with creating man, and I'll go down to see that none will be lost, and none will become the destructive force you fear.

GOD: How will you accomplish such a tremendous feat?

LUCIFER: I'll go to them as God, and make them all bow down to me. Not one will dare disobey; I'll see to that. Of course, you will have to give me your power and glory.

CHRIST: That would defeat our purpose in giving man agency, and he would be in worse condition with agency, and not allowed to use it than if he never had it given to him.

LUCIFER: I think you are making too much over a little thing like agency. With God's power and glory, I would make all their decisions for them and your problem would be solved.

HOLY SPIRIT: Why that would make man a creature of misery. It would be like locking him in a prison cell, then telling him he is free to do whatever he wishes.

LUCIFER: (Retorts angrily.) Who cares about man's misery or agency? You wanted to keep him from using his agency in the wrong way, so send me and I'll see to it that no one will dare think of disobedience. Just give me glory so I can be God to them.

CHRIST: There must be a better way.

# KEYS TO THE HIDDEN MYSTERIES

GOD: Man needs a way of getting experience in the use of his agency so he can develop his love and wisdom as Christ pointed out. He needs the experience of using his creativity and intelligence in a way that does not release his power in a destructive manner until he learns how bad that can be. He must be able, through choice, to use it only for constructive purposes. So, suppose we design a laboratory in which he can experiment. We will call the laboratory "Mortal Life," and he will be given a physical body to lock him into the lab. Then we can reduce his power while he is there so he will only have enough power to experiment with. In that way, we can let him exercise his agency where the damage can be confined to the lab. He will make a lot of mistakes and get himself into deep trouble. In fact, I'm sure he will try every conceivable wrong way, but given time, he should make himself so miserable he will finally learn to follow the instructions we give and live the right way.

HOLY SPIRIT: That sounds like a great idea. We can send him instructions on how to live the kingdom way, but he will have freedom to do whatever his scheming mind will suggest.

GOD: Yes, we will give him the freedom to reject our instructions and do as he chooses. In that way he will gain experience and see how destructive his agency can be and how imperative it is for him to follow instructions.

CHRIST:        That must be the way. However, when we turn him loose in the lab, he is bound to make so many serious mistakes he will become too corrupt for the kingdom. As his creators, we have a responsibility to him, so at the meridian of time, I'll set aside the glory you have given to me, then I'll go down among them and be one of them to show them the way. I'll not experiment. I'll do exactly as you my God, instruct me. I'll demonstrate the kingdom way of life. All who have faith enough to do as I demonstrate will be prepared for entering the celestial kingdom. As they enter, the glory will be yours, God, because yours is the power, the intelligence, and love that makes this all possible.

GOD:           Yes. That is the way.

LUCIFER:       (As he angrily stomps out of the room.) If you are going to give them instructions and the freedom to reject them, then I'm going to prepare some instructions for them myself.

HOLY SPIRIT: Where do we start?

GOD:           (Pointing to a spot on the blueprint) Let's put man here in the Garden of Eden by the Tree of Knowledge of Good and Evil.

CHRIST and HOLY SPIRIT:
               (Smile and nod agreement)

# EFFECTS OF ROLE PLAYING

As the play concluded, John commented "It is surprising how much is revealed to us when we see events from the perspective of the people involved.

"An interesting thing happened that allowed me to see that an individual can get extremely involved in the role he plays. I once used this play during a sermon. I asked people to act the various roles. A man was assigned the role of Lucifer. The expression on his face when he stomped off the stage after the play revealed he was extremely depressed and miserable about the part he had just played. I had another play with me which I had not intended to use, but I called on the same people to act it and I assigned the man the role of an angel. He finished with a changed attitude and a cheerful smile."

# THE PLAY BASED ON SCRIPTURE

"You know, that was a provocative play," Don observed "I had never thought of such a thing as God as an engineer, but it's true someone had to devise the system."

"We don't intend to depreciate the holiness of God and Christ and The Holy Spirit, with plays like this but in order to understand God's plan better we need to make a situation which we as humans can understand and relate to," Lilli explained.

"Oh, I understand that," Don responded to Lilli's comment, "but it had never occurred to me that our agency was a problem to God. Its obvious there is more to our creation than I had supposed. How did you learn of this?

"The setting for the play came from this scripture," John answered as he turned to Gen. 3:1-6.

"I, the Lord God, spoke unto Moses, saying, That Satan whom thou hast commanded in the name of mine only begotten is the same which was from the beginning; and he came before me saying, 'Behold, send me, I will be thy Son, and I will redeem all mankind that one soul shall not be lost, and surely I will do it...' Wherefore, because that Satan rebelled against me, and sought to destroy the agency of man, which I, the Lord God, had given him, and also that I should give unto him mine own power; by the power of mine. Only begotten I caused that he should be cast down; and he became Satan; yea even the devil, the father of all lies, to deceive, and to blind men, and to lead them captive at his will, even as many as would not hearken unto my voice."

John finished the scripture and added, "It is shown in the play that an almost insurmountable problem arose from granting to man creativity and great power along with agency, or the freedom to do whatever his imagination might suggest."

"Hey, releasing such a person in the Kingdom of God would be as destructive as freeing an arsonist in a fireworks factory," Art exclaimed. "I see why God sent Adam and Eve out"

Fran continues reading:

There was no escape from granting man agency if he was to be made into the image and likeness of God. So God chose to give man freedom and the opportunity to exercise it, but not in the kingdom. He created a laboratory beyond the gates of the kingdom; then he said in effect, "Do anything you wish in the laboratory and see for yourself what happens. We will send you instructions on how to live, but you can make your own rules if you wish. Either way, you will learn a lesson you will never forget."

KEYS TO THE HIDDEN MYSTERIES

Genesis 4:13 tells of the "Carnal, sensual and devilish" condition many people adopted as a lifestyle. This testifies to God's wisdom in preparing a place outside of his pure kingdom for this part of our creation.

# GOD PLANNED IN DETAIL

"It is difficult to imagine," John broke in, "where the thought came from that God's planning was without definite direction concerning mankind, because God knew precisely what he was going to do and how he would proceed. His plans were set and prepared eons before Adam was given his body and the process started."

Fran continued reading:

We note that during the planning for creation man had not yet been created physically but all humans who were ever to live in mortal life were created. All animals and plants had been created. The scriptures sound like these were all in preparation for millenniums before Adam, in readiness for events to begin. In Gen. 2:5-9 God told Moses:

"For I, the Lord God, created all things of which I have spoken spiritually, before they were naturally upon the face of the earth; for I, the Lord God had not caused it to rain upon the face of the earth. And I, the Lord God, had created all the children of men, and not yet a man to till the ground, for in heaven created I them, and there was not yet flesh upon the earth, neither in the water, neither in the air... And I, the Lord God, formed man from the dust of the ground, and breathed into his nostrils the breath of life; and man became a living soul; the first flesh upon the earth, the first man also; nevertheless, all things were before created, but spiritually were they created and made, according to my word."

When God revealed to Enoch all the inhabitants of the earth he said:

> (Gen. 7: 39-40) "They are the workmanship of mine own hands, and I gave unto them their intelligence in the day that I created them. And in the Garden of Eden gave I unto man his agency; and unto thy brethren have I said, and also gave commandment, that they should love one another, and they should choose me their father."

> (Gen. 2:4-5) "I The Lord God made heaven and earth, . . . For I the Lord God, created all things of which I have spoken, spiritually before they were naturally upon the face of the earth". . .

> (II Timothy 1:9) "Who hath saved us and called us with a holy calling, not according to our works, but according to his own purpose and grace, which was given us in Christ Jesus before the world began."

John smiled, "There was an important tipoff in the play that lets us know God absolutely knew that man would fall. Did any of you happen to pick up on it?

Bob answered, "I expect that when he gave man agency to make choices God, could assume that man would make the mistakes you call sin."

"That's true, but there was something even more definite than that."

"I know, John." Lilli said, "He won't tell you. He will keep you guessing until you get this one. It was something to do with Jesus."

Sandy said, "Well—Jesus said he would come as our saviour."

John said, "True, but when was this said?"

"I see what you are getting at." Don caught on, as he reviewed the play script, "This was during the planning for the Garden of Eden. It was planned for Jesus to come at the meridian of time."

"Exactly." John answered, "There were no surprises to God. It was fully expected and provided for."

Reading continues:

God deliberately devised a plan by which man can exercise his intellect, imagination, creativity, and agency. Upon entering mortal life man came into an environment of both good and evil. It was not only God's love for his creatures, but his sense of responsibility for putting us into this situation that caused the most significant event in the millenniums of history to be written into the scheme of things. Jesus was foreordained to be "The Lamb slain from the foundation of the earth." In other words, the moment the plan was initiated, even before the earth was made, Jesus knew he would come at the meridian of time and be murdered to redeem us. This knowledge is a key in letting us see that God was sure we would sin and get into serious trouble needing help. This knowledge is our assurance God is not mad at us because we have sinned, or made mistakes, even though these cannot be tolerated in the kingdom.

Because we are aware this process is going on, we can observe how God is working in our lives. We can see the things he brings to pass, and the problems we must surmount, to learn to work with him in our own creation. But we see them as temporary character–forming problems.

"Tell me," Jan began, "Why is it that we never knew of this? I went to Sunday school when I was younger but they always made things seem so complicated that I thought you had to be a trained preacher to understand about God. Why didn't we know about this?"

"Originally God's plans for mankind were given in a straight forward manner, which was simple to understand," John answered, "but through the years, transcribers, preachers, theologians and others have twisted and distorted and taken from it until now it is difficult to understand and nearly impossible to follow."

"Yes," Lilli added, "It would be ridiculous to think our creator is working against us. He wants us for his highest kingdom, so we can expect him to make the directions as easy as he can. We sometimes forget that God is on our side. It is too bad so many people think of God as the opposition."

"One of our greatest hopes with this study," John continued, "is to regain the simplicity of what God has determined to accomplish in our lives."

# SUMMARY

God has determined to make man in his image and likeness. This requires a process. Mortal life on earth is the process.

God knew man would fall and Jesus would have to come so man could understand that instead of being cast off as worthless, he was actually of great value to God and could be redeemed.

# LESSON PURPOSE

To emphasize the vital role of our agency.

## THE MASTER KEYS:

1. (Gen. 1:27), " I, God, said unto mine only begotten which was with me from the beginning. Let us make man in our image and after our likeness."

2. (D.C. 22: 23b), "There is no end to my works neither to my words; for this is my work and my glory, to bring to pass the immortality and eternal life of man."

# CHAPTER 3

## LABORATORY IS PREPARED

The study group gathered for their second meeting at the home of Jan and Bob. The key to be studied is the creation of the laboratory:

Key to life
as a laboratory

Don said, "You know, that creation play has been on my mind all week. It certainly gave me a lot to think about."

"Yes," Bob agreed, "it enlarged my understanding of the importance of our agency."

"What are we going to study tonight?" Fran wanted to know.

"Tonight we will talk about the box God built." John answered.

"Oh, no?" Jan said, "Last week you had God as an engineer. I suppose you are going to have God as a carpenter this time."

"No" John laughed, "The box he built was an enclosure for the laboratory. We call it Time."

"Would you like to start reading for us?"

Jan begins reading:

## CREATION OF THE LABORATORY

Planets were spinning like marbles in the universe, but when he was preparing a place for man apart from the pure Celestial Kingdom, God did not pick one and say, "Ah! this will do just fine." As a good engineer he drew up a careful list of specifications for a new planet designed especially to meet the needs of the creatures he planned to place upon it.

Arguments have gone on endlessly about certain parts of the creation story. But one factor in creation, however, is seldom addressed although it may be of greater importance to us than others. That is time.

# THE CREATION OF TIME

Certain facts seem so apparent we take them for granted without examination, so we miss their importance and implications. God, Christ, the Holy spirit, the angels, and Lucifer already existed before the creation of man. They dwelt in a timeless realm about which we know little except that it existed. The one thing which should stand out clearly is, that the earth and its total environment were created as a special place for mankind. God's statement to Moses is of particular interest.

**"In the beginning I created the heaven and the earth."** This was not the beginning of God. It was the beginning of time. Not only was the earth created, but all the means by which we measure time were put into motion. The earth was spun into orbit around the sun and given its twenty-four hour cycle. The moon was placed in orbit around the earth. God said, "Let there be light..," and the blue oceans, the green meadows and the purple and white mountains were bathed in light letting the splendor of their colorful creation shine forth. The Lord continued, "I, God, divided the light from the darkness...

"I, God, called the light day and the darkness I called night ...and the evening and morning were the first day." (Gen 1:6-8.) His work of establishing time went on, God said: "Let there be lights in the firmament of the heaven, to divide the day from the night; and let them be for signs and for seasons, and for days and for years...I, God, made two great lights, the greater light to rule the day, and the lesser light to rule the night; and the greater light was the sun and the lesser light was the moon." (Gen. 1:18-19.)

"Why, there has always been time. " Bob exclaimed, " I can't imagine anytime without time, We would have terrible confusion without it."

"I can't either, but read on and see what the scriptures say about time." Lilli answered "What we just read tells about God establishing all the things we measure time by such as days, nights, seasons, years etc."

## A BOX CALLED TIME

Our lives have been so regulated by sunrises, sunsets, days, nights, weeks, months, seasons, and years that timelessness is incomprehensible to us. Such a condition is beyond any experience of mortal life, yet God is not mortal, nor subject to time. Since time is nonexistent in the Eternal kingdom of God, God sometimes speaks of things yet to come in the past tense as though they had already happened. This is because they have already happened on the plan he has drawn. For example, he speaks of having created man, but we are still in the early process of being created. Once God had determined he was going to create man in his image and likeness, and prepared a plan to do so, it was, as far as he was concerned, done. He could say, "I **created man**, despite the fact that we are still in the process he established for our creation, and a major part of our creation cannot take place until we enter paradise.

It is comparable to an architect who may tell a friend, "I have just built a beautiful new office building," while the contractors, carpenters, masons, and plumbers are only beginning the construction, because the architect's design work and plans have been completed. The great architect of human creation completed his plans for the entire project before Adam was sent upon the earth.

It is not surprising that science which likes to chop things up into sectors of time and put labels of years or light years on the pieces, has difficulty with the creation story. What is a hundred million years to God who is not limited by time? When he had prepared the plan for the creation of the earth, and set the plan in motion, it was completed. Time was not a factor. He said he did it in six days, and science argues with the concept. If he had said he did it in six stages, the meaning would not have changed, but science would largely agree. Science cannot conceive a timeless situation. In timelessness the period over which events occur is of no importance, it is the sequence in which they occur. The Genesis story is the relating of sequences.

"I always wondered about how he created the earth and everything in six days. Six periods make more sense, but it seems that even six periods would be measured in time. Even the speed of the fastest computer is measured in nanoseconds and that's time. How can things happen without time?" Art wondered .

"The scriptures tell us there is no way we can comprehend even the least of God's kingdoms and this is a good example of it." Lilli said.

"Then, when the geologists say the earth took hundreds of millions of years to be formed, they could be right, but it could still be only a snap of the fingers, or six snaps of the fingers, for God if time does not exist," Don said thoughtfully.

"The following scriptures may give some insights on this. Let's continue reading." John directed. D.C. 2:1 points out:

> The works, and the designs, and the purposes of God, cannot
> be frustrated, neither can they come to nought, for God does
> not walk in crooked paths; neither doth he turn to the right

hand nor the left; neither doth he vary from that which he hath said; therefore his paths are straight and his course is one eternal round.

Genesis refers to God as Him who was without beginning of days, or end of years.

Alma 19:38 repeats, All is as one day with God; and time only is measured to man.

John 8:58, Jesus said unto them: Verily I say unto you, before Abraham was, I am.

Moses was caught up to an exceeding high mountain and he saw God face to face. God spake unto Moses saying,

"Behold I am the Lord God Almighty, and Endless is my name, for I am without beginning of days or end of years; and is not this endless...There is no God beside me; and all things are present with me for I know them all."

God created time as a kind of box to contain mankind until the problems associated with agency were worked out and we could see the results of using it against God's wishes. Time is not endless. It will not be for eternity. It will end when God's work with man on earth is concluded. This is indicated by scriptures, particularly Rev. 10:5-6:

The angel ...sware by him that liveth forever and ever, who created heaven and all things that therein are, and the sea, and the earth and the things which are therein, that there should be time no longer.

The following figures attempt to illustrate the relationship between God's endless path where time does not exist and Time which is a temporary appendage attached to the kingdom, but separated from it. This appendage will eventually be disconnected and eliminated.

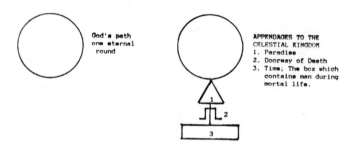

The works, and the designs and the purpose of God cannot be frustrated, neither can they come to nought, for God doth not walk ln crooked paths; neither doth he turn to th right hand nor to the left; neither doth he vary from that which he hath said; therefore his paths are straight and his course is one eternal round (D.C 2:1)

# A TIMELESS DISPLAY OF HISTORY

A wondrous experience was given, at different times, to Moses, Enoch, Nephi, and the brother of Jared. They saw all human life from God's timeless perspective. They saw Adam at the beginning of time and every succeeding individual until the end of time. The amazing thing is that they did not see them as a replay of a video tape, one generation after the other, but they looked down upon a living, moving event as though it were spread out on a table top. All parts of the picture, and all people who ever lived were present and living as were those yet to live. This being true, then what we call time would be to God as distance or space in his picture. Adam would be living near the border where time began. Jesus on earth with the twelve apostles would be in the center, or "The Meridian of Time" and we must be somewhere near the border opposite Adam.

To visualize time from God's perspective, imagine a draftsman's table with a blueprint spread out on it as shown in the illustration.

God's work table and his plan for time. He can look down and see all of time from the beginning to the end at the same moment

God looks down on his plan and sees everything from the beginning to end as a modern architect looks at the floor plan for a building. The architect's drawing, however, has fixed lines. If God's plans had fixed lines, it would mean predestination for us. To illustrate the difference, picture an aerial traffic reporter flying high over a city. When he spots an accident he radios to motorists who cannot see over hills or around corners and warns them of the accident suggesting they choose other routes to avoid entanglement and delays.

We cannot see beyond this moment, but, from God's vantage point, he sees what lies ahead of us in time and he "radios" to us through the prophets or by other communcation means to warn us. If we do not change our ways we are bound for destruction. We are free to plow straight ahead into trouble or take an alternate route with our lives.

## THE PURPOSE OF TIME

You may ask, "Why did God create time? What is its purpose?" The master key tells us it was necessary in order to "bring to pass the immortality and eternal life of man."

Since we could not exist in our present condition within the Kingdom of God, he established a temporary location for us outside the confines of the eternal kingdom. This emphasizes the fact mortal life is a process within a laboratory. When this part of God's creating has been completed, all people will have been taken from the earth and time will end. It will no longer exist. Time is the box in which the preparatory work of creating man in God's image had to be done outside the purity of the heavenly realm.

"Do you realize you may be taking away one of the atheist's major arguments," Bob asked "and perhaps adding power to the evolutionists? "

"In what way?" John asked.

"Through the years," Bob continued. "there have been atheists who based their disbelief in God upon the idea of the impossibility of a God without a beginning. They may see in this that God could have had a beginning because God did not tell Moses he had no beginning. He said he had "no beginning of days, or end of years." Since days and years exist only to man, this could offer a glimmer of light to them and the evolutionists . "

"However, the creationists who find it inconceivable that man, let alone God, could in any way have evolved will be just as adamant in refuting this." Lilli affirmed.

"And, the scriptures offer little to resolve their arguments."

John smiled, "God said, in effect, don't worry about it; it is not your concern. This life is enough for you to struggle with for now."

"Fran would you continue reading, please? Start where it speaks of Moses."

The record of the time Moses stood before God tells:

It came to pass that Moses called upon God saying, tell me I pray thee, why these things are so, and by what thou madest them...And the Lord God said unto Moses, for my own purpose have I made these things. Here is wisdom, and it remaineth in me...Worlds without number have I created and I also created them for my own purpose...but only an account of this earth and the inhabitants thereof give I unto you. God went on to tell Moses, The heavens, they are many, and cannot be numbered unto man, but they are numbered unto me, for they are mine and I know them.

In his book, *GOD'S SPIRITUAL UNIVERSE*, Arthur Oakman wrote, "Time had a beginning, and it will have an end." He added. "We may illustrate this by drawing upon a paper twelve inches square a straight line one inch long. The straight line represents time—It begins and ends on the paper. The paper represents eternity which encompasses time, wholly contains it..."

We can expect that in the numberless worlds God created there will be found other beings created for his own purposes, but these are of no concern to us. Our mortal life and the use of our time is our major concern. We will not leave this life in the image and likeness of God, but if we use time properly, we will graduate from a most important class in becoming so.

# ENCOUNTER WITH SIN

Adam and Eve had no idea how far-reaching their choice would be. They brought us into this life through an encounter with sin. Since then, every person has had to face the same, or similar temptations. I cannot face sin for my children, they must face it personally and individually. By the choices they make they will receive lessons of both failure and success.

In other areas of life, such as science, we can grow from the experience and knowledge of our predecessors. Through schools, television, and writing, a young person can gain the knowledge of centuries and add more to it with his own life. This is not true in facing the questions of choice in following either God or Lucifer. Each person stands with Adam and Eve working out his individual decisions from the same level. This is the only way everyone can be judged equally.

In mortal life we must make the most of our encounters with Lucifer and sin. The first step to our being shaped into the likeness of God is to resolve the question of to whom we will submit ourselves. The process is often compared to a potter making a vessel on his wheel. Only when the clay is pure and free of lumps can the potter shape it into an article of beauty and value. We cannot begin to be made into the image of God until our flawed dedication is purified and we are totally God's. Time is the period in which we will meet Lucifer. At the conclusion of time we will either belong to Lucifer, or we will be so dedicated to God that Lucifer could not in any way find temptation which would draw our slightest interest. We will be like Moses after his meeting with God.

(D.C. 22:8a,b,c, 9a,b,c) Satan came tempting him saying Moses, son of man, worship me. And it came to pass that Moses looked upon Satan and said, Who art thou, for behold I am a son of God in the similitude of his Only Begotten; and where is thy glory that I should worship thee? for, behold, I could not look upon God except his glory should come upon me, and I were transfigured before him. But I can look upon thee in the natural man. Is it not so, surely? Blessed be the name of my God, for his spirit hath not altogether withdrawn from me; or else where is thy glory; for it is darkness unto me and I can judge between thee and God. For God said unto me Worship God for him only shalt thou serve. Get thee hence, Satan, deceive me not; for God said unto me, Thou art after the similitude of mine Only Begotten.

Those who come forth in the first resurrection are they who have gone from this life to Paradise. They will have no fear of the judgment.

(Rev. 20:6) Blessed and holy are they who have part in the first resurrection: on such the second death hath no power...

The decision must be made in time. Even temptation will not exist in the Celestial Kingdom. This is the purpose for which time was created.

"You mean," Fran asked, "that if we make it through this life we won't have to worry about Lucifer again? What about temptation; will it be gone, too, or do we lose our agency so we can't go wrong again?"

"I think it will be wonderful to be free of Lucifer," Sandy remarked, "John said we could not comprehend the wonders of God's realm. I think we cannot comprehend the evil black terror of Lucifer and his realm either."

"There are a couple of other points involved here." John added "First you will not lose your agency. Mortal life has been spent training you to use it in a manner ordained of God, and he will not take it from you. The second is that Lucifer will not be present in that kingdom, but even if one such as Lucifer should arise, you would by then understand the awful destruction he

51

would create if he could win souls to follow him, and since there will not be a hint of disloyalty to God in the kingdom, none would follow him anyway.

"These things are to be worked out in this life. That is why it is so tremendously important whom we choose to follow right now. Choose God and never deviate from following him."

"Can you imagine someone who has had the experience of seeing the havoc wrought by the devil in this life, then seeing the wonders and beauty of the Celestial kingdom, ever **being tempted to turn from God?" Lilli asked.**

# CHAPTER 4

## IN THE GARDEN OF EDEN

Eve: Oh what a beautiful place. This is wonderful!

Adam: You mean this is all ours?

God: Yes. This is the Garden of Eden; it was prepared especially for you.

Eve: Look at all that fruit. Is it all good to eat?

God: Yes, I created it myself, and I'll have to say it is very good.

Adam: I think I'll just go around and try some from each tree.

God: Oh, don't do that.

Adam: Why? You said it is all good.

God: Yes, Adam, it is all good, but there is one tree you must not touch. See that one over there? You are absolutely forbidden to eat of it.

Eve: Oh, come on, God, If that fruit is good, why can't we have some? It looks beautiful.

God: Just remember, I forbid it.

# KEYS TO THE HIDDEN MYSTERY

Eve:            Not even a little bit? Just a bite?

God:            I have said you are not to touch it. You are not to take one bite.

Eve:            Oh, God—that's not fair.

God:            I've given you all the other trees in the garden to use. I only forbid you to use this one, the Tree of Knowledge.

Adam:        I don't understand why.

God:            You will have to decide for yourself, but remember this, you have been warned. You know I forbid it. In fact if you do eat of it, you will die on that very day. You have to make the choice yourself.

God leaves and Adam wanders around looking at other trees until he is out of sight. Eve stands looking at the Tree of Knowledge.

Lucifer:      (Steps up and taps Eve on the shoulder)

Eve:            (Startled) Oh!

Lucifer:      Don't be frightened Eve. I'm your friend. I just stopped by to get acquainted and tell you how happy I am that you have come to the Garden.

Eve:            Do you live here?

Lucifer:     Oh yes, I'll be your neighbor. Tell me, why are you looking at this tree so intently?

Eve:     I am just wondering why God forbids our eating this fruit. He said it would cause us to die.

Lucifer:     He didn't! Why, he just wants it all for himself— That's the best tree in the garden and he is just being selfish. Why that tree will give you knowledge like God has and he just wants to be the only God around. You go ahead and have all of it you want. It won't hurt you one bit.

Eve:     Do you really think I should?

Lucifer:     Of course. It didn't hurt me did it? You just show God you are big enough to do as you please.

Eve:     Well, maybe just a little taste at least.

# CHAPTER 5

## EVICTION FROM PARADISE

Tuesday evening at the home of Bob and Jan.

"You know", Don began, "I've been thinking a lot about our last two classes. The idea that I am in the process of being created now has changed my whole outlook on life. I see things going on which I never dreamed of before."

"What kind of things?" Sandy asked.

"You know, before this I supposed the creation part was all done so all I had to do was try to be good until I died. I didn't understand that I was being created now and could participate in it myself. I just accepted that if I believed in Jesus and was good enough I would go to heaven. Now I sense God actively at work in my life, and it affects the decisions I make and my plans for the future. It even affects how I look at my job and other people."

"I've been thinking about the study about time. I still can't understand timelessness" Jan confessed, "but somehow I picture time as a sort of corral for us, like God has a corral for training wild horses; once they are trained and disciplined he will open the gate and let them go out to green pastures. Does that make sense?"

"Yes," Fran agreed, "I like the idea of a laboratory where I can experiment and, even if I make mistakes, it doesn't mean I have to be thrown into hell forever. I'm even expected to make mistakes. After all, Christ said to either be hot or cold but if you are lukewarm he will spew you out of his mouth. I'm expected to be doing something. Even if I'm wrong, I will learn from it. Of course I think it's a good idea to find out what the directions are and follow them, but I had never thought of it that way before." As everyone began taking places around the dining table, Fran said, "The first night you had God as an engineer, the second night he was a carpenter building a box, what will he be tonight, an electrician?"

John chuckled, "No, tonight we are going to see how Adam and Eve were set up."

"Set up? You mean framed!" Art exclaimed in amazement. "I never read anything about that."

"Sure you did," John grinned as he opened his book, "but it was done so cleverly that you never realized what happened. For that matter, Adam and Eve never seemed to realize they had been set up either.

"Let's look at what happened. Go ahead and read it for us at the start of the chapter, Art."

# EVICTION FROM PARADISE

The Garden of Eden charade was a drama for moving man from God's kingdom into mortal life using man's right of choice. Elaborate arrangements were made to insure there would be no failure, because it was a vital part of man's creation.

What would have happened if Adam had been obedient to God and not fallen? This is explained, in part, in 2nd Nephi 1:111-114: "If Adam had not transgressed, he would not have fallen; but he would have remained in the Garden of Eden. All things which were created must have remained in the same state which they were after they were created; and they must have remained for ever and had no end. They would have had no children; wherefore they would have remained in a state of innocence, having no joy. for they knew no misery; doing no good, for they knew no sin. But behold, all things have been done in the wisdom of Him who knoweth all things." Verse 120 continues: "They are free to choose liberty and eternal life, through the great mediator of all men, or to choose captivity and death, according to the captivity and power of the devil."

Lehi called his family about him when he was on his deathbed. He wanted to be sure they understood the way to the kingdom and the works of God. His message is very revealing of God's ways. It is too long to be quoted in its entirety here. However the following excerpts reveal much about the purpose of our lives, II Nephi 1:94-100

> "Now my son, I speak unto you these things. There is a God, and he hath created all things, both the heavens and the earth, and all things that in them are; both things to act, and things to be acted upon; and to bring about his eternal purposes in the end of man. It must needs be that there was an opposition; Eden the forbidden fruit in opposition to the tree of life; one being sweetened the other bitter; Wherefore, the Lord God gave unto man that he should act for himself. Wherefore he could not act for himself save it should be that he was enticed by the one or the other."

Inexperienced, naive, Adam and Eve who had never dealt with deception were now subjected to the full devilish cunning of Lucifer.

## THE PLAN PUT INTO MOTION

God tells of how he created the setting to initiate his plan, and how he put man into it to get the work started. Gen 2: 18-22 "I, the Lord God, took the man, and put him into the Garden of Eden to dress it, and to keep it. And I, the Lord God, commanded the man saying, of every tree of the garden thou mayest freely eat; but of the tree of the knowledge of good and evil, thou shall not eat of it; Nevertheless, thou mayest choose for thyself, for it is given unto thee, but remember that I forbid it; for in the day thou eatest thereof thou shalt surely die."

## ADAM AND EVE WERE SET UP

Adam and Eve had been warned and told of the consequences of disobedience; they could never claim God made them do it. However it is obvious they were set up to fall. God situated them in an environment where he knew they would disobey his instructions. Still, their disobedience was an exercise of agency for which they had to accept responsibility.

Art, pausing in his reading said, "Hey, I never would have guessed that was a setup. I always thought God warned them and then was angry when they went ahead and took the apple anyway."

"There is infallible proof God knew man would fall," Lilli said, "as we pointed out last week, Before man was even created God had the plan prepared for Jesus to come at the meridian of time to redeem man. The plan to recover fallen man was prepared before mortal life began. This emphasizes even more that their eviction from the kingdom and their mortal life which followed that sin was an important step in their creation."

"I didn't think God would ever play a dirty trick like that and then punish Adam and Eve for it," Art said.

John smiled in amusement at Art's lively response. "I don't think of it as a dirty trick," he said, "because it proved to be a blessing for them. You remember from our first play they were going to put man into the laboratory? The trouble was that man had to choose to go into the laboratory and God would not take his agency away and force him to go. How do you get someone to choose to go from Paradise into the world and work for a living?"

" I understand, and you are right, it was done so cleverly that I never realized what happened," Bob joined in, "I had always blamed Eve without realizing God had planned it."

"Don would you take over the reading for awhile?"

Adam and Eve were innocent in the garden; they were not perfect, they were still being created and would not be perfect until their creation was completed. Many people feel we should strive to achieve the state they were in the garden, but this is not true. We are born in that innocent state. We must still be transformed into the image and likeness of God, and he is working on us. That's the purpose of this life. This requires thousands upon thousands of decisions. Some decisions are seemingly minor, of little significance, others are soul-searching and life-changing decisions. They spring from all kinds of motivations from self interest and greed to generosity and compassion.

## LEARNING TO BE LIKE GOD

Those who achieve the Celestial Kingdom will have great powers bestowed upon them by God; these powers will never be for personal aggrandizement or for control over other people, however. Those who are granted such power must work within God's intent. They will see other people as God sees them. More and more they will be fashioned in the likeness of God so they will act only as God acts and administer power only as God would. We have witnessed, even in today's study, the restraint God exercises in the use of his power. Instead of evicting man from the Garden by force, he allowed Adam and Eve to choose and to accept the consequences of their choice. External restraints will not be placed upon man when he is fully perfected and accepted into Celestial Glory, he must develop internal restraints based upon wisdom in the use of his powers. They must be used only in the way and for the purposes for which God would have used them. This requires man to come into complete harmony with God's will.

Developing such harmony demands a close relationship with God through prayer, meditation, and the experiences of this life. One gains and practices wisdom with every decision made. Each decision adds to one's store of knowledge and wisdom whether it proves right or wrong.

When you understand this concept, it permits you to plot the course to your celestial goal avoiding many of the serious misadventures of life.

Sandy, unconsciously fingering the pendant on her necklace, said in an awed voice, "I never realized the wisdom and compassion, and planning that God put into this. It does something to me that I can't express."

With moist eyes, Lilli reached out and laid her hand on Sandy's, "I know exactly how you feel, Sandy, and it is even more touching when we see that God has always worked this way, and is doing so with us even today."

## ADAM AND EVE CHOOSE DEATH

After Adam and Eve had eaten of the forbidden fruit, The Lord God said, (to Christ) "Behold, the man is become as one of us, to know good and evil; and now, lest he put forth his hand and take also of the tree of life, and eat, and live forever, therefore I the Lord God will send him forth from the Garden of Eden... Gen 3:28-29.

Death is a doorway between Paradise, or the Garden of Eden, and mortal life. You passed through it once. You were created spiritually before Adam came on earth, but you died to the presence of God, as Adam did, and came into mortal life. You will pass through it again going back to God.

The gateway of death is not like a gate in the walls of Jerusalem as it is generally portrayed. It has special qualities. Perhaps it can best be compared to an air vent of the type engineers use on pumps or steam lines. These allow air to freely pass through, but prevent the passage of water or steam.

"Hey," Art said, "That sounds like a logic gate used in computers and electronic controls which only pass a signal when certain predetermined conditions are met."

"That's a good comparison," John agreed. Lilli continues the reading:

We are locked into mortal life, in the laboratory as long as our bodies and spirits are bound together. Death allows our spirits to pass through when conditions are right, but prevents the passage of our bodies or any temporal things which we accumulate. This not only magnifies the folly of dedicating our lives to stockpiling wealth, which will be left at the gate, it also raises a thought about Adam's death on the other side. Each of us were created and present with God before we came into this life. It is expected that we had a body which could not be brought through the gate, so when we came from the presence of God it was left there in death. There are indications this is true, and it will be the body we left there which will be our resurrected, eternal body, not the mortal body we have here. (We will look at this more closely when we study Life After Death in a later key.)

At the end of our period in mortal life we return to where we came from. This is known because we return to where the Tree of Life is, and the Tree of Life is near The Tree of Knowledge. Rev. 2:7

"To him that overcometh I will give to eat of the Tree of Life which is the midst of the Paradise of God."

# GOD NOT ANGRY

Adam and Eve's eviction from Paradise was not the act of a vengeful God. If they had not been drawn out of the garden they would have lived forever in God's presence, with the knowledge of their guilt making it a burning hell for them. Even worse, they would be helpless to change the situation or make amends. God's plan to make them into his image and likeness would have been frustrated. Alma offers Additional information about this in the ninth and nineteenth chapters of his book, from which we quote the following excerpts:

> What does the scripture mean which saith he placed cherubims and a flaming sword on the East of The Garden of Eden, lest our first parents should enter and partake of the Tree of Life and live forever?...Now I say unto you, if it had been possible for Adam to have partaken of the fruit of the Tree of Life at that time there would have been no death, making God a liar; for he said, If thou eat, thou shall surely die...Therefore this life became a probationary period, a time to prepare to meet God...If it had not been for the plan of redemption which was laid from the foundation of the world, there could have been no resurrection of the dead; but there was a plan of redemption laid which shall bring to pass the resurrection of the dead...Now if it were possible that our first parents could have gone forth and partaken of the Tree of Life, they would have been forever miserable having no preparatory state Never-the-less, there was a space granted unto man in which he might repent; therefore this life became a probationary state, a time to prepare to meet God. Alma 9:35-41

"This reminds me of a disturbing experience I had some time ago." Bob interrupted as he laid down his book and nervously tapped it with his pencil. "I had to drive out on a country road one rainy evening. Just after sunset as it was getting dark the car's engine quit and wouldn't restart. I checked under the hood and got myself greasy. I found the trouble was with the fuel line, so I slid under the car and got myself muddy, but I couldn't fix it. I needed help. Looking about in the darkness I saw a light from a farm house in the distance. I walked to it and knocked on the door. A kindly couple opened the door, and even though I was standing there oily, muddy, and rain-soaked they invited me in.

"After asking if I could use their telephone I saw the room was beautifully furnished with white shag carpet, and furniture with lovely white linen padding. Everything was spotless. I declined to enter, preferring to remain outside, but they would not hear of it, knowing it would be some time before my help arrived, they insisted that I come in where I would be warm and have a hot drink.

"I felt terrible as I walked on that white carpet and sat on the white sofa in my muddy clothes. They did everything to make me comfortable but I was totally miserable. As gracious as they were it was almost unbearable for me.

"I understand the hell it would have been for Adam and Eve in the Garden after their transgression."

"Yes," John responded, "and eternal judgment will be like that. Our gracious God wants us in his beautiful, pure kingdom but if we are filthy it will be a hell for us so we will accept a lower glory more fitting for our condition."

## BARRED FROM THE TREE OF LIFE

Adam and Eve were barred from the Tree of Life until they completed their mission here. When they returned, they were free to go to the tree and partake of it.

It is interesting how testimonies of people in our time confirm the words of scripture concerning events in Paradise in the time of Adam and Eve. There are books, such as *LIFE AFTER LIFE* and *REFLECTIONS ON LIFE AFTER LIFE* by Raymond A. Moody Jr. and *LIFE AFTER DEATH* by David R. Wheeler, which relate the experiences of people who have died but for some reason, they were returned to mortal life. They often relate similar experiences. They tell of a boundary which they were not allowed to pass because if they crossed over it they could never return.

The boundary was presented in various ways, but a common understanding was, that once they crossed that barrier, there could be no return to this life. Apparently they were experiencing the same thing Adam and Eve experienced when they were prevented from partaking of the Tree of Life and living there forever.

Another significant thing which many who returned from death reported was that they knew they had been there before and it proved to be a pleasant feeling of returning home.

As a footnote John said, "One of the happy experiences Lilli and I encounter in our speaking engagements or classes is when the revelation breaks upon a person that God already knew he would fall into transgression, yet God loved him anyway and had prepared a way for him to return. This is usually accompanied by a joyous, tearful admission he has sinned so badly he was sure God could never forgive or love him. It is a dreadful, lonely thing to think you have been cast off eternally with no possible hope of redemption."

Bob smiled thoughtfully, "Like standing alone in the rain on a dark lonely road, knowing you can't get home without help. Then you see a light- - -"

# CHAPTER 6

# THE SIMULATOR

"Tonight I would like to present a paradigm which may have a profound influence upon your concept of life," John announced. "I shall not attempt to convince you that this concept is accurate and true, however, it may be." Certainly the principle involved is true whether or not the method is. And whether or not the method is accurate does not really matter because the end result is what is important and the end result will be the same whether it is achieved in the way I'll outline here, or not. That is what we are each working toward.

"Before this hypothesis is presented I would like for you to consider some of the wonders man has accomplished. The Boeing company developed a simulator to train pilots who fly the Boeing 747 jet liner. As a pilot steps into the simulator his senses tell him he is in the cockpit of one of the huge airplanes. He sees all kinds of equipment as found on the real airplanes. The scenes outside the windows and windshield are of actual fields he is to fly into. The voices on the radio, the vibrations of the simulator the power of the engine thrust on simulated takeoff, and the speed at which the runway goes by are all so real that if he did not know he was in a simulator, he would be convinced he was flying a real 747.

"The simulations are all computer controlled, as are the emergencies, such as wind shear, near collisions with other aircraft, engine failure, fire, etc.

"The pilot may have flown the machine perfectly, or he may have crashed. He may have responded well to emergencies, or he may have panicked. The computer has perfectly recorded everything so both he and the company he flies for will know the kind of pilot he will be on a real flight. The computer is an impartial recorder.

"The simulator is a marvel of ingenuity, it permits training pilots to fly the great airplanes without the disasters and loss of lives that might occur in actual flying. Pilot errors, which could be disastrous for a real flight, are simply a computer record of what the pilot did wrong, and there are no passenger lives endangered by the training flight.

"The story of technology does not end here. The American Telephone Company has a wonderful movie presentation at Disney Land in California entitled AMERICA THE BEAUTIFUL.

"The audience stands in a theater and watches the show projected onto the lower walls of a dome, making a complete circle. The movie had been filmed by a pod of eight cameras synchronized so each camera captured forty five degrees of the scene being filmed, making it a complete circle. The pictures are then shown by eight projectors at forty five degree angles to each other. The effect is that the viewers are standing in the middle of the scene. They can turn completely around and see what met the camera's eyes in any direction, just as though the viewers were standing in the center of a field and by turning around they see in any direction.

"Looking in the direction the pod of cameras were traveling the viewer sees the approaching scene. He can turn to the side and watch the scenery go past, then he can turn about and watch it recede. The observer has the feeling he is actually passing through the country where the pictures are being taken.

"The stage for our hypothesis will be set by two more examples of technology.

"Place a taped movie into a VCR and watch it on your television set. You feel you are seeing people, hearing their voices, and looking at colorful landscapes. However, there are no people, or sounds or scenes on the video tape. You are actually seeing the response of your TV to magnetic impulses on the tape. These impulses create a convincing illusion that you are watching and listening to people.

"Finally, consider computers, They can design all sorts of things from cars to music. For example a computer programmed to use a mathematical system called "fractals," can create colorful scenes of mountains, lakes, highways, or cities which look so real it is like someone had taken colored photographs with a camera. The scenery for the movie, Star Wars, is said to have been made this way.

"Technology of this kind can certainly fool us into believing we are seeing, hearing, and doing things which do not exist; they are only computer programs.

# GOD'S TECHNOLOGY

Surely God also has the technical ability to produce even greater marvels. He stimulates our minds and plants visions, ideas, and knowledge beyond our rational thinking.

He opens experiences to us which enlarge our understandings and change our lives. Certainly the technology of a great simulator is within his power.

God has revealed to us that his objective is to create us in his image and likeness. This implies he will put us through some kind of process to accomplish it. What better method could he use than a simulator programmed to bring to us every conceivable type of experience to train us and to check our progress? So the hypothesis is this: suppose, instead of your being in mortal life on a planet whirling around the sun to keep you isolated from his kingdom, he has placed you in a simulator. Suppose, also, that everything, and everyone around you is not real, but only part of your computer program. Think of the thousands of situations you have faced and the multitude of people you have met under an infinite number of conditions. Every person you have known may be only part of your program which is designed to make you into the likeness of God.

Your program has written into it everything from ecstasy to grief, successes to disasters. You are put through every possible emotion, joy, anger, happiness, love, jealousy, greed, and hate. It will bring into your life all kinds of people, some you love, some you may not love, but when your program is played back to you it will be very apparent what your response was to each person. Your program will lead you to people who are in desperate need of your help, to see if you have compassion, or if you will turn them away with a shrug. It will put you into worrisome conditions to see if you try to fight your way through by yourself, and maybe panic, or if you will put your trust in God. Anything you have experienced in life could be only a part of a computer software program designed to take you step by step through a procedure to prepare you for celestial glory. If there was ever a true candid camera program, this is it. You may think nobody is watching, but according to some of the reports of people in the book *LIFE AFTER LIFE*, even their thoughts had been recorded.

Jesus said, "Have faith in God," but how many times have we worried and fretted? Stress from worry and fear, impatience and anxiety is one of the major medical problems today. Imagine living most of your life under such stress. Add to that envy, jealousy, anger, and hate. Then imagine your feelings at the end of your simulator session when you step out the door and learn all the situations were just parts of a program you were put through.

When your tape is replayed the Lord might say, "It looks like you crashed."

You may want to excuse yourself by saying, "I didn't know that was just a simulator to test me. I thought it was real life. What difference does it make? It is still the way you actually responded. You may have worked hard all of what you thought was your life, to get ahead, and accumulate wealth and position. Perhaps you ignored the scriptural instructions to "Have faith in God—Put the Kingdom of God first—Love one another." Now Your time in the simulator is past and you discover you were flying a course of your own choosing, but it was in the wrong direction for getting to the kingdom.

Suppose you have really built up a case of hate toward some individual who has come into your life; later you learn the one you hated so much was only a blip on your program to check your response to certain situations? When your tape is played back and you find the one you hated was only a part of a program, you suddenly discover it was you, not he, who was on trial.

# KEYS TO THE HIDDEN MYSTERIES

I cannot prove you are in a simulator, nor can you prove you are not. That, however, is not the point. The important thing is that it does not make any difference whether you are alone in a mechanical simulator, or whether you are living among others working your way through the laboratory of mortal life on earth. The purpose and results are exactly the same, and the scriptures say it is all recorded in each person's book. It is vitally important how you have submitted to God's will (instructions) and responded to situations and people, in a manner acceptable to God.

The main purpose of this study is to present the concept of life as a process God is using to create you in his image and likeness. When we grasp the simulator concept, it can have an impressive impact upon our lives because we are aware that we are in a process, being trained and tested and watched for the celestial kingdom. We either fly it right, or crash. Everything we do is recorded for all to see. We need to realize whatever comes to us in life is a part of our total training, which we need to learn well and to respond in the way Jesus would have.

"John, that idea is as far out as any I've ever heard," Jan said. "I don't think it can be that way. I'm sure that Bob, and for that matter the rest of you are real. I don't think I just imagine you."

"But suppose you are lying all alone on a great celestial couch," John answered. "You are surrounded by a program which is much better than the American Telephone Company scenes. They are so real that I doubt if you could tell they are only blips on a program."

Lilli said, "I doubt if God would work with just one person at a time. I think that even if he uses a simulator he would be more efficient than that. Perhaps his simulator processes millions of people at one time. In that case at least most of the people we meet could be real. Maybe just the situations are programmed."

"That is an interesting paradigm," Bob said. "It might answer the question about angels. Maybe they are attendants watching from outside the simulator and they step in sometimes just when someone is getting into serious trouble."

"Oh man!" Art said, "last year someone did something that made me so angry, I'm still mad at him. Now you are telling me that when I step out of this life a computer may show me that all those mean things I said were just spoken to an impulse on a tape, and not to a real person I'll sure feel stupid. I wish I hadn't acted the way I did. Come to think of it, it doesn't seem that important now."

"On the other hand," Don observed, "you might avoid anger, just by telling yourself the person who offended you is just a blip on your tape and pass it off as though nothing had happened. In fact you might even feel good about getting through the simulated experience in a manner acceptable to God."

"This could help in some ways," Sandy offered. "For example when I am tempted to do something I know isn't just right, I'm going to be thinking, 'I sure don't want that on my tape,' so I won't do it."

"Not only that," Fran added, "just think of all the time and effort Art and I have spent trying to get a lot of things to be successful. I guess we really want to get a little ahead of other people, but if this is true we have wasted our opportunities to be trained by the simulator, and when our simulated session is over everything stays in the machine. We step out and find we are just like everyone else."

"Ya, we'll probably be with the others who crashed," Art said.

Lilli jumped up, "I have an idea, you know a simulator doesn't have to be the size of a room. Maybe the whole world is a great simulator for training us for celestial glory."

Perhaps it is," John replied, "I guess we will know when we step out of it, won't we?"

# CHAPTER 7

# EMIGRANTS FROM JERUSALEM

## SESSION FOUR

As the members of the group took their places around Bob's and Jan's dining table, John asked, "Have you reviewed the first three sessions? Do you have any questions on the material we covered?"

Emigrants from Jerusalem

Bob answered, "I went over the material from last week and found several interesting quotes from Nehi, and Lehi, and Alma. Who are these people?"

"Lehi was a prophet in Jerusalem at the time of Jeremiah, about 600 B.C., shortly before the Babylonians destroyed the city. Nehpi was his son, and Alma was a descendant about eight or nine generations later," John explained.

God led Lehi, his family and a few others in a group out of Jerusalem about fifteen years before the Babylonians came in. They kept written records of their travel halfway around the world to what is now Central America. The Bible records their leaving, and the *BOOK OF MORMON* is an abridgment of the records they kept."

"From what I have heard about the *BOOK OF MORMON* I have some reservations about it." Bob said.

"I don't blame you." John replied, with an understanding smile. "Many people who have not read it tell us that. There have been some horrible things written about it. Lucifer uses every means he has to discredit or destroy anything which reveals truth or the way to the kingdom. People who know what the book is and have actually read it don't have a problem with it, so Lucifer tries to keep people from seeing it by frightening them with false stories about it. I don't want to get sidetracked onto it tonight, because we will look into it in depth farther down the line. However I would like to ask you to just put your reservations on a mental shelf until we get to it, then you can take them down and we will study them. Okay?"

"Okay," Bob replied.

"I might add just a thought or two though," John said, "The bible has quite a lot to say about the people who were led away. One whole chapter is devoted to them, and especially to the *BOOK OF MORMON*. There were other people who were led away also besides this group. The scriptures tell us that they also kept records, and Jesus visited them after his crucifixion. As far as I know, we don't yet have any of those records, but it is promised that in time we will have them. I'm anxious to see them.

"Anyway, until we make a study of that, you might circle any quotes from it. For now, judge them for yourself and ask yourself if they conflict in any way with what you have read in the Bible. We will go back and examine them. Fair enough?"

"Okay, " Bob said, "I'll use my red pencil . "

"Hey, isn't that the book that teaches polygamy?" Art asked.

Taking a copy of the *BOOK OF MORMON* from his briefcase, John said, "let me read to you exactly what the book teaches on that subject: Jacob 2: beginning with verse 33 says,(God speaking)

> 'David and Solomon truly had many wives and concu-
> bines, which thing was abominable before me, saith the
> Lord...Wherefore, I, the Lord God will not suffer that this

people shall do like unto them of old...there shall not any man among you have save it be one wife; and concubines he shall have none; For I, the Lord God, delighteth in the chastity of women. And whoredoms are an abomination before me: Thus saith the Lord of hosts.'

" That is found on pages 171 and 172 and there is no place in the book where it teaches any different." John said. "The book does not teach polygamy in anyway, except to condemn it." John added.

"Maravilloso, estupendo," Fran exclaimed slipping into Spanish. "That's one for our side."

"Then where did they get the polygamy idea?" Art persisted.

"They didn't get if from this book" John said, holding up the *BOOK OF MORMON*.

"And they didn't get it from Joseph Smith, " Lilli contributed.

"Incidentally, you might like to get the book to study. You would find it interesting reading. You can get it from the Deseret Publishing Co. in Salt Lake City, Utah, or from the Herald House Book Store in Independence, Missouri. The books are nearly identical except for the divisions of chapters and verses. Mine came from the Herald House, so the texts I have quoted will be under the locations in my book. You would find the references much easier to locate if you had the same book," John explained.

# DOCTRINE AND COVENANTS

"This is not the direction I had planned to go with tonight's session," John said, "but while we are on the subject, there is another book quoted in our studies which you might want to get from the Herald House. It is *DOCTRINE AND COVENANTS* (D.C.),. When it is quoted, ask yourself if it changes anything you have studied in the Bible, or just enlarges upon what you have in the Bible.

"Incidentally," John continued, "this is the major test of truth about revelation and scripture; it can enlarge on past scripture and it can offer clearer detail so you know much more about the subject, but it can never be in conflict with what God has previously given because God does not change and the truth never changes."

"You know, I've always wondered how they know what is true revelation and what isn't," Don said.

"Just this one illustration, then we have to get on with our class," John said. "I often think of truth like it was a huge megaphone. You can crawl into the small end, the mouthpiece end, and you can touch the truth all around you, but as you go farther into it you have to stand up and reach farther and farther to touch all the truth. Finally you go so far that you cannot reach all of it. It is still truth, but it is beyond your capability to grasp it.

"Okay, let's get on with the class. Sandy, would you begin reading for us tonight?"

# CHAPTER 8

## COMMUNICATIONS DRAMA

## COMMUNICATIONS

SETTING:   Adam and Eve have just been sent from the GARDEN of EDEN. God, Christ, and Holy Spirit are watching from the window of their work shop. They are concerned for these new innocent beings they have just been creating.

GOD:   Apparently we understood man's weakness perfectly. The first time they faced Satan's temptations, they chose to disobey. It is fortunate that we made provision to send them to a laboratory and keep their sins out of the Holy Kingdom. Now they have been sent to the laboratory to learn to use their gift of choice to choose what is right.

HOLY SPIRIT:

That's not going to be a picnic for them. They will get themselves so mixed up and miserable they will be knocking on the door to get back into here.

GOD:   No, I don't think so. We turned off their memory banks for the time they are in the lab so they won't remember us at first. Anyway, they will only be in the lab for about a hundred years.

# KEYS TO THE HIDDEN MYSTERIES

HOLY SPIRIT:

Well, all they will have to do is look around the lab and they will know it didn't just happen. Somebody had to make it. They sure couldn't have done it.

GOD:

Oh, in time they will figure that out but by then one of them will surely come up with a silly thought like, I know there must be a supreme being who made us but why did he abandon us ?

CHRIST:

This is an especially dangerous time for man . While he is trying things out in the lab Lucifer is going to be right there tempting him all the time. He will have man so mixed up he will think up is down.

HOLY SPIRIT:

Yes, he is so sneaky and slick he'll have them thinking the road to destruction is the bridal path to Paradise.

GOD:

Wait a minute, you two. You are starting to sound like you think we have abandoned them, too. Surely you didn't forget that we have a plan for man to help him find the way back to the kingdom, and we will beat Lucifer at his own game.

CHRIST:

I haven't forgotten. We will send man instructions and tell him how he should live; but it does not seem quite fair that we have to be so careful about his agency when Lucifer doesn't have to.

HOLY SPIRIT:

> Lucifer never worries about those rules. It would help if we could at least give man a little shove in the right direction from time to time and a good hard kick when he goes the other way... Besides that I'd like to boot Lucifer into orbit around Jupiter and get him out of the way.

GOD:

> I understand how strongly you feel about man, and our plan will work—unless of course, you protect man too much so he can't get into trouble or you get rid of Lucifer. Remember, there has to be opposition in all things.

CHRIST:

> Yes, we should get our plan going so man can have direction right from the start. Should we send angels to talk to them first or should we have Holy Spirit go slip some understanding into their minds?

GOD:

> First, I'll call to Adam from the way of the Garden.

HOLY SPIRIT:

> That's great for Adam, but what about those who are clear down at the other end of time? They can't hear what you say to Adam.

GOD:

> Look, Holy Spirit, let's go back to the table and review our plan to be sure all men get the message. Hand me that portfolio marked "Communications With Man."

# KEYS TO THE HIDDEN MYSTERIES

HOLY SPIRIT:

> Here it is.

GOD:

> Look at this index. You can see there is plenty for each of us to do. See, Chapter 1, "God's Part," Chapter 2, "Christ's Part," Chapter 3, "Holy Spirit's Part," Chapter 4, "The Angels' Part," Chapter 5, "Man's Part."

CHRIST :

> I remember the plan very well. You, Father, will speak to man from time to time and bring about the miraculous events that keep the plan on schedule, and Holy Spirit will inspire men to understand and know things they could not have known on their own, and lead them into all truth.

HOLY SPIRIT:

> That's not all, I'll inspire them to speak and write prophetically.

CHRIST:

> And I'll go talk with them personally and show them how to live. I'll even let Lucifer inspire men to do their worst to me so they can see what Lucifer's way leads to. I'll lay down my life for them to show them how great our love for them is, and to show them the way to eternal life.

HOLY SPIRIT:

> And we will inspire men to go out and spread the story to others.

GOD:          And along with all this, we will send the angels to communicate with them, not just to Adam, but all along the line of time even to those at the end of the line.

HOLY SPIRIT:

          Let's get to work. I can hardly wait to start getting man back on the path to the kingdom.

# CHAPTER 9

## MAN'S ENTRY INTO MORTAL LIFE

God, Christ, and Holy Spirit agreed that man should be placed in a laboratory. The laboratory was an ingenious display of creativity stocked with every conceivable thing man could need or want. This was not to be a weekend camping trip; it would be for all of time, and supplies had to be packed for millions upon millions of individuals. So God packed very carefully. Everything was created and stockpiled in readiness for the great event of natural creation, but they were already created spiritually.

Each little pansy and each giant redwood were prepared as spiritual beings, as were each ferocious tiger and little puppy, and the spirits of all men and women who would live upon the earth.

King David considered the beauty and fullness of the earth and wondered in awe at how bountifully God had prepared it for man's habitation. His heart opened in a song, "The heavens declare the glory of God; and the firmament showeth his handiwork . . ." Ps 19:1.

God's compassion for the men and women he brought upon earth was so great he did not commit them to just a spartan existence in a barren land devoid of anything which would be pleasing for a happy comfortable existence. He did not grant them only the necessities for survival, which would have left them as creatures of misery. He provided surroundings of exquisite beauty which stimulate man's finest instincts. He provided means of joy, and comfort, which may spill over in happiness and humor. He put into his created man the capacity for tender love, so man can have a happy mortal life despite the required trials and decisions he must endure. When a person walks in faith and obedience to God in this life he has love for others and the world about him. Even the plants and the earth itself with its snow-capped mountains and streams, its prairies and forests seem to speak to him of a providential God.

"Isn't that wonderful," Lilli's voice revealed her emotions, "After Adam and Eve were disobedient, God still took such tender care of them and provided for them, and gave them a wonderfully beautiful world, so they might have joy."

"Oh yes, when I look at the ocean and mountains and valleys I feel like King David felt when he wrote that psalm," Sandy replied. "I never understood how people could really love God but I do now."

Lilli looked around at the little group at the table. "This always seems to happen at about this point in our classes."

"What happens?" Fran asked."

"We find ourselves getting strong ties of affection for everyone in the class. John and I talked about it and decided it is because we see the love of God given so freely that it seems to flow among us."

"I think it started last week," Jan joined in.

"Back to the reading—there's more to come," John said.

It is God's will that we have joy. "Man is that he might have joy." "There is, however, a tragic side to this," John continued. Whenever a person will not respond to God's invitation to come to him that person lives in a spiritually dark world. He walks in gloom and depression, never seeing the beauty and wonder others share. Ignorance and pride and greed and lust created misery in the world although it is the will of God that we have peace, love and joy.

"Oh, how awful that would be," Fran said, "just think of looking at something like a beautiful Gladiolus and never being moved by it."

"Would you begin our reading here, Art," John asked.

God provided means for his creations to sustain and feed themselves, to replenish and reproduce. As some become old and fade away, a new generation appears. Even the earth was made so it is continually destroying and renewing itself by winds, rain, erosion, and raising up out of the oceans to flood the lands, then subsiding again. Volcanic action replenishes the minerals and huge glaciers compress the earth, pushing up mountains and grinding the mountains down spreading them as soil in the valleys (See Gen 2:5-9).

"It sounds like the earth is a living being with feelings too," Jan observed.

"It really does," Lilli agreed.

## THINGS PRECREATED

I The Lord God created all things of which I have spoken, spiritually before they were naturally upon the face of the earth; for I, the Lord God, had not caused it to rain upon the face of the earth. And I, the Lord God had created all the children of men, and not yet a man to till the ground, for in heaven created I them, and there was not yet flesh upon the earth, neither in the water, neither in the air; but I, the Lord God, spake and there went up a mist from the earth and

> watered the whole face of the ground. And I Lord God
> formed man from the dust of the ground and breathed into
> his nostrils the breath of life; and man became a living soul;
> the first flesh upon the earth, the first man, also; Neverthe-
> less, all things were before created, but spiritually were they
> created and made according to my word (Gen 2:5)

When all was in readiness, God gave a series of great commands, beginning with Gen 1:6:

> I God said, Let there be light...Then Let there be a firmament in the midst of the waters... Let it divide the waters from the waters...and on until the earth was prepared for man's habitation.

Following this, God prepared a special place for a special purpose:

> Gen 2:10-12 I, the Lord God, planted a garden eastward in
> Eden; and there I put the man whom I had formed. And out
> of the ground made I, the Lord God, to grow every tree
> naturally that is pleasant to the sight of man, and man could
> behold it, and it became also a living soul; for it was spiritual
> in the day that I created it; for it remaineth in the sphere in
> which I, God, created it; yea even all things which I prepared
> for the use of man; and man saw that it was good for food.
> And I, the Lord God, planted the tree of life also in the midst
> of the garden; and also the tree of knowledge of good and
> evil...

## PROBLEM WITH MAN'S ENTRANCE

The stage was set for man to come as a mortal into the laboratory Earth, but a major problem remained. Since man had the right to choose for himself, Adam could be expected to say, "I'm perfectly happy right here with you in Eden" had God said, "Go forth into the earth and work for a living." Knowing this to be the logical result, God set up a charade by which man would move out by choice, but one in which he could never say, "God made me do it."

> Gen 2:18-22 I, the Lord God, took the man and put him into the Garden of Eden to dress it and keep it. And I, the Lord God commanded the man saying, of every tree of the garden thou mayest freely eat, but of the tree of knowledge of good and evil thou shalt not eat of it. Nevertheless, thou mayest choose for thyself for it is given unto thee; but remember that I forbid it; for in the day thou eatest thereof, thou shalt surely die.

Adam was as innocent as a baby at this time, and God set a prized toy in front of him and said, "Don't touch it. Of course you can choose for yourself, but remember I said don't, and if you do I'll punish you." There is no question that this was a setup.

Disobedience and evil cannot exist in the Celestial Kingdom so the necessity for man to meet Satan head on and learn to reject his temptations in favor of obedience to God was a vital element in the creation of man. God could not hold man responsible for the act which sent man out of the Garden if God forced him out. Therefore it was necessary to allow Adam to encounter Lucifer and make the wrong decision when tempted. This was the beginning of a process which would prepare man, through repentance, and the Grace of Jesus Christ, to return to the kingdom. It would be a difficult experience for man, but upon returning he would be a wiser, experienced person dedicated to God

These preparations were all taken to protect man's agency but still get him to move out of Paradise and into the natural world. Adam and Eve's choice led them here, but it was engineered by God. And it was a blessing for men because it was the only way in which they could be given agency and be allowed to exercise it. They could never be created in the image and likeness of God without this gift of agency, nor could they be in the kingdom if through their agency they did not learn to reject Satan and obey God.

# EVICTION FROM THE GARDEN, A BLESSING

Adam and Eve could never have been created in the image and likeness of God without partaking of the Tree of Knowledge. But after partaking of it in disobedience to God's command they would have been forever miserable with the knowledge of their disobedience if they were forced to remain in the presence of God. If they had not been led to leave the Garden, they would have lived forever in God's presence with such a sense of guilt it would have been hell for them. Worse, they could never have changed their situation or made amends for their error, and God's plans to make them into his likeness would have been frustrated.

> Gen 3:22 The Lord God said, behold the man is become as one of us, to know good and evil; and now lest he put forth his hand and take also of the Tree of Life and eat and live forever; therefore, the Lord God sent him forth from the Garden of Eden."

"See that illustration?" Jan squealed, as she turned the page, "that's just the way I had it pictured last week when I said I saw mortal life as a corral of wild horses . "

"I can almost see angel cowboys riding herd on them," Don joked as he studied the illustration.

Alma in the *BOOK OF MORMON* enlarges upon this. "Now we see that Adam did fall by the partaking of the forbidden fruit, according to the word of God; and thus we see that by his fall all mankind became a lost and fallen people. If it had been possible for Adam to have partaken of the Tree of Life at that time, there would have been no death, and the word would have been void making God a liar: for he said If thou eat thou shalt surely die. And we see that death comes upon mankind, yea the death which is the temporal death; nevertheless there was a space granted unto man, in which he might repent...Therefore, this life became a probationary state granted unto man in which he might repent...a time to prepare to meet God; a time to prepare for that endless state which is after the resurrection of the dead....If it had not been for the plan of redemption which was laid from the foundation of the world there could have been no resurrection of the dead...If it were possible that our first parents could have gone forth and partaken of the Tree of Life, they would have been forever miserable having no preparatory state;..." (Alma 9:38-44)

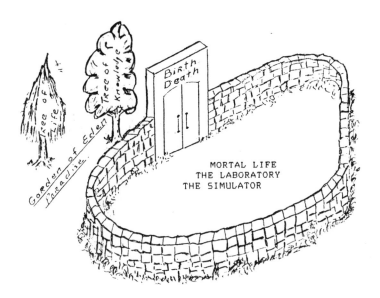

# CHAPTER 10

## DEATH IS A DOORWAY

Death is simply a passage between Paradise, or The Garden of Eden, and mortal life. Like Adam and Eve, you have been through it once. You were created spiritually and present with God before you were separated from him to enter this life. You died from God's presence to get to this life and you will die from this life and go back through the same passage to return to God.

ADAM'S DEATH IN THE GARDEN AND BIRTH TO MORTAL LIFE

At the end of our period in mortal life we return to where we came from: we return to the Tree of Life.

> Rev. 2:7 To him that overcometh, I will give to eat of the Tree of Life which is in the midst of the Paradise of God. This comes as an additional testimony that this life is only a temporary time of our being processed for the kingdom. We were with God; he sent us here for the experience, then, each who will follow his instructions, will return to him.

## ADAM AND EVE WERE NOT PERFECT

The death Adam and Eve endured on the day of their disobedience was a separation from God; it was also an actual death of their spiritual being.

John interrupted, "We will study this in detail when we study baptism."

Art wondered, "Earlier God said that on that day they would die, but it looks as though they lived on, only in a different location, Why is that?" .

John explained: "They did die an actual death. They lost that special life which God had breathed into Adam and they were removed from the Garden of Eden. They passed through the doorway of death to come into mortal life. Then they awoke in physical bodies without the spiritual life with which they had been endowed. It was their physical being that lived on, like other animals. They were especially gifted animals, of course, but the spiritual life had died. We will return to this later when we study baptism."

The Garden of Eden experience was not the end of a period of perfection in the presence of God. Nor was being forced out of the Garden the act of an angry, vengeful God. It is apparent that although Adam and Eve were innocent when placed in the Garden, they were far from perfect and would not be perfect until they were created in the image and likeness of God. To be made into such an image and likeness required a process. Mortal life is a beginning step in the process, and the Garden of Eden charade was the means of moving man out of Paradise and into the laboratory by man's choice. This was a first step in starting the process.

## GOD'S LOVE DISPLAYED

Except for sending his son, Jesus, to die in our behalf, there is no place where the love of God is so evident as the events immediately following Adam and Eve's eviction from the Garden. If we could imagine God with human-like emotions, we would see him anxiously concerned about the young couple he had sent out into the world to face not only the rigors of survival in a hostile environment but also the machinations of an evil, wily devil who would try every diabolic stratagem to destroy them, and God's plan as well.

God knew that man had to have the mortal life experience as a vital part of his creation but God did not thrust man into this life and abandon him. God not only taught them how to provide for their needs; he also sent the gospel to teach them how to prepare to return to Paradise.

We gain keen insight into the nature of God as we see his concern and care for Adam and Eve. Gen 3:27

"Unto Adam and also his wife, did I, the Lord God, make coats of skins and, clothed them."

Gen 4:4 Adam called upon the name of the Lord and Eve also, his wife; and they heard the voice of the Lord from the way towards the garden of Eden, speaking unto them, and they saw him not; for they were shut out from his presence... and he gave unto them commandments...

Gen 5:1 The Lord God called upon men by the Holy Ghost.

Gen 4:1 And thus it came to pass, that after I, the Lord God, had driven them out, that Adam began to till the earth, and have dominion over all the beasts of the field...as I the Lord had commanded (taught) him.

Gen 5:44 And, thus, the gospel began to  be preached from the beginning, being declared by holy angels sent forth from the Presence of God and by his own voice and by the gift of the Holy Ghost. And thus, all things were confirmed unto Adam by an holy ordinance; and the gospel preached; and a decree sent forth that it should be in the world until the end thereof...

Gen 6:5 Then began these men to call upon the name of the Lord; and the Lord blessed; them; and a book of remembrance was kept in which was recorded in the language of Adam for it was given unto as many as called upon God to write by the Spirit of inspiration; and by them, their children were taught to read and write...

Gen 6:8 Now this prophecy Adam spake as he was moved upon by the Holy Ghost;

"God was very busy making sure Adam and Eve and their children were cared for and taught," Lilli pointed out.

Fran laughed and chided, "First you had God as an engineer, then a carpenter, and an electrician. Now you show him as a seamstress making clothes for Adam and Eve. What will he be next, a coal miner?"

"That's coming," Lilli joined in the joke, "but isn't it wonderful, the kind of care God gave to them? He really loved them."

"I wouldn't have believed it if I hadn't seen it with my own eyes," Art exclaimed with delight.

"How could you see it with your own eyes?" Fran teased. " I mean I saw the scripture, but it seems so real I can almost see God making clothes for them." Alma again fills in more details for us:

Alma 9:47-49 and 54 After God had appointed these things that should come unto man, behold, he saw that it was expedient that men should know concerning the things whereof he had appointed unto them; therefore, he sent angels to converse with them who caused men to behold his glory. And they began from that time forth to call on his name; therefore, God conversed with men and made known unto them the plan of redemption which had been prepared from the foundation of the world;...and "God did call upon men in the name of his Son,...saying: If ye will repent, and harden not your hearts, then will I have mercy upon you through mine only begotten Son;...

Finally, in the Book of Jacob's, parable of the Lord's vineyard we can feel the anguish in God's heart as he sees how men have turned to evil despite all he has done.

"What could I have done more in my vineyard? Have I slackened my hand that I have not nourished it? Nay, I have nourished it, and digged about it, and I have dunged it; and I have stretched forth mine hand almost all the day long..." Jacob 3:101-102.

God had done everything a loving creator could do; now it was up to man to choose between God and Satan.

# CHAPTER 11

## GOD'S DILEMMA

SETTING:    Christ and Holy Spirit are entering the engineering office. God is at his desk. Papers in front of him indicate he has been at work for some time.

HOLY SPIRIT:

Good morning God. You certainly are up early today—couldn't you sleep.

GOD:    Morning.

CHRIST:    Are we starting a new project?

GOD:    No, I'm still studying the problems caused by man's agency.

HOLY SPIRIT:

I thought you solved that by putting him in the laboratory and letting him do whatever he chooses.

GOD:    It is really not that simple; we are also trying to make him into our image and likeness, which means he has to learn what we are like.

HOLY SPIRIT:

Why don't we just go show him? Then he will know what he is working toward.

GOD:

I'm afraid the problem is much deeper than that. We put them into the lab to let them use agency and if we are not very careful in the use of revelation we can take their agency away. The problem is that every bit of truth revealed to man requires him to live at a higher level of responsibility. If we appeared to him in such a way that he is forced to believe in us it will destroy his right to choose to accept us.

No, I will not even make man believe that I, God even exist. He must choose to believe, and choose to accept and follow our directions.

CHRIST:

(Grasping the magnitude of the problem) That's right. If we just reveal ourselves to them they will have no choice but to believe in us. It will be overwhelming. The only choice they would have would be to become immediately submissive and totally obedient to our instructions—or rebel against us—which of course means they join Lucifer's bunch. Either way it destroys our efforts.

HOLY SPIRIT:

Say, that's right. This is really a delicate situation. I knew we were going to have trouble with this job. Man has to know us and what we are like so he can become like us, but that knowledge can destroy him because he has to live up to the revelation he receives. What can we do?

GOD:            I think we will have to reveal ourselves through
                the choice of man.

HOLY SPIRIT:
                How in the world can we do that? Do you
                mean we go down and say, "Hey look at us, we
                are God, Christ, and Holy Spirit, but you don't
                have to believe it if you don't want to!"

GOD:            In a sense that is what I mean but not the
                method I had in mind.

CHRIST:         I'm not sure I understand what you mean.

GOD:            Suppose we surround man with testimonies that
                we as supreme beings, or creators, had to have
                created the laboratory in which he lives; even his
                own body will provide outstanding evidence that
                it did not just happen. We will put him amidst
                such marvelous wonders he will almost be
                compelled to see the hand of a creator at work. But
                we will give him the freedom to say, "It is just a
                series of coincidences—it just evolved." if he
                wishes to. There will be many who will be
                discerning enough they will begin a search for the
                creator of all the beauties and wonders around
                them. As they search they will find more and
                more testimonies of our creative work, so their
                faith will grow until, by their own choice they will
                proclaim "We are the created beings of a great
                God."

CHRIST:    Then those who have discovered the truth will share it with others so their testimonies can bring people to an understanding.

## GOD'S DILEMMA

The group was informally visiting in Jan's and Bob's living room, and John asked, "What were some of the high points for you from last week?"

"I had had no idea that God was so involved in watching out for Adam and Eve and taking care of them." Sandy said.

"Yes," Fran agreed, "Even making clothes for them and teaching them how to raise crops for food, and sending angels to teach them."

"I always thought God was only interested in great spiritual things beyond our understanding.

I had never supposed he would be concerned with our day to day things like that." Art joined in. "It makes him seem like a totally different God. I like him better this way."

"How do you feel about our studies?"

"The Bocas told us it would change our lives, and I think that has already happened," Bob said. "At least it has changed my outlook on life. I used to think I knew quite a lot about God." "Now I feel I know God."

Fran hesitantly offered, "I have a strange feeling I can't quite describe."

"What do you mean?" Lilli asked

"Well, it used to be that I might not even think of God for a month but now I have a funny feeling that he is right with me all the time, like I could just start talking to him, or if I turned around real fast I could see him behind me."

"How do you feel about it?" Lilli continued. "Does it worry you?"

"Oh no! It seems kind of nice. Maybe reassuring would be a better word."

"I know how you feel Fran, because I have felt the same way," Don assured her, "but I read in the Bible where it says, 'Draw near unto me and I'll draw near unto you,' so I assumed that since we have been drawing near to God in these studies that he was making his presence known to me."

"It sounds like everyone has had positive experiences," John said, then asked, "Has anyone had a negative experience or do you have questions now?"

"Just one," Fran said. "Is God going to be a doctor tonight?"

"Let's gather around the table and find out."

## REVELATION, GOD'S DILEMMA

Madylyn Murray O'Hare is a name which always produced a mental image for me of a hateful, miserable, spiteful, vicious, mean woman, because of her campaign against anything addressing itself to a belief in God. She is best known to the public for taking the school prayer issue to the Supreme Court. She was the keynote speaker televised from the 1990 world conference of atheists in Florida.

I listened intently, and was surprised to find she came across the air as a warm, fluent, excellent speaker. She used rational argument, sarcasm, and wit effectively. I was also surprised to note that many of the arguments she used to support disbelief in God and to portray how atheists are discriminated against are the same arguments we use to support faith in God, and discrimination of atheists against Christians. The similarities were so striking that I wondered if she may have been a dedicated Christian at one time who, for personal reasons reversed herself and went the other way. Whether or not this is true, two things stood out from her two-hour talk:

1. Science has never been able to prove there is no God. She claimed some of the best scientific minds in the world were among the atheists there, but with all of their science. The best they can offer is "We don't believe."

2. Believing scientists have also tried to prove God exists and even though statistically, the preponderance of evidence is in their favor, they have not been able to prove the existence of God. One scientist claims he can prove the existence of God statistically; but in the end, all he or the others can definitely say is: "We do believe." God is infinite and spiritual, not subject to microscopic investigation or physical measurement. Just as God is outside of time, and not subject to that dimension which is so important in the lives of men, he is beyond any scale of measurement or proof. God is known and proven only to individuals through revelation. The proof which comes through revelation is positive to the person receiving it. When one is spoken to by the Lord, there is no question or doubt in his mind that God has spoken to him, and he can rely totally upon any message presented to him including all promises. When the Lord speaks to you, you don't need further proof that God is or that he has spoken to you. People who have had the experience can understand but others cannot because, like many experiences, they can only be understood by those to whom they have been given. The spiritual world is beyond the capability of our words to explain, nor can we, without divine enlightenment, conceive the things

the Lord would show us .

Following a transcendent revelation shared by Joseph Smith and Sidney Rigdon about the glories after this life, they declared: "Great and marvelous are the works of the Lord and the mysteries of His kingdom which He showed unto us, which surpasses all understanding in glory, and in might, and in dominion, which he commanded us we should not write, while we were yet in the spirit, and are not lawful for man to utter, neither is man capable to make them known, for they are only to be seen and understood by the power of the Holy spirit, which God bestows on those who love him and purify themselves before him, to whom he grants this privilege of seeing and knowing for themselves." The part of this sublime experience which they were permitted to write is found in D.C. 76.

## ATHEIST'S DILEMMA

Atheists have a serious dilemma. They are like deep sea divers with their air lines pinched shut. They cannot believe in God without revelation; and by denying the existence of God, they close the channel through which the spirit of revelation comes; so they are spiritually strangled. Revelation comes only to those who have faith in God; it is understandable why any who do not believe cannot receive revelation. To them, miraculous events are only interesting coincidences. Then they allege that God does not exist because they have not seen him. It is like a blind man who argues sunsets do not exist because he has never seen one. In reality, they don't exist for him.

Those who cannot see God in the testimonies of all creation and the environment in which they live are blinded in that God does not exist for them, even though God is sustaining them and blessing them.

> Mormon in Ether 5:7 instructs us, "Dispute not because ye
> see not, for ye receive no witness until after the trial of your
> faith...."

The atheist cuts his own lifeline when it's needed most.

Bob said, "I had never thought of that, but I know it is true. I once hired a man at the restaurant to do repair work but whenever a problem came up he would swear that the work could not be done. He was so positive that he would not even attempt it but I would ask someone else to do it and they would go ahead and do it. That man couldn't do it only because he didn't believe he could. and he would never make an attempt, so it confirmed for him that the task was impossible."

"It would be the same way with faith in God. A person who is sure there is no God would find it impossible to believe that anything God did to reveal himself was a revelation of God because he is positive there is no God to reveal or to be revealed. So without a revelation it confirms his belief that God does not exist. His mind is closed. He would not believe if he had watched God create the world."

Don said, "One of my college instructors warned us that it is not the things we don't know that get us into trouble, but the things we know for sure that aren't true."

> In his letter to the Hebrews, Ch. 11:6 Paul explained:
>
> "Without faith it is impossible to please him; for he that
> cometh to God must believe that he is and that he is a
> rewarder of them that diligently seek him."

Faith is so basic in our relationship with God that we will not even attempt to come to him if we don't have it. Why try to contact God if we don't believe he exists? But to help us build a faith, God will move in our behalf if we will only demonstrate a hope that he is.

# FAITH WILL NOT BE FORCED UPON US

Pam, a young lady on a youth caravan, bore a testimony and spoke about her fiancée's inability to believe in God. He had been reared in a non-believer home, and though he could see, with envy, the joy, the freedom, the hope in the lives of his believing friends, he still could not force himself to cross over the line his parents had embedded in him, and believe in God. One day, in frustration he demanded, "Pam, make me believe."

The young man was asking Pam to do what God refuses to do. God invites us to believe. He calls us to faith, he promises revelation to those who do believe, but he never compels a person to believe. God may yearn to reveal himself to you, or speak to you, but you must first have faith in him. He will not force you to believe in him? Recall that in our first study, the major problem in man's creation was the agency which he must be granted to become like God. This put God in the position of having to respect man's agency, not even insisting on what man should believe. A person would be forced to accept God if God appeared before him in a sudden puff of smoke or in any other way in which the person could not deny a supernatural being had spoken to him.

## GOD'S DILEMMA

On the one hand. God must refuse to reveal himself to a person who does not already have faith in him, but, or, the other hand, he must reveal to man what he, God, is like in order to build within man the faith needed for belief.

Adam and Eve had a son named Seth who was so much

like his father in every way, it is said, they could only be distinguished from each other by the difference in their ages. This indicates not only a physical resemblance much like identical twins, but Seth must also have mimicked his father's actions in the way he walked, talked and thought. He would appreciate the things his father enjoyed and abhor those things his father disliked. Seth walked and worked and lived with Adam. He was taught to see things from Adam's perspective and think as Adam thought. Their close relationship allowed Seth to see his father and absorb his ways.

God, our Heavenly Father, would establish the same relationship with us; and if we are to become like him, we must learn what he is like. He longs to be revealed to us to satisfy the plan for our eternal life because we cannot absorb his likeness if we cannot have a close enough relationship to see what that likeness is.

Arthur Oakman, in his book, *HE WHO IS* wrote: "If we believe in God at all, what we believe about him matters more than anything else which goes to make up our lives. To believe in God falsely conceived may very easily be worse than to disbelieve him altogether. For we become like the thing we worship."

The true God must be revealed as a pattern for us. Even the marvelous experiences of the twelve who walked with Jesus was not enough to let them see beyond the physical person of Jesus until their eyes were opened by the divine influence of the Holy Spirit which bears testimony of Jesus. Jesus asked, "whom say ye that I am?" Peter replied, "Thou art the Christ the Son of the living God." Then Jesus said, "...Flesh and blood hath not revealed this unto thee, but my Father who is in heaven." Although they were with Jesus daily, it was the revelation from God that revealed to them who he was.

# MUST BELIEVE BY CHOICE

To attain the Celestial Kingdom, we obviously need to believe; but God is very, very careful never to impose a revelation upon us. We must believe first. The revelation of God comes in ways which allow us to believe or not. We can either accept it as of divine origin or we can say the experience was just a coincidence; it just happened. We may reject the natural elements of nature, which testify of God, and say they just evolved.

To establish an initial faith in him without forcing us to believe, God has placed us in an environment where all of creation bears testimony of him.

> (Gen 6:66), And now behold, all things have their likeness; and all things are created to bear record of me; both things which are temporal and things which are spiritual; things which are in the heavens above and things which are on the earth and things which are in the earth, and all things which are under the earth, both above and beneath, all things bear record of me.

We are in a world which virtually shouts of a supreme creator. The more we learn about the earth and the creatures upon it the more we see God and witness his creations causing our faith to enlarge. The fascinating, wondrous world upon which we stand and depend upon for our survival and sustenance declares the creator's presence. King David with his boundless faith, saw the hand of God in everything.

> Ps 19, The heavens declare the glory of God, and the firmament showeth his handiwork.

I held my newborn daughter's tiny hand on my huge construction worker's palm and savored that moment because I held in my hand a revelation of God's creativity.

# FAITH OPENS A DOOR

Faith is demonstrated in our response to the will of God. Whenever a person yields to the commandments of God, the results which go with obedience are seen and faith increases until it leads to baptism. Baptism turns our life over to God and gives him permission to begin work within us. Then God can unfold revelation to us without force as we grow in faith and understanding because we have invited him to do so.

An important promise is stated in D.C. 50:6.

> That which is of God is light, and he that receiveth light and continueth in God, receiveth more light, and that light groweth brighter and brighter, until the perfect day.

Faith and revelation are balanced. As we add to our faith, God adds more revelation, so the scale remains in balance.

Arthur Oakman, in the book previously mentioned wrote, "In learning more about the world we are learning more about God...Therefore, all science could and ought to be a divine service, a reverent following of the alignments of God's creation."

# FAITH IS NOT REVELATION

Faith is built up by many things which testify of God, but faith in itself is not revelation. It is the path leading to revelation. God did not shove Adam and Eve out the door and abandon them. He had a purpose. "My purposes fail not..."

God offered every assistance to build up Adam's faith. He spoke to Adam "from the way of the garden," he sent angels, he worked through the Holy Spirit, yet everything was channeled through Adam's faith.

Earlier we discussed that it was for Adam and Eve's benefit for God to put them out of the garden and into mortal life. Alma 9:41 called this life "our days of probation, a time to prepare to meet God." He also states, "It is a time to prepare for that endless state...which is after the resurrection of the dead." In verse 47 Alma continues,

> ...God appointed that these things should come unto man,...it was expedient that man should know concerning the things whereof he had appointed unto them; therefore he sent angels to converse with them who caused men to behold his glory. And they began from that time forth to call on his name; therefore God conversed with men and made known unto them the plan of redemption which had been prepared from the foundation of the world.

Probation is given to prisoners to see if they are capable of living within the law. It is necessary that God reveal his law and kingdom to us if we are to learn to live by that law. God, as both the law-giver and righteous judge, cannot hold man responsible for a law he never revealed.

## GOD WANTS US TO FIND HIM

In chapter three of his book *FUNDAMENTALS*, F. Henery Edwards points out that God is personally concerned about us. All his plans and self sacrifice point toward our molding. God is revealed in his work and he wants us to find him there.

"...There can be no true revelation except to those whose own lives point the way to understanding. The more we are like God the more readily he can make himself known to us. The less we are like him the more difficult it is for him to really communicate with us."

James 1:5 reinforces the message that God wants to reveal himself to us.

"If any of you lack wisdom, let him ask of God, that giveth to all men liberally, and upbraideth not; and it shall be given him."

# INSIGHTS AND CONDITIONS FOR RECEIVING REVELATION

Alma 9:50 And this He made known unto them according to their faith and repentance and their holy works. 9:15-19 It is given unto many to know the mysteries of God: nevertheless they are laid under a strict command that they shall impart only according to the portion of his word which he doth grant unto the children of men; according to the heed and diligence which they give unto him; and therefore he that will harden his heart, the same receiveth the lesser portion of the word, and he that will not harden his heart, to him is given the greater portion of his word until it is given unto him to know the mysteries of God; until they know them in full; and they that will harden their hearts, to them is given the lesser portion of the word until they know nothing concerning his mysteries; and then they are taken captive by the devil and led by his will down to destruction. Now this is what is meant by the chains of hell ...

The Book of Ether 1:101 In that day that they shall exercise faith in me, saith the Lord, even as the brother of Jared did, that they may become sanctified in me, then will I manifest unto them the things which the Brother of Jared saw, even to the unfolding unto them all my revelations, saith Jesus Christ the Son of God, the Father of heaven and of the earth, and all things that in them are. And he that will contend against the word of the Lord, let him be accursed and he that shall deny these things, let him be accursed; for unto them will I show no greater things, saith Jesus Christ, for I am He who speaketh;...*and if it so be that I do not speak, judge ye; for ye shall know that it is I who speaketh at the last day. But he that believeth these manifestations of my spirit; and he shall know and bear record. For because of my spirit he shall know that these things are true for it persuadeth men to do good; and whatsoever thing persuadeth men to do good is of me; for good cometh of none save it be of me.*

# INDIVIDUAL RESPONSIBILITY FOR REVELATION

The responsibility for lack of revelation is placed directly upon the person who does not receive it. God makes it available, but to receive it a person must prepare himself.

"You know," Don began, "that is pretty direct. It means that if I don't receive revelation it is my own fault because of my lack of communication with God. God says, 'Have faith and talk to me and I'll talk with you,' so if we don't have experiences of inspiration from God it must be because we don't have faith, or we don't seek his direction."

John considered this for a moment, then said, "I think that is true, however, it goes farther than that. How many things do you already know that God would have you change in your life which you have not yet changed? You see, If God has made you aware of imperfections in your life and you don't do anything to correct them, don't you think it is unlikely he will offer you further instructions? It wouldn't be a blessing to give you even more revelation. It would only place a heavier burden of guilt upon you. In other words, why should God give you instructions for what to do after you get over a hill, if you have not followed the instructions for getting to the hill?"

"That ties in with the scripture from Ether that we read earlier that we don't see the evidence until after a trial of our faith. I guess that means we have to live and move forward in faith, then God gives us the revelation," Bob said.

# CHAPTER 12

## PRAYER AND MEDITATION

"Prayer and Meditation," Fran read from the top of the pages John handed out. "That's our subject tonight?" she asked.

"Yes," John replied. "This is one of the most important of our studies."

"But I've known about prayer as long as I can remember," Art said, "My mom taught me to pray as soon as I could talk."

"Most people find there is more to this study than they had supposed," Lilli told him. "Perhaps you will find something more in it tonight."

Sandy set down her coffee cup and joined in. "It seems that every place we go they have classes on prayer. Not long ago we were in a class that seemed to tell us all that could be said about it. I remember the first of your prayer should be praise and worship of God, then thanksgiving for past blessings, followed by confession of your sins, and finally your list of requests that you are praying about so God will know your needs."

"I've read quite a lot of scripture about prayer." Don added. "It always seemed to me that the most important part is to pray with a broken heart and contrite spirit and to pray in faith. The part I have trouble with is the contrite spirit because I don't really feel that way."

"One thing I've learned from our studies," Bob said, "Is not to prejudge these lessons. I have always received far more from them than I had expected, and I have a hunch tonight will be the same."

"I think the studies you have been referring to are the mechanics of praying, rather than prayer," John suggested. "We want to look at prayer and meditation and its purpose rather than praying. I think you will find it worth your attention."

"Jan would you begin our reading tonight?"

## IMPORTANT KEYS TO PRAYER AND MEDITATION

Why pray? You cannot escape God's presence and power and knowledge; it is everywhere. Scriptures such as the 139th psalm tell us God is where we are, we cannot avoid his presence. Moreover, Matt. 6:6 tells us:

"Your Father knoweth what thing ye have need of before ye ask him." And Isaiah 65:24 reveals, "Before they call I will answer and while they are yet speaking I will hear."

"The 139th Psalm offers some provocative thoughts about prayer," John said. "Listen as I read it."

## THE 139th PSALM

O Lord thou hast searched me, and known me.
Thou knowest my downsitting, and mine uprising;
thou understandest my thought afar off.
Thou compassest my path and my lying down,
and art acquainted with all my ways.
For there is not a word in my tongue,
but lo, O Lord thou knowest it altogether.
Thou hast beset me behind and before,
and laid thine hand upon me.

Such knowledge is too wonderful for me;
it is high, I cannot attain unto it.
Whither shall I go from thy Spirit?
Or whither shall I flee from thy presence?
If I ascend up into heaven, thou art there;
if I make my bed in hell, behold thou art there.
If I take the wings of the morning,
and dwell in the uttermost parts of the sea;
even there shall thy hand lead me.
And thy right hand shall hold me.

So why pray when God knows your need and answers your prayer before you pray?

We have repeated the master key throughout our studies. Now we need to look at it more closely. We are prone to accept the idea that Satan is energetically working to win us to his side. But we tend to think of God as passive, just waiting and hoping we will want to go to him. This is an illusion, however, when we put the proper emphasis on the wording of the master key, it reads like this,

This is *MY* work and it is to *MY* glory to bring to pass the immortality and eternal life of man.

God is very definite that man cannot save himself, but he, as our creator, has vigorously undertaken the work of preparing us for eternal life as a work he is actively engaged in.

This study of prayer and meditation spotlights his deliberately planned effort in our behalf and makes clear he is active in our lives.

It is unfortunate that there was no tape recorder to capture for us what Jesus said about prayer. The scriptures record the Lord's Prayer and a few others, but they do not answer why we must pray, how prayer works, how to pray, what to

**115**

expect of prayer, or when prayer will be answered. Undoubt-edly, Jesus told much more about prayer than that which is recorded, but those who did the recording were more impressed by the prayer than by the instructions concerning it. The instruc-tions were lost to us and we must rediscover them.

The foundation we have gained in our studies of God working in our lives through a process gives us the essential basis in understanding prayer. We will focus on three facets of prayer which are of major importance, yet often overlooked:

1. The place of meditation in prayer
2. The prayer of submission, and
3. God views us from the eternal life viewpoint, and answers prayer in a manner which best facilitates our being molded into the image of God and prepared for the Celestial Kingdom.

## UNDERSTANDING AND RETAINING INFORMATION

Information which comes to us through a sermon or lecture is often misunderstood and usually quickly forgotten, but the information we have worked to discover and have studied to understand generally stays with us for life. God knows of our need to discover truth and study it through to an understanding; so it becomes the foundation of our life, never to be forgotten. He is also aware that we go about our daily lives without giving much thought to anything except routine matters. To bring about growth in us, he meets us at the intersection of our needs, the point at which we turn to him in prayer.

# PRAYER IS FOR THE PERSON WHO PRAYS

If God is always near and knows our needs and answers before we pray, it cannot be to inform God. He is not swayed by our begging or our excuses, so our prayers apparently do nothing for God. We must accept, then, that prayer is for the person who prays, and not for God.

The experiences of prayer recorded in scripture often involve action such as "going out," or "going up into a high mountain," or other action which implies going to meet God, but if God is everywhere, and always present with us, what is the purpose in going out to meet him?

# ABRAHAM

A study of the following examples offers a solution. Consider Abraham, who in his old age was commanded by God to sacrifice the most precious thing he had, his son Isaac, as a burnt offering. He could have proven his loyalty to God by stepping out of his tent, and sacrificing Isaac on an altar in his backyard, completing the awesome task quickly, but God would not have it this way. He sent Abraham to a mountain which required a three-day journey.

It is not difficult to imagine the questioning pain in Abraham's heart as they traveled. Abraham, who had been promised that he would be the father of many nations loved his son dearly. But now was instructed by God to lay his son on an alter and slay him with a knife, then offer him as a burnt offering to God. Knowing the tragedy that lay ahead must have made traveling with his son at his side and camping with him at night almost unbearable for Abraham. Certainly he had time to consider every aspect of his situation and savor every remaining sad moment he had with his son. Any wavering in his dedication and loyalty to God would surely have surfaced as they walked together. The three days and nights of meditation proved there was nothing in the world Abraham would withold from God. He could have refused to go through with the instructions. He could have questioned how he could become a "father of many nations" without an heir. He could have made excuses not to complete the dreaded journey. Undoubtedly, these and many more concerns were in Abraham's mind as he traveled to the mountain, but still his faith was such that he was determined to follow God's instructions regardless of the cost.

It was not until the moment he took up the knife to slay his son that God rescinded the order. Abraham had proven his faith and obedience to God despite having three days to think about it. God had devised this drama to force Abraham to meditate, to think, and to search his soul.

"My what a terrible test of his faith," Jan paused in reading. "I don't think I could have done what Abraham did."

"You will probably never be tested as Abraham was," Lilli pointed out, "but you will be tested and you need to be prepared to respond as he did."

"Brrr," Jan shivered at the thought, then continued reading.

## MOSES

Moses climbed a mountain and spent seven days there before God came to him and then another forty days before God gave him the tablets. God could have come to Moses the first day but he wanted Moses to meditate. Moses was to be a great leader of God's chosen people. His loyalty to God had to be assured. This time was not spent in talking with God. It was spent in prayer and meditation in preparation for meeting God.

Moses had ample time to review the thankless task assigned him as the leader of constantly complaining people. It may have been tempting to him to yield to their cry to allow them to return to the relative security of slavery in Eygpt rather than face the unknown. Moses was keenly aware that he was helplessly dependent upon God, and the only hope for the survival of the frightened people he had led out of Eygpt was with God. The thought may have appealed to him to let the people go their way; then he could return to the peaceful family life of a shepherd.

At the end of his long period of meditation, he met God with a determination to fulfill God's purpose in him, and because of his faithfulness, God spoke to Moses face to face, and revealed to him all of his work with mankind from the beginning to the end of time.

## ENOS' WRESTLE

Another classic illustration is that of Enos, in the Book of Enos in the *BOOK OF MORMON*. It illustrates how God induces us to greater spiritual stature through prayer and meditation, using it as a means of changing and molding us. Enos records that he went into the forest to hunt beasts, but the onus of his spiritual condition bore heavily upon his mind. He said,

"I will tell you of the wrestle I had before God before I received a remission of my sins."

He began praying early in the morning and prayed late into the night before God responded.

God could have answered early in the morning when Enos first lifted up his voice, but he was silent. Enos needed time to reflect upon his lost condition and the need for God in his life. As time went by with no response from God, Enos, undoubtedly, considered his unworthiness and began to probe the depths of his aching heart.

**119**

We can easily read into the account the soul searching of Enos as he reached for God. He was driven to review his sinful life and come to repentance. He longed for God's touch, but God remained silent. So Enos laid bare his sins before God. With a sharp image of his failures confronting him. He dedicated himself to the hand of God and a new life, opening his heart to receive the message of revelation. His wrestle to throw off the old life separate from God and to exchange it for a new, enduring dedication did not end until late at night. His meditation finally brought him to plead for just God's acknowledgment of him. Then the voice of God came:

"Enos, Thy sins are forgiven thee and thou shalt be blessed." Enos said, "I ...knew God could not lie, wherefore my guilt was swept away and I said, 'Lord how is it done?'"

Enos' vital meeting with God was through meditation and prayer; the two being so much an interwoven fabric that the words of prayer without meditation would not have brought the insights and understandings which opened to Enos the doorway to God's presence. This was a prayer process which God put Enos and Abraham and Moses through.

Since God does not need our words to know of our needs, it is clear that our prayers are for us, and meditation is the greatest part of prayer. It is meditation which leads us to examine ourselves and to make the required decisions to change.

The revelation of God's plan for us in eternity comes through prayer and meditation. Meditation is not passive It may contain the emotional elements: love, anger, compassion, thoughtfulness, fear, frustration, dedication, and more. These are intrinsic facets of the meditation part of prayer. They surface in our struggle to grasp a revelation of understanding and truth.

# THE HEART OF PRAYER

When we have finally learned that meditation, not asking, is the heart of prayer, we expand our wonder at our communication with God. We discover why God instructs us to pray even though he already knows our need.

Oliver Cowdery wanted to be able to translate, so he asked for the gift of translating but did not receive it. Later the Lord spoke this message of explanation to him:

DC 9:3 Behold you have not understood; you have supposed I would give it unto you, when you took no thought save it was to ask me; But behold I say unto you, that you must study it out in your mind; then you must ask me if it is right, and if it is right I will cause that your bosom shall burn within you; therefore you shall feel it is right; but if it is not right, you shall have a stupor of thought, that shall cause you to forget the thing which is wrong.

The key element here is Oliver's lack of meditation. The message should be very clear to us from these three experiences. God knew meditation to be so vitally important that he put Abraham, Moses, and Enos into situations in which each of them was forced to meditate and think through the implications of their relationships to the Eternal, and finally come to a deep and lasting dedication. It seems probable that some of the difficult situations in which we find ourselves, such as sickness, might be allowed to come upon us to force us to suspend our hectic activity long enough for serious meditation.

Many stories in magazines, like guideposts, are told by people who were too busy for God until they were struck by a disaster which forced them to interrupt their activities and consider their lives and their relationship with the Eternal. When they finally turned to God, they were richly blessed. This being true, it would seem to behoove us to spend time daily in prayer, and especially meditation, so we do not have to be stopped long enough to think seriously about our condition.

"Does that really mean that if we don't go to God voluntarily that he will put us flat on our backs to make us take time to talk with him?" Bob wondered.

"There seems to be compelling evidence that this happens," Lilli said. "At least that would be one way to get our attention, wouldn't it?"

"I'm going to pray and meditate an hour every day from here on," Sandy declared.

Jan continued reading:

The prophet Isaiah also tells of the spiritual growth which comes through prayer and meditation.

Is. 28:10 "...precept must be upon precept, precept upon precept; line upon line, line upon line; here a little, and there a little...that we might know the word of the Lord.

## GOD SEES US FROM AN ETERNAL PERSPECTIVE

Our life span is only a flyspeck on the great wall of eternity, and during that speck of time we are being prepared for life in a kingdom greater than our hope allows us to believe. When we can see ourselves from this perspective our prayers take a step upward and become prayers of praise and thanksgiving, and we seek deeper understanding. Our relationship with God turns to a loving relationship. This in turn creates appreciation and as though murky waters are becoming crystal clear we fathom truth to greater depths of meaning. Prayer becomes a channel through which God's transforming will is revealed, and the eternal secrets we have sought begin to unfold to us.

Also through this channel we gain a peaceful assurance which overcomes the trauma of life's trials, and we experience the peace of God that passeth all understanding. Phil 4:7

We need to remember that we do not view our situation from the same perspective as God views it. Everything is distorted when we look at life and its problems from the perspective of this life only, as though everything ends at the end our mortal life. When we are hurting or we feel our needs pressing upon us for immediate relief we don't even think of this lifetime, we think of this moment, right now! Our preconceived idea of how we want our prayer answered is, "I'm hurting; do something now!"

God may take care of these immediate needs; nevertheless, he sees our problems from the eternal life point of view. He is working to bring about our immortality and eternal life, so he will bring into our lives those things which cause us to grow in the eternal picture. Sometimes it is the very problems which he has brought to us to shape us that are hurting us now.

To remove them would destroy the progress he is making in building our eternal life.

God's great plans and purposes for man extend far beyond mortal life, which is only the initial step in our preparation for an infinitely greater role in a concept called "Eternity". Mortal life is only a seed buried in the soil of earth, but the blossoming and fruit which springs from the seed transcends the limitations of this life. The slightest stain of disloyalty to God is equivalent to a fungus which can destroy the seed and also spread to destroy the crop. Therefore, it must be quarantined here and prevented from entering the fields of glory. In mortal life we must be tried, tested, and our initial spiritual sprouting begun before we are transplanted to richer eternal soil.

The preparations made in this life are for the life beyond, so God answers prayers and molds us with that in mind, rather than just the present. The Lord also sees us in the eternal environment. If the request we make in prayer here will destroy us for the role he has pending for us, the request will not be granted. If we could view beyond the wall of death, and see from God's perspective, our prayerful plea for the life of a loved one might turn to a joyful bon voyage.

## A KEY PRAYER, THE PRAYER OF SUBMISSION

Jesus summed up the subject of faith and trust, with four simple words to his father, "Thy will be done." It may be difficult for you to repeat these words with full commitment when you recognize the implications. Through these words you lay your life at the feet of God, saying, "I give myself to you. Use me in any way you wish." It may be a frightening thing to think of the possibilities this statement opens, but we cannot reach the heights in our prayer experience or fulfillment of the purpose of our creation until we can say them with our full intention of letting God take control. They permit the Lord to bring about what is needed to form us into his likeness.

We usually have some kind of mental picture of how we want our prayers answered. Sometimes we become insistent upon things happening in the way we wish. An example is when we have a loved one, perhaps a child, who is critically sick, there is only one way we want our prayer answered. We virtually demand having our way and we want it now. But often the healing process seems to be delayed and the child drifts farther away, so we finally beg God for a healing, then when there is no response, we may find ourselves angry with him for not responding. When we finally submit to God's will and pray, "Thy will be done," it is amazing how often there is a miraculous turnaround, not only in the condition of the child, but in our own attitudes. Our heart is at peace as though God has spoken assurances to us.

# DELAY MAY BE NECESSARY

This delay may seem severely unjust, but it causes us profound meditation. It is the same as required of Abraham when he laid Isaac on the altar to die. Even God's own son was sent to die on the cross; he knows the anguish you feel. To be judged with Abraham and Moses you must be tried as they were. When you can come to the point that the life of someone dear to you is in the balance and you can turn to God with the words, "Thy will be done," you have demonstrated there is nothing in this life you would withhold from God. You lay bare your heart and place that life upon the altar, releasing to God that which you have loved, the one for which you would lay down your own life. At that moment, you have fulfilled the first great commandment. You have totally placed your trust in God in a way surpassing all the words and promises you could express. You have released the last of your reservations and opened the locks of God's love to you, so his spirit can flow out in peace and love, and the works of eternal life which will lead you to celestial glory take place.

# DIFFICULT EXPERIENCE MAY BE AVOIDED

If you had known what to expect, you might have saved yourself weeks or even months of distraught worry, demanding prayers and agonized pleading by submitting to God in the beginning. But it is a difficult thing to turn someone dear to you over for "God's will to be done."

"How could you know in advance that you would have to go through all that?" Jan asked.

"You may not know in advance just what to expect, but you should always be prepared to submit to God. In order to know how to submit, you need to go back to prayer and meditation." Lilli answered.

125

"It might appear that you are stone-hearted and uncaring If you turn a loved one over to the will of God like you really don't love her, or him," Don said as he considered the idea of turning all care over to God.

"Yes," Jan said, " it might seem that way to someone but it is the most loving thing you can do."

# SUBMISSION

Once again we consider the testimonies of people in publications such as guideposts and note that they seem to have a common theme. Presented in different ways, they repeat, "I was in a very desperate situation which was growing increasingly grave, until I remembered God and prayed for help. Then things changed."

In every great experience of your life God has a lesson for you. It is not mandatory for them to be learned through traumatic problems. Many of the lessons can be learned from studying the scriptures regularly to learn how the Lord has led other people and how he will work with you. You can learn from the testimonies of others, and you learn through meditation and communion with the Lord. Finally, and most dramatically, learn by the very difficult experiences that come into your life, in which you are absolutely dependent upon the mercy of God. At this point of intersection with your need you may find God is using your need to slow you down enough to get your attention. This is a drastic way to learn, especially considering that you might have learned the same through quiet meditation and submission to God.

# WHAT HAPPENS TO THE PERSON WHO PRAYS?

We are always keenly aware of what happens to the person for whom we pray, but we don't give too much thought concerning what happens to the one who prays, yet the whole drama may have been staged to bring to pass submission in the life of the concerned one who is laying his heart on the altar of prayer.

# REACHING BEYOND OURSELVES

God wishes to reveal himself to us so we may more readily be made like him. Through meditation and prayer we make the connection and reach beyond ourselves. It becomes the conduit through which we tap into the eternal omniscience. Sometimes knowledge comes to us in dramatic ways as we pray. At other times our knowledge grows imperceptibly, but continuously, as we submit our lives to God and communicate through prayer. You cannot always explain how you know something; you just know it is true. As our meditations continue we become aware of truths we had never known. Our daily living carries meanings we had not realized previously; scriptures we study, open with light not seen until now, and decisions we make seem to be guided.

# A PROCESS REQUIRED

We may unwittingly bring about many of our own problems by our prayers. Prayers require a process in order to be answered. The process may take years of difficult experiences. If you cannot see what God is working to accomplish, the experiences become hard to bear. An example is the simple prayer,

"Lord make me worthy of thy kingdom." The person who offers such a prayer may soon forget it, but to God, this is a serious matter, and it is one of the things he wants us to request, so he begins working on it. The fulfilling of this prayer could, and no doubt often does, require us to be laid upon the anvil and pounded into shape and dragged through a process taking the rest of our lives. If the person offering such a prayer is selfish, proud, or arrogant, for example, he could very well become destitute as God leads him into poverty so he can learn humility in answer to his prayer to be made worthy. That is what is needed, so that is what he should be expecting from such a prayer, unless he can learn through study or meditation or submission. Until he has learned humility he may be hurting and probably complaining about what is happening to him as a result of his previous prayer—which he has likely forgotten by now. So now he prays, "God help me overcome the impoverished circumstances I'm in."

# SCRIPTURE THOUGHTS

He that cometh to God must believe that he is, and that he is a rewarder of them who diligently seek him. Heb. 11:6

Wherefore dispute not because ye see not; for ye receive no witness until after the trial of your faith. Ether 5:7

The natural man receiveth not the things of the Spirit. They are foolishness to him. I Cor. 2:14

# CHAPTER 13

# INTRODUCTION TO STAGES OF LIFE

The women of the study group chose to meet at noon Friday at Bob's restaurant for visiting and a no host luncheon.

Jan was idly stirring her shrimp cocktail with her demitasse fork when she thoughtfully revealed to Lilli, "I've learned more these past few weeks than I ever thought there was to know about life. It had never occurred to me that life was a programmed affair.

I had always thought you were born, and lived, raised your children and died. Along the way you just tried to be good to each other and honest, and accept Jesus as a savior. The Idea of this life being our time of creation is fantastic, but I can see it so clearly now."

"I would never have considered God having a problem to be solved, like being careful about how he revealed himself to us," Sandy added. "I wonder how many other things there are about life that we just take for granted but they are actually part of the plan?"

Lilli set down her cup and said, "Mortal life is an amazingly wonderful process; even more amazing when we recognize it is a planned process. We have found that if you are alert to what is happening in your life you begin to see a continuing evolution of changing events which are most certainly a process. We begin to realize the events in our lives are not just random occurrences."

"I think it is exciting," Fran joined in, "I find myself thinking so differently than before our classes. I see things happening that I never saw before. I can understand how those who are faithful and submissive to God inexorably become endowed with the character of the creator."

"It's strange," Jan added thoughtfully as she sipped her coffee, "I could see that those who followed evil always seemed to become more devilish but I had never applied the opposite and noticed that those who follow Christ become more God-like."

"That's right." Sandy was struck by Jan's comment, "Things seem to drift to evil so easily, but it always seems such a struggle to be good. Maybe it's because we make excuses for our weaknesses, but not for what we do that's right. Isn't there some kind of study to prepare us for what is coming next in our lives so we can recognize it when they come?"

"That is just what John has scheduled for next Tuesday evening. There are general stages and patterns in our lives which emerge as we go through the process of living," Lilli explained. "They are different steps in God's process for teaching us. It is a very definite program. Of course, just as there are dropouts in school, some people never follow through the entire program, so they never mature spiritually. On the other hand, many people tend to grasp the lesson of a step in the process very quickly and move ahead."

"That's what I need," Fran said, "a curriculum I can follow."

"That may be a better term for it than we have used," Lilli responded. "We never called it a curriculum. We just called it stages of life."

"I wonder what stage I'm in." Sandy said, "Can you tell me?"

"By the time we finish the series on stages of Life, you will be able to tell for yourself quite well. Of course, you are seldom actually in just one stage because you don't reach a cutoff point from one and then begin another. They seem to merge so you evolve from one into another at the same time. Also, I think we all have a little of previous stages clinging to us as well, but you will be able to get a good estimate of your progress toward perfection and an idea of what might be coming next."

"Oh, I was starting to feel pretty good about myself until you spoke of perfection." Jan laid down her fork and looked closely at Lilli, "Perfection is a depressing word for me because I don't think I can ever make it. In fact I wonder if it is possible for anyone."

"Yes, Jan, it is possible, and you will learn that you can make it. Each of you can," Lilli added. "You see it is God's work to lead you into immortality and eternal life. He makes it as easy as possible, then helps by showing you how. You are nearer perfection than you think already.

"Blindness to life as a process creates misconceptions about God. He never was an angry vindictive power determined to tame the wild rogue within us. His commandments are strict and must be obeyed, but obedience to each one proves to be a blessing. I expect you will soon be looking for his commandments just so you can obey them and draw closer to him, actually our studies of stages of life will list some of them."

Our concepts of God's love and forgiveness get all tangled up in a mixture of human emotions when we fail to see that God acts with purpose. We must remember God is firmly committed to elevating us to Celestial Kingdom level. Forgiving us in our sins would allow us to settle for a level far below the glory he has planned for us.

"Lilli, if only I could have the confidence you have—I do want to believe what you say is true," Jan said, " but for me it seems like a dream, an impossible dream."

Lilli leaned forward, her voice soft with emotion, "Do, believe, Jan and each of you." Because if you believe it and want it you can have it. It is not only what you do for God that is important but what you refuse to do for Lucifer as well.

"I wondered why John gave me this paper to review before he left home, but now I think he must have been inspired to give it to me. Let me read it to you." Lilli took a few sheets of paper from her purse.

# GOD'S INTENT HAS NOT CHANGED

God's intent through the swirling mists of time has always been to create man as a mirror image of himself, lighting in us the flame of godliness. To accept us in our reprobate condition would destroy any hope of fulfilling his plan, so he cannot accept or forgive the unrepentant. However, he loves us at every stage of our development, but he cannot rest or find us acceptable until his purpose in us has been achieved, and we are like him in every way.

His love for us is not based upon our "goodness" or "badness." His love is given to us freely. Just as we have prepared an educational program by which our children can develop into knowledgeable adults, God has prepared a program, or process, by which we grow into the "stature and fullness of Christ."

To become his heirs sharing in all he has is God's fervent desire for us. D.C. 76:5h speaks of those who attain the Celestial Kingdom.

"Wherefore all things are theirs, whether life or death, or things present, or things to come, all are theirs, and they are

Christ's, and Christ is God's: and they shall overcome all things."

# GOD'S LOVE IS FREELY GIVEN

Blessings occur as the result of the heavenly instructions given to us. We will be loved by God as much if we refuse to follow the instructions, but the results will be different. It is as though God has sketched a map for us to get to his house. We can turn the map upside down and get lost, or take shortcuts which lead to dead-ends but that does not affect his love for us. His love is as compassionate while we are lost, as when we faithfully follow the map. Forgiveness means that when we turn the map rightside up and follow it, it still leads us to his house, and we will be welcomed when we arrive.

The prophet Isaiah declares that God is much more dynamic in leading us to his home than just sending us a map. He says God lays out a path then gets behind us and tells us to walk in it without turning to the right hand or the left.

> Thine ears shall hear a word behind thee, saying this is the way. Walk ye in it, when ye turn to the right hand and when ye turn to the left." Isa. 30:21

It is only when we can see God working in our lives this way that we understand it is a blessing when the Lord gives us "The bread of adversity, and the water of affliction," (Isa. 30:20.)

# ONLY GOD CAN JUDGE

In our judgment we would consign a 'good' person to paradise, and a 'bad' person to hell. But our judgments are based upon assumptions that may be disastrously wrong. We seem prone to overlook the good in a person who annoys us somehow.

133

Also we lose track of what God is working toward. God is not busily trying to find compartments to segregate us. He said, "My work and my glory is to bring to pass the immortality and eternal life of man." So he will use methods which may seem strange to us to accomplish that objective, and God can bring out goodness from those we supposed were completely devoid of anything worth saving. It is God's will that all be saved for his kingdom, and no matter how bad we think someone is, God is still working to salvage that person, and he still loves him.

# MAN'S ERRORS EXPECTED

We are not condemned for experimenting and making mistakes. Condemnation comes when we fully learn the truth, then return to our old wrong ways by choice. God put you into a situation in which he knew you would make many mistakes and be unfit for the kingdom, but he takes full responsibility for redeeming you. He has set up an elaborate system for this purpose. He sent his son to be our savior, he has sent the Holy Spirit to be our guide leading us into all truth. However, it is incumbent upon us to follow that which he has given and Yield ourselves to Christ who is "the way, the truth, and the light.

"That is wonderful," Sandy murmured. "I wish I could express how I feel."

"There is more," Lilli said.

# COMMANDED TO BE PERFECT

Scriptures such as Matthew 5:50 tend to make it seem impossible to achieve the level demanded of us.

"Ye are therefore commanded to be perfect, even as your Father who is in heaven is perfect."

134

However, Jesus came to show us this can be done D.C. 90 explains how to follow Jesus' steps to perfection,

> "I John saw that he received not the fullness at the first, but received grace for grace; and he received not the fullness at first, but continued from grace to grace

Isaiah 28:9-10 adds to this progressive understanding of spiritual growth.

> "Whom shall he teach knowledge? And whom shall he make to understand doctrine?...Precept must be upon precept, precept upon precept, line upon line, line upon line; here a little and there a little;...wherefore hear the word of the Lord.

We grow in understanding and compliance step by step, and decision by decision; each adding a little to our mountain of experience. These steps, or stages, of human life emerge in general as outlined here. An awareness of the stages allows us to examine where we are, the stages we have passed through, and what may be coming next . A serious problem in our public schools is caused by students who drop out and fail to graduate. The same thing happens in our spiritual preparations. Some become distracted by other things and never complete the course so they never mature spiritually. The result (as we shall see under a later key) is that they never receive their full share of wisdom, and gifts, or the glory which could be theirs .

"Why, that is what we were talking about," Fran exclaimed, "It is just as though that was written just for us today."

"God works in wonderful ways, doesn't he? Let me finish the paper," Lilli added.

## ADVANTAGE IN KNOWING ABOUT STAGES

It is a great advantage to be aware life is a continuing development involving many changes. Since there is no set time or age for completion of any stage, the person determined to follow Christ and attain the Kingdom of God is never held back; he can learn the lessons of his level and move on. The Holy Spirit is sent to "lead us into all truth" ( John 16:13). Those who are discerning of the spirit's guidance through the stages learn to respond quickly to the lesson, then because he does not have to be put through a long difficult lesson, he can avoid some of life's most traumatic experiences by skipping over to the next stage, but the person who does not realize he is in a training process may never move beyond a certain level. The one who does not move up, usually complains bitterly because life is treating him so outrageously. Misfortunes are repeated over and over in his life with slight variations, but until he learns from the experiences, he continues to relive them.

The Holy spirit will not drag, or push. He is sent to lead, and you must choose to follow. We are not forced to move on, and because many become satisfied and comfortable, they fail to progress. This occurs when they begin looking at other people rather than to God. They observe that they are on approximately the same level as others who are respected, so they don't have motivation to continue on to perfection.

## SEQUENCE MAY VARY

The stages we will outline are in the usual logical order, but dependent upon circumstances, they do not always follow this sequence. For example, a person raised in a Christian home with loving parents may well skip over the rebellion stage, only to fall into it at some later time in life. The child who is raised in a large family with many exchanges with others may learn very early to socialize and share and be concerned with others and by this avoid the infant stage of Christian growth. However he may fall into it later in life due to pressures upon him to compete and achieve.

As a rule people do not recognize these stages and never examine their lives to discover where they are.

"More coffee anyone?" the waitress interrupted.

"Oh No!" Fran exclaimed, "I'm late for my class. The time went by so fast I hadn't even noticed. Bye, see you Tuesday," she said to the group.

Sandy, also hurrying to leave for an appointment said "Let's do this again next week."

Jan reached out and took the papers from Lilli's hand and asked, "May I have these so I can make a copy?"

"Of course," Lilli replied, "but John will have a copy for everyone Tuesday evening."

"I don't want to wait until Tuesday," Jan smiled.

## STAGE NUMBER ONE

Tuesday evening at Bob's and Jan's home.

"Hey, we're going to have to do something about these Friday women's luncheons," Art was saying. "Fran has not talked about anything else all weekend. She thinks she is about to be processed into a golden goddess. I can just see her with swept back wings and flowing hair like a hood ornament on an old Terraplane."

"Oh, Art, you are exaggerating again." Fran pretended to hit him. "You know that I was just talking about God leading us through a training procedure to make us more nearly perfect. Besides that you enjoyed our discussions. You wanted to come tonight as much as I did."

"You have nothing to worry about; you are already perfect . Haven't I always told you so?"

"Don't be silly, Art. I'm a long way from perfect, but Lilli says the Holy Spirit will lead us into perfection."

Realizing his humor was not having the effect he hoped for, Art changed his approach. "This idea about stages we are in is okay. I'd like to find out where I am on God's plan and what I have to do to move along."

"I had thought of joining the ladies on Friday, but when I looked out of the office and saw how deeply engrossed they were in their discussion I decided not to interfere," Bob said. "But Jan gave me a copy of the paper they had and I've been reading it. It has caused me to do a lot of thinking about my own situation."

Sandy joined in, "I wonder why I had never heard of a process God has for preparing us for eternal life. I've gone to church most of my life, but no one ever told me there was anything directing my life except what I directed myself."

"I think it is a good indication of the value of the keys. Without them there are many important things we totally miss and others which we would not understand," John suggested. "This process works quietly and continuously throughout our lives. The important thing, now that you know about it, is to work with it. Study and meditate. Pray and talk with God about your situation, and obey everything God reveals to you as his will. Finally, be submissive to God in all things. I think that as we go along this will become more apparent."

"It might be easier to keep in mind what is being said in our study tonight if we read first, then discuss the material. Okay?" John asked. "Bob, would you like to begin?"

# CHAPTER 14

# STAGE OF LIFE NUMBER ONE: THE INFANT STAGE

The infant cradled in grandmother's arms and receiving her practiced inspection was only hours old. Folding the blanket back, grandmother exclaimed, "Oh! Isn't he beautiful? Look at his eyes, they are just like mine, and that cute little nose is the image of my sister Joan's. Don't you think those sweet little rose-petal lips look like my mother?" Then turning to her husband, she asked, "Didn't your brother James, have rather large ears?" The life-long comparison and competition has begun in this new life.

## COMPARISONS AND COMPETITION

The child will be compared with others for the age at which the first tooth came, when he was potty-trained, his first step, first words, and so on. When school begins, he soon discovers it is more important to bring home top grades and excel in sports than to enjoy learning and developing non-competitive skills. To be acceptable to teachers, parents and peers, he must compete and be a winner.

The drive to be best is imprinted upon the child as he becomes adult, but even then he is not free of the struggle to be most important. The terminology changes from "being best" to "being successful," but it is only a change in wording. The idea of being successful in the eyes of others dominates the choices of careers, homes, and even eligibility as a marriage partner.

Careers which people would enjoy very much are shunned, and others more stressful to them are entered because they offer greater earnings, more prestige and, perhaps, more power. Businesses use the compulsion of people to be number one to push them to greater efforts. They imply that you are nobody unless you are the best. Sales people are instructed to "Crystallize your thinking upon earning a million dollars." They portray the winners as living in mansions and enjoying cruises on the company yacht. Those who attain the top echelon are held up as people of great importance, but those who are not in that elite circle are scorned.

The natural demands of infancy for care and feeding by others embed the idea that others are here to serve them, so it is little wonder that so many grow up believing they are the center of a private universe in which all things are satisfying their individual needs and desires. The greater some people's achievements and worldly glory, the less sensitive they become and the less caring of others. Self-interest becomes the construction material of thick walls between people. It is difficult to truly wish the best for those you are competing against.

The infant stage, or the "adult-infant," is not dependent upon tender years. Some people never mature or leave it behind, and some of it clings to most of us throughout life.

## KING SAUL

Saul was a tall, genial, somewhat naive, farm boy when God sent the prophet Samuel to appoint him as Israel's first King. Despite Saul's humble beginning, he slipped into the mantle of authority quickly and the adult-infant in him surfaced, taking control.

Two years after becoming king, Saul grew impatient in waiting for the prophet, Samuel, to arrive to make a burnt offering. Samuel was late, so Saul took the priest's authority upon himself to make the burnt offering. Saul did not have the priestly authority for this act, but after all, he was king, and who could be greater than this? Saul was soon to learn, because almost immediately Samuel arrived and proclaimed,

"Thou hast done foolishly; thou hast not kept the command-ment of the Lord thy God which he commanded thee; *for now would the Lord have established thy kingdom upon Israel forever... but now thy kingdom shall not continue..."* (I Samuel 13:13-14).

Saul was also disobedient to God. He was told to utterly destroy the "sinners, the Amalekites, and fight against them until they be consumed..." They were to take no spoil for themselves, and to destroy everything, but "the people took of the spoil, sheep and oxen, the chief of the things which should have been utterly destroyed" and spared Agag the King of Amalek. Then, in an attempt to justify what they had done, Saul lied and told Samuel they were taken to offer sacrifice to the Lord.

I Samuel 15: 22-25 "And Samuel said, Hath the Lord as great delight in burnt offerings and sacrifices as in obeying the voice of the Lord? Behold, to obey is better than sacrifice, and to hearken, than the fat of rams. For rebellion is as the sin of witchcraft, and stubbornness is as iniquity and idolatry. Because thou hast rejected the word of the Lord, he hath also rejected thee from being king."

# GOD'S SPECIAL SPIRIT TAKEN FROM SAUL

> The Lord said unto Samuel, How long wilt thou mourn for
> Saul, seeing I have rejected him from reigning over Israel?
> Fill thy horn with oil and go, I will send thee...for I have
> provided me a king...I Samuel 16:1; vs 13, Then Samuel took
> the horn of oil and anointed him in the midst of his brethern;
> and the spirit of the Lord came upon David from that day
> forward...vs 14, but the Spirit of the Lord departed from
> Saul...."

While Saul still held the throne, David was returning from battle, and Saul overheard the women of the city happily singing, "Saul hath slain his thousands, and David his ten thousands." King Saul's infant being rose up in jealousy at the singing, so from that time forth he dissipated the power of his kingdom by dragging his army around the country trying to destroy David, who was actually the most loyal subject Saul had.

Jealousy and other evils related to self aggrandizement destroy people of all levels. Saul not only lost the kingdom, but in the end, his life as well.

# THEY DO NOT KNOW GOD

The competitive, self-centered life creates extreme deviations from the likeness and image of God. It brings to pass the very thing which was anticipated by our creators in giving us the freedom to use our agency. Man becomes an evil god to himself. We see examples everyday in all degrees. The person who is guilty of greed lacks compassion for others and walks a path leading to destruction. Consider the unscrupulous salesman whose only interest is his commission at whatever loss to the customer. It is this same selfish attitude which prompts some people to sell drugs for money, despite their knowledge they destroy innocent children's lives. These people demonstrate the extremes of the infant stage of life. They become patently evil through greed and they walk away from God. They have not and cannot build a faith which opens their eyes to all the testimonies of God surrounding them. Without this faith, God does not have permission to work in their lives, so they become subject to their carnal, sensual, and devilish desires and nature.

## GREED IS NEVER SATISFIED

The adult-infant longs for the joys of the world, but his greed drives him farther from its source. He tries to grasp as many of the world's treasures as he can get, but they bring less and less satisfaction to him. The price he pays is the quality which makes life beautiful and pleasing. The wonder of sunsets and flowers no longer touches him deeply, nor does he enjoy the stirring emotion coming from sacrificial giving; they are blocked by his overriding resentment.

Avarice is never satisfied. It leads step by step into deeper depths of evil. James 4:2-4 explains,

"Ye lust and have not, Ye kill and desire to have and cannot obtain, ye fight and war, yet ye have not...whosoever therefore will be a friend of the world is the enemy of God."

The paraphrased Living Bible words it this way:

"The evil pleasures of this world makes you an enemy of God...if your aim is to enjoy the evil pleasures of the unsaved world, you cannot also be a friend of God."

## JESUS' WAY

Jesus clearly saw this condition as a gurgling wellspring of division among people. It creates jealousy and pride which in turn cause wars. Just as important, it has always prevented the coming of Zion and the kingdom on earth, where (Gen 7:23) "They were of one heart and one mind...and there were no poor among them..." The Lord further emphasized the problem when he said, "I say unto you, be one, and if ye are not one ye are not mine." The problem is that while we are in the infant stage of life, it is impossible to truly be one, since each person is attempting to rise above his neighbor.

## THEY CANNOT SEE THE KINGDOM OF GOD

Jesus explained the way to Nicodemus, who came to him at night, John 3:3, "Jesus answered and said unto him, verily, verily, I say unto thee, except a man be born again he cannot see the kingdom of God." The portrayal of our infant stage clearly reveals Jesus' meaning. He was saying, "From the world's perspective of a successful life you cannot even conceive such as the Kingdom of God. You must return to the inception of life and rebuild your total concept, your ambitions, your desires and those things to which you dedicate your life. You must be born again"

> Jesus directly addressed this problem, John 12:25, "He that loveth his life shall lose it, and he that hateth his life in this world shall keep it unto life eternal."

Jesus repeatedly told his apostles, "Love one another." In his prayer in The Garden of Gethsemane, he prayed,

"That they may be one as thou, Father, art in me, and I, in thee, that they also may be one in us; that the world may believe that thou hast sent me, and the glory which thou gavest me I have given them, that they may be one, even as we are one... I in them, and thou in me, that they may be made perfect in one...(John 17:21-23).

He also gave them another concept which was foreign to the world. He told them to come out of the infant stage, in which they felt they should be served, and serve others.

Matt. 20:26-28, *"But whosoever will be great among you, let him be your minister...and whosoever will be chief among you, let him be your servant...*even as the son of man came not to be ministered unto, but to minister and to give his life a ransom for many."

He said Luke 12:17,

*"...Beware of covetness, for a mans life consisteth not in the abundance of things which he possesseth."*

In instructing us to be reborn, Jesus did not discourage our seeking success, but he reverses man's idea of success. Man sees success in great wealth and acclaim from the masses. Jesus' definition of success was 180 degrees opposite the definition the world uses.

In D.C. 6:3, he said, "Seek not for riches, but for wisdom, and behold the mysteries of God shall be unfolded unto you, and then shall you be rich. Behold he that hath eternal life is rich."

# A NEW WORLD SOCIETY

Stage one of life, the concept that we are the center of the world and need to subject all things and all people to us, needs to be erased and a new concept built using Christ's definition of love for all people and the glory be to God.

Our vision of the Kingdom of God on earth is obscured by a world in which each person attempts to gain advantage over others, where deceit is an homogenized part of society, and greed and pride are the norm. Jesus said we cannot even see the kingdom, because we cannot imagine such a condition as would exist if love and caring replaced greed and self interest. However, we get a notion of the contrast between the kingdom and our world when we consider the money we spend on locks for our doors, arms for protection, prisons to protect society, lawyers and courts, police, insurance, wars and weaponry, dishonest officials, and public graft.

Bob sat erect in his chair and slightly raising one hand said, "I understand that nearly three-fourths of all the money we spend is spent for some form of protection. Do you have any idea how much I spend for insurance alone? My business liability insurance takes a big share of the profits; then there is the cost of the security patrol; part of my fire insurance is for fear of arson, and the list goes on. I can name at least ten inspectors who come around to check on us, and whether they are paid directly or by taxes, they are a cost of operating the business. If something does go wrong, even if caused by someone else, I have attorney fees and court costs. I would guess we could easily live on one forth what it costs us now if we didn't have to protect ourselves from others."

Sandy stared at John in disbelief. "You mean all that is caused by the infant stage, by people who put themselves first?

That must be the root of all crime and deceit. Everything from simple lies to murder must start there."

"Hey, I used to leave our house and car unlocked, but no more," Art affirmed. "Now there are too many thieves around."

## THY KINGDOM COME

Jesus told us to pray, "Thy Kingdom come," but it is difficult to realize the scope of change the kingdom would make. Individually, it is impossible to turn the world about and usher in a kingdom so marvelously conceived. However, we can individually begin casting off the bondage of our infant stage of life and become compassionate and caring to others. We can learn to be forgiving. We can join with other individuals in becoming one, then groups of individuals can join, spreading the move to be one. In short, we can follow Jesus who came to show us the way.

Don leaned forward and raised his hand, "You know," he began, "I have competed all my life. I've always tried to be a winner and I've taken courses on how to be successful. Is this wrong? Everyone seems to have more respect for a successful person."

The serious meditation Jan had been doing the past few days prompted her to say, "What I get from this is that when you are competing you are working against others so you cannot truly have their best interest at heart, but in God's Kingdom there will not be competition because you will be working for the benefit of others. You can, however, compete with yourself in trying to always do better.

"I've been trying to imagine what that kind of world would be like. I know I cannot fully conceive of such a world, but I also know it would be a wonderful, loving and peaceful place."

Jan summed up the problem saying, "And there will be one fold and one shepherd, so there can be no one in the infant stage in the kingdom. It just won't work."

## THE WORLD COULD BE CHANGED

"Isn't that marvelous, Jan?" Lilli said. "If we could have that condition on earth, think how wonderful it would be. We could love and trust everyone and the whole world would be at peace."

"Just because of the infant stage?" Sandy was awed at the thought.

Rereading part of the text, Don observed, "Old King Saul is a good example. He could have had the support of all the nation of Israel, and could have become a great king. He had even been granted a good portion of the spirit of God to direct him and he had the opportunity to make it the greatest nation of its time, but he was destroyed by vainglory. It's ironic that, if his jealousy had not blinded him and he had worked to uphold the nation before God, he would have gained ten times the glory he worked so hard for but failed to win."

"Yes," Bob agreed, "if he had overcome his infant stage he would have gained all the things he fought so hard to get and never got. This is true on all levels from kings to petty thieves. When their only interest is themselves they don't care who they hurt if they can get what they want."

"And I wonder how depressing it must have been for Saul when he saw that the special spirit of the Lord was transferred from him to David, and it was replaced in him with an evil spirit which was not of the Lord."

Sandy was still awed, "It would be so simple to change the world just by everyone leaving their infant stage."

"And what a wonderful world it would be." Fran added.

# CHAPTER 15

## REBELLION STAGE OF LIFE

John and Lilli arrived at Bob's and Jan's home at the same time Art and Fran drove up. After an exchange of greetings as they walked together to the door, Fran said, "I can't think of any stage worse than the infant stage we studied last week. What stage will we be in tonight?"

John grinned at her comment and replied, "Tonight we will be in rebellion."

"Oh! that sounds even worse than the infant stage."

"Ha, that's one I won't have to worry about," Art declared, "because I'm not ever going to rebel against God, no way."

Lilli glanced at John with a slight smile as they entered the house.

Sandy intercepted Lilli on the way to the table and spoke in a near whisper, "I've been struggling with my infant stage all week. I thought it should be easy to get out of something as destructive as that."

"How did you do?" Lilli asked.

"I'm hopeless," Sandy replied, "I never realized how self-interested I am, but every time I turn around I find myself doing something selfish. If you had asked me last week, I would have denied having a problem, now I don't see how I can overcome it."

"Keep working on it, Sandy, your heart has been opened and you will overcome it," Lilli assured her.

At the table Fran fumbled with her papers and sipped the punch Jan had passed around, then hesitantly interrupted the small talk by asking, "How can rebellion be worse than the infant stage? Aren't they the same thing?"

"Not exactly," John said, "But they do go hand in hand. You can't think in terms of better or worse between them, because either one keeps you from the kingdom, and that is as disastrous as it can get, isn't it?"

"It seems to me," Fran returned, "that the infant stage is something you just fall into but rebellion is something you deliberately do in opposition to God. So it seems you would be punished more for rebellion."

"That sounds reasonable doesn't it?" John answered. "Perhaps our understanding will expand as we study tonight."

"That's the reason I know I don't have to worry about this one," Art stated. "I'm not doing anything against God. I'm sure of that."

"Sandy, would you begin reading?" John asked.

## STAGES OF LIFE NUMBER TWO
## REBELLION

It was murder; premeditated and for gain. He had been warned, but he was in league with the devil and would not be deterred. Cain was as rebellious and guilty of murder as it is possible to be. Those who suggest, "Poor Cain" should receive mercy because his offering to the Lord was rejected while his brother's offering was accepted, have not done their homework. Cain was rebellious from the beginning. See Gen 5:4

"Adam knew Eve, his wife, and she conceived and bare Cain,
and said I have gotten a man from the Lord; wherefore he
may not reject his words. But Cain hearkened not, saying,

152

who is the Lord that I should know him? Vs. 6 Cain loved Satan more than God. And Satan commanded him saying, make an offering unto the Lord...Cain brought of the fruit of the ground...Vs 8 Now Satan knew this (that Cain's offering would be rejected) and it pleased him. Cain was very wroth and his countenance fell. And the Lord said unto Cain, Why art thou wroth? Why is thy countenance fallen? If thou doest well thou shalt be accepted, and if thou doest not well sin lieth at the door; and Satan desireth to have thee..." Vs 11, "Cain was wroth and listened not any more to the voice of the Lord, neither to Able his brother who walked in holiness before the Lord." Vs 12, And Adam also and his wife mourned before the Lord, because of Cain ... Vs 14-21, Satan said unto Cain, swear unto me by thy throat and if thou tell it thou shalt die; and swear thy brethren by their heads, and by the living God, that they tell it not; for if they tell it they shall surely die; and this that thy father may not know it; and this day I will deliver thy brother Able into thy hands. And Satan swear unto Cain that he would do according to his commands. And all these things were done in secret.

And Cain said, *Truly I am Mahan, the master of this great secret.,that I may murder and get gain. Wherefore Cain was called Master Mahan and he gloried in his wickedness.* And Cain went into the field, and Cain talked with Able...and it came to pass that while they were in the field Cain rose up against Able his brother, and slew him. *And Cain gloried in that which he had done, saying, I am free: surely the flocks of my brother falleth into my hand.* And the Lord said unto Cain, where is Abel, thy brother? And he said, I know not, am I my brother's keeper?

## INSTRUCTION REJECTED

Cain's parents had taught goodness to him. They explained the way of God; they prayed for him, and mourned for him. Still Cain chose to go his own way. He said, "who is the Lord that I should know (or listen to) him?"

Cain's example of rebellion against God seems extreme, but actually three typical elements were working:

1. He wanted to go his own way.
2. He refused to listen to counsel from parents, brother, or God.
3. He longed for the things and glory of the world, so he turned to Satan. His greed negated any compassion he might have had for any person in his way.He was even willing to kill to get his brother's flocks and then glory in what he had done.

## CAIN WAS NOT UNIQUE

Unfortunately, Cain's example is not unique. In July of 1990, Stanley Allan Dodd of Vancouver, Washington, was sentenced to die for killing three young boys. His diary told of how they had been sexually abused and tortured. He kept photographs of them in various degrees of mutilation, and he wrote of his plans to do experimental surgery on the next boys he molested. In addition, he wrote of a pact he had made with Satan.

Each day's newspaper seems to recite other terrible examples, and certain individuals and groups are boasting of devil worship.

# REBELLION: A STAGE OF LIFE

We are shocked by horrendous acts like these, but despite our shock at what others have done we have the same three elements of rebellion in our lives. Rebellion is a major stage of life, and it is a primary reason we are in mortal life. As long as we have the freedom to choose, we have the potential of choosing just as Cain did, to tune out God, refusing to listen, then aspire to worldly, carnal, sensual, even devilish, things.

We must remember we are in an early stage of being prepared for the Kingdom of God, and a starting point in our preparation is to rid ourselves of the inclination to turn our backs on our creator and to become gods ourselves. Submission does not come easily to most of us. Social conscience about evil has faded, allowing reprehensible acts to take place without public outcry. People in this stage are often still in the infant stage in which they are the center of their own world, so it is natural for them to long for glory and things of the world for themselves. They refuse to listen to counsel from any source which would prevent their attaining what they have set their hearts upon.

When King Saul disobeyed the Lord and was rejected as king by God, Samuel the prophet asked Saul:

> Hath the Lord as great delight in burnt offerings and sacrifices as in obeying the voice of the Lord? Behold to obey is better than sacrifice, and to hearken, than the fat of rams, *for rebellion is as the sin of witchcraft, and stubborness is as iniquity and Idolatry.*

## UNRECOGNIZED REBELLION

Through the years, Lilli and I have taught many classes. We have held renewal retreats, and spoken to groups. We have found that the one thing more people deny than any other is their rebellion against God. We concluded that this is because many do not recognize rebellion. They believe that since they are not overtly against God, they must be in accord with him; nor do they realize the joy they would have without this barrier between them and God. Romans 3:23 says,

"All have sinned and come short of the glory of God."

This began with the parents of the human race, Adam and Eve. They did not kill. They did not fight against God, they failed to obey one commandment, so they were no longer worthy of Paradise, and were driven out.

Others might also say, "we are not against God, and what we stole was of very little value," but the point is, if it breaks the truth, and bars us from Paradise, what difference does it make whether it was the theft of a penny or millions of dollars? The result is the same. It is like saying a person "is only a little bit dead."

## THERE ARE NO MINOR SINS

We don't have to kill to be guilty of rebellion. The truth and the way to the Kingdom of God is like a bridge across a deep chasm supported by a chain of many links. When one link is broken, whether it is because of greed, or pride, or killing, or other sin, the chain is broken, the bridge collapses. There is no rating to the degrees of rebellion. In Rev. 22:15, lies, whether of the little white lie, or the bold black variety, are rated along with murder.

> For without are dogs, and sorcerers, and whoremongers, and
> murderers, and idolators, and whosoever loveth and maketh
> a lie."

The ultimate test is: will the door to the kingdom be closed when I get there? Any sin we carry will cause the door to remain closed. There can be absolutely no stain of sin in the Kingdom of God. Therefore, our rebellion has locked us out.

## GOD PROVIDES A WAY THROUGH CHRIST

John Newton was the captain of a slave ship when he came to a realization of his wretched condition and turned to Christ. He submitted himself to Christ's service, eventually becoming an effective minister, but he was never able to overcome his amazement at how Christ was willing to redeem someone with his kind of past. He wrote the hymn Amazing Grace. The first line of this hymn reveals how overwhelmed Newton felt at the wonderful redeeming love of Christ. He wrote: "Amazing grace, how sweet thou art, that saved a wretch like me..." When he gave his life to the Lord God accepted him and completely changed him from a dealer in human lives and flesh into a child of the kingdom. His hymn was written as an attempt to express his amazement at the wonder of the transition the Lord had made in him.

A general theme runs through the testimonial stories in the guideposts magazine and others of the same genre. The theme is: I went my own way, rejecting the teachings of my youth, and forgetting God. I even believed God would never again accept me if I did turn to him. I finally became so low and destitute that I had no hope other than God. In misery, I finally called out, "God help me," and God responded to this simple prayer in miraculous ways.

Near the close of world War II, Lew Miller was wounded by German machine gun bullets, two in the head, as well as bullets in his hand, arm and shoulder. He lay in the hospital month after month with no apparent improvement. He finally discovered how to communicate with God, and the man who should have died came back to life. His story was written in a guideposts article called in tune with the infinite March 1978. Later, Lew wrote a book about the experience which he titled prayer through mental imagery. He testifies he was too weak for deep prayer so he visualized himself healed and asked for God's help. God responded to his need with healing.

The radio program, unshackled has, through the years, told the stories of people who walked away from God. Their lives became so wretched and miserable that they had given up hope, but when there was nothing else they could possibly do for themselves, and they were cast off by society and had no one to turn to, when, almost as a dying thought they asked God for help, their lives began the long trip back from the depths of despair.

# KEEPING GOD ON CALL

Some of the people whose lives are told in these stories, who openly rejected God and scorned the thought of calling upon him for help, were not aware that they were in rebellion. They had not consciously chosen to be in opposition; they simply had too many things in their lives with higher priority than God. They did not have time to seek or serve the Lord, so they put God on hold.

Some ways of rebellion seem too innocuous for serious thought, things like, 'It will have to wait until I finish college,' or 'I'm too busy now getting my business off the ground'. Some people think "Everything is going fine; I don't need God's help just now." Many simply closed their eyes and ears to God, expecting to call on him if they ever needed him, but for now they had more important things. Then when the need arose they did not know him.

Rebellion is not always acts committed. Just as often it is the failure to follow the commandments of God. Whatever the reason or way of rebellion, it is always self-defeating. Rather than putting God first in our lives, we often seek riches and pleasures and a happier life, thinking religion a burden. In doing this, we close the way to the richer, happier life we seek because Christ is the way to the kingdom and to peace and to happiness in this life. The commandments so carefully ignored are the instructions on how to gain our greatest success.

"Say," Art said, as he underlined much of the last two paragraphs, "I'm never going to make another statement in this class. I've been in rebellion for years and didn't even know it. I've put everything ahead of God and closed my ears to him. I've kept him on hold for years."

Everyone remained thoughtfully silent.

## RETURNING FROM REBELLION

I've written much about rebellion and it is important to know the way back from it. God has called you to repent, and he has promised you celestial glory if you will turn from evil. But he has been careful not to violate your right to choose to walk alone on your own until you have been baptized and born again. He does not prevent your going on to destruction if you choose. He will not intervene until you invite him by turning your life over to him. When the quicksand of despair is closing over your head, and in desperation you cry out, "God help me" you have given permission for him to intervene and he reaches down to snatch you out.

The testimonies of wise people who have faith in God are that. You do not need to get into such a dreadful condition, or go through such severe processes because you can learn to submit quickly to the will of God and follow his directions whenever you recognize that you are in a trying experience. Give God the right to lead your life. Then, after you have learned the lesson from an experience there is no need for you to continue to be put through this process. Practice recognizing the process you are going through and quickly learning the lesson of each event that takes place in your life. Seriously consider the lesson of each experience, submit to God in a "Thy will be done" attitude. When you can do this, there is no need to be taken into the bitter depth of hopelessness before you get the message.

This is not a secret. There are a multitude of scriptures which testify of this.

I John 3:9 "Whosoever is born of God doth not continue in sin, for the Spirit of God remaineth in him; and he cannot continue in sin, because he is born of God, having received that Holy Spirit of Promise."

II Chron. 26:5 "As long as he sought the Lord, God made him to prosper."

Prov. 3:6 "In all thy ways acknowledge him, and he shall direct thy paths."

Don looked up from his paper and asked "Remember how God told Adam that on the day he was disobedient he would die? Well, I must be dead. I've been guilty all my life."

"If that is true everyone is dead," Bob mused. "Because we have all made the same kinds of mistakes. Isn't there  a scripture somewhere that says, 'All have sinned and come short of the Glory of God?'"

"Actually, everyone in the rebellion stage is nearer to eternal death than they realize," John said. "Fortunately, God knew this was going to happen and he prepared a way for them to turn the disaster of rebellion into dedication and faithfulness."

**BLANK**

# CHAPTER 16

## STAGE OF LIFE NUMBER THREE

## TENTATIVE REACHING OUT

Tonight the study group is meeting at the home of Don and Sandy because Bob's and Jan's living room is being re-carpeted.

"Oh, smell that home baked bread!" each couple said as they entered.

"What will you have, hot bread and butter, or cookies?" Sandy asked.

"Who wants cookies when there's fresh home baked bread?" Art spoke for the group.

"Good," Sandy laughed as she put the hot bread, and raspberry jam on the table, "because I didn't make cookies, I was just teasing. I'll get the honey for those who don't care for the jam."

"Don't spread your papers out until we take care of this bread and jam," Lilli warned John, "or we'll have them all stuck together."

"Who could think of papers at a time like this?"

"I'm going to be glad to get out of the infant and rebellion stages," Fran was almost pleading. "Where are we going tonight?"

"Tonight we are going to start leaving those stages as far behind us as we can. Of course, I can leave them behind in our studies," John teased, "but you may still be struggling with them in life because they have a tendency to hang on."

"I have been working on getting rid of them," Jan offered as she displayed a long list she had made. I've been thinking of some of the ways I have to change to leave them behind. Would you believe how long this list is. I think I'm going to have to change my whole life."

"I think you have already done the hardest part," Lilli told Jan. "You have changed your attitude, so the rest will follow. In fact you may be well through the stage we are going to study tonight."

Art grabbed the last heel of bread saying, "This is my favorite piece," then added "The state I want to get into is the one the people of Enoch's Zion were in."

"That would be great, and maybe you will make it," John said, "Of course, it took the people of Zion three hundred and sixty years to get it all together, but maybe we can work faster now that we have their example."

John began laying out papers as Sandy cleared the table of bread crumbs and jam. Art assured her he could enjoy eating hot bread all evening.

Lilli said, "Okay, I'll start reading tonight."

Sandy in the kitchen called, "Don't start. I'm coming."

## STAGES OF LIFE NUMBER THREE: TENTATIVE REACHING OUT

Hear the first prayer of the Lamanite king. (Alma 13:52) "...the king did bow down before the Lord, upon his knees; Yea, even he did prostrate himself upon the earth, and cried mightily saying, O God, Aaron hath told me there is a God, and if there is a God, and if thou art God, wilt thou make thyself known unto me..."

One day Lilli and I watched the birth of a baby deer. We saw the mother nuzzle the little fawn to its feet for its first steps on long, untried, trembling legs. The drama reminded me of the first tentative steps and reaching to God by a desperate person who has reached the end of a wayward path. The Lamanite king's prayer, "O God, if there is a God" is typical of the person who has reached this impasse. Some have heard of God but have never known him. They question if he really exists, and if he does, will he respond to their need. Others have known God but have wandered so far away they are sure they are condemned forever and they only turn to him in desperation, hoping to beg for mercy and be spared by God's benevolence.

A person is in this condition usually as a result of his infant and rebellion stages. Often he is physically sick and or destitute, he has become so miserable, frustrated and wretched that life seems to have nothing to offer. He may even contemplate suicide. Finally in the hopeless situation he is in, he cries out, "God help me." God responds to even this feeble prayer with an answer that brings a gleam of hope.

**Footnote:**

The king had been reared in a culture that did not recognize God. The teachings of Aaron the Nephite missionary was his first introduction to the concept of a supreme God. Contemplate on how many suicides were people who came to this point and never called for new hope in Christ Jesus who would have reached out to save.

God has been waiting on the sideline, wanting to help, but unable to do so without violating the person's right to reject him. The lost person has been sure he could be a self-made man without the help of God and be his own person, reaching heights of worldly praise and glory. He is too far down the wrong track to turn back without divine help by the time he finds he has made a mistake. No matter how great his error has been, if he looks to God with a desperate prayer, "God help me," The Lord responds.

People are awed by the wonder of God's grace in reaching down in their time of need when they are totally unworthy, and keenly aware of their past rejection of God.

It is an astonishing experience. They are accustomed to the human response in which they might expect the answer to their plea to be, "You got yourself into this trouble. You have had plenty of opportunity to call on me, but you always rejected me. Now I am justified in rejecting you." However, God does not operate through human emotions, and certainly not with spite. We forget that God's work is to bring to pass our immortality and eternal life, but God never forgets.

A time of human desperation is the intersection of a person's need, and is a divine opportunity for God to answer a plea so God reaches out to help and win this soul for eternity.

The mercy God has extended to a despairing person becomes the foundation of a tentative seedling faith.

## AGENCY REMAINS

A person is free to go his own way, even after this kind of experience. However, he may find himself going through crisis after crisis until he builds his tentative reaching out to God into a faith to live by.

Some of the most powerful testimonies of God's love and mercy come from people who had become so debouched and corrupt that society would have turned them over to Satan, but God never abandoned or rejected them.

"Do I understand you to say that a person can go as far into trouble as he can, then all he has to do to turn his life around is say 'God help me' and all is forgiven?" Don asked.

**166**

"Let's put it this way," Lilli suggested, "If a child of yours whom you loved dearly got into serious trouble, you would do everything you could to help, wouldn't you? The thing that surprises people is that God's love never fails no matter how rotten you may become; even when someone puts his hand into Satan's and turns his back on God and is walking into hell, God still loves him."

"That is true," John added, "but when a person is just reaching out from his stage of rebellion his faith in God is so tentative that he really is not expecting anything to happen. What does happen is often very dramatic as God uses the opportunity to bless him."

Lilli brushed her hair back and said, "We have known people who have gone through severe experiences before they finally reached out to God but when they finally did they were astounded at how God blessed them."

"Why would it be so dramatic at a time when he has been in rebellion?" Bob asked.

"Remember, God has been waiting for the invitation to work in that person's life and this is his first invitation," John responded.

"So he moves right in to let the person know he is there," Don added, to complete John's thought.

"It sounds like the story of the prodigal Son," Sandy said. "His father had good reason to kick him out, but he welcomed him back and had a big party for him."

**BLANK**

# CHAPTER 17

## STAGES OF LIFE NUMBER FOUR
## THE ANCIENT AMERICANS

"Here they come," Don called to Art and John who were in Art's inflatable boat fishing a little off shore. John pulled the anchor in because the arrival of Jan and Bob in their motorhome was the signal that the campout dinner being prepared by Sandy and Fran would be served soon.

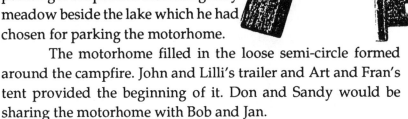

Don was waving his arms and pointing to the place in the small grassy meadow beside the lake which he had chosen for parking the motorhome.

The motorhome filled in the loose semi-circle formed around the campfire. John and Lilli's trailer and Art and Fran's tent provided the beginning of it. Don and Sandy would be sharing the motorhome with Bob and Jan.

"Those last two miles were pretty crooked and rough for a big rig like this," Bob said as he swung out of the drivers seat.

"That's what keeps it so quiet here," Don said. "Most people go where they can drive on pavement right up to their campsite."

"My this is beautiful," Jan said strolling past the campfire to the narrow beach where the waves made by Art's oars were gently rolling up the sand. "Just smell those ponderosa pines," she added looking at the forest around the lake. "I'd like to have a cabin right here. It's so quiet and peaceful."

"That's a real estate broker for you," John said as he stepped out of the boat. "Always wanting to develop any nice piece of ground."

"That's a good idea," Lilli laughed, "I can paint a cabin right here. It will be the perfect finishing touch for my picture." Lilli had been painting a picture of Mt. Achoon's snow peak rising above the pines beyond the lake.

The study group was spending a weekend at Big Dipper Lake in the mountains. Big Dipper is somewhat isolated, being seven miles of uphill grade from the nearest paved road and without developed campsites, so it does not attract the crowds found at some of the better known spots. Just now the smell of freshly brewed coffee and bacon fried with fresh trout was drawing attention to the most important business at hand, dinner. Don retrieved the foil wrapped potatoes from the fire embers and threw on a couple more logs to keep the fire up.

"The only thing missing for this dinner," Art said, "is Sandy's homemade bread and jam."

"Art! Didn't you see the cornbread Fran made?" Sandy asked. "With trout it's better than bread and honey and jam in that picnic basket."

Everyone had filled a plate and found a camp chair or log to settle on for dinner, foregoing the luxury of the tables and cushions in the motorhome and camper. The blessing had been asked on the food when Art exclaimed, "This is the best part of camping."

Shortly they heard a call from down the shore of the lake. Two men were emerging from the pines just beyond the edge of the meadow and came toward the campers. As the men drew near they called "Hello, can we join you?"

Without answering Don waved them into camp.

"You are the first people we have seen for two days," the taller one said as they took off their packs and leaned them against a log. Then holding out his hand to Don who was nearest them he said, "I'm Ted," and motioning to his companion added, "this is Paul." "We have been hiking the trail from Canada to Mexico. We knew someone was near because we could smell coffee for the last mile. Do you mind if we cook some fish on your fire? We have only eaten freeze-dried food all day."

"Better yet, why not take one of those paper plates and join us," Bob said. "I'm sure these cooks fixed enough for all of us."

"That would be great," Paul was already reaching for a plate and cup. "We could build a fire and cook, but it would take an hour, and I'm starved now."

Ted chuckled. "Paul's appetite goes up with the altitude. We haven't stopped to cook today; we've eaten right out of the packages. Say this coffee sure hits the spot."

"How long have you been on the trail?" Jan inquired

"Two weeks this time," Ted replied "We planned to walk from Panama to Nome Alaska. Last winter we spent three months in Mexico and Peru. We gave up on going all the way to Panama."

"Those Sierra Madre Mountains in Mexico proved more of a challenge than we had counted on," Paul explained. "At one place we had to go up to nearly sixteen thousand feet. They are unbelievably rough. We learned a lot, and I'm glad we went, but I'd never want to do it again. Now I think the trail and snow in Alaska would kill us off before we reached Nome so we will probably settle for Valdez."

"Those are pretty ambitious hikes," Bob said.

"Yes," Ted agreed, "We take part in it each year. This year we are trying to go border to border through the states, and next year we will take on Canada."

"We have had a good time and seen a lot. We have met a good many nice people. We usually try to camp at night with other people if we can. I hope you don't mind if we camp with you tonight."

"There's a nice spot for a tent right over there," Art pointed out a likely place.

## THE CAMPFIRE

The dinner dishes were washed and the food put away for the night and Sandy was humming 'Amazing Grace' as Don put more wood on the fire. Others joined in with Sandy until they broke out in singing the song. This was followed by 'This Is My Father's World'. Ted and Paul joined in readily as other hymns followed.

As the pastel blue of the sky gave way to ribbons of gold and red, and violet rays of the setting sun reflected off of Big Dipper Lake, Jan turned to John. "How did you get into the ministry? Was your father a minister?"

"No," John answered "He was a faithful Christian supporter of the Restoration Gospel but not a minister. I came through a roundabout way. It's probably a longer story than you would care to listen to."

"I love to hear stories like that around a campfire," Sandy encouraged. "We have all evening—not even a TV to bother with."

"It is an interesting story." Lilli said, "You had really ought to share it with them."

With more encouragement from Bob, John began. "Some people like to trace their geneology back to royalty; but if I traced mine, I'm sure it would lead me to the Prodigal Son."

"We must be brothers," Art laughed.

"Now you know how he knew so much about the Rebellion Stage," Lilli joked.

"I went through every day of World War II, and even though I had been a fair Bible student, and always had a strong faith in Christ, by the time of my discharge in 1946, I had become case hardened. Few feelings or emotions could break through. Except for Lilli, I could no longer love deeply or appreciate beauty. I found it difficult to feel compassion. Lovely things like roses and sunsets no longer touched me. Emotionally, I was dead to them. I was aware that my feelings were shallow; I had lost something precious, a critical element that made life rich and beautiful, but I knew of no way to regain it."

Art had been listening carefully and now spoke earnestly, "I know just what you mean. After my tour of duty in Vietnam nothing has seemed important anymore. Things I used to really care about, things that touched me right here," he said, putting his hand on his heart, "just don't matter anymore. I know something is wrong and I would like to get back what I used to have, but I've never been able to go back."

"Maybe John's story will help you find it again," Lilli told him.

"Lilli and I began attending churches trying to find God, but discouragement set in more deeply each week. In my search, more questions arose but no light came through to bring answers. The day came when I told Lilli, "These preachers all have one theme: 'Christ died for your sins, so give us your money'. I'm not going to church again until God himself calls me."

"Lilli made a few attempts to get me to church, but I was adamant. My brother made several trips of over three hundred miles to get me to church. I refused to go. In the meantime, I had become a third-year engineering student at Oregon State University, but spiritually I was in a long dark tunnel."

"My two evangelistic sisters tried to coerce me into reading the BOOK OF MORMON, a book about the colony of people who came to Central America from Jerusalem, and the history of God leading them. They said these were the 'other sheep' which Jesus referred to (John 10:16) other sheep I have, which are not of this fold—

Ted and Paul sat up visibly interested.

"I had read some horrible things about that book, and had no intention of reading it," John continued. "Finally, to satisfy them, I agreed to look through it. Secretly, I felt that as a knowledgeable college student I could find enough in it to refute it in short order. As I read, it soon became apparent that the horror stories I had read about the book must have been written by prejudiced people who had never even read it.

"They were not close to the truth. The book was a straightforward history of people of faith who God had led out of Jerusalem to a promised land and another group led from the Tower of Babel when God said, I, the Lord, will scatter them abroad from thence, upon all the face of the land, and unto every quarter of the earth (Gen. 11:5). It told of blessings upon them when they clung to his ways, and the darkness that overtook them when they turned from him. It wonderfully illustrated things I had read in the Bible. Reading this added testimony by ancient people halfway around the world from Jerusalem, but living under the same God, I gained more understanding of the Bible than from reading the Bible alone. It didn't change what I had read in the Bible. It enlarged it.

"I had said I would not return to church unless God himself called me. Now, as I read the Book of Mormon, the Spirit of the Lord gripped me with a power that bored to the center of my heart and opened a well of conviction and feelings which I thought had been dried up forever. I discovered that he who seeks God has already found him, and my soul was expanding.

"The ancient people of this land came to life. They were real and and they were struggling with eternal issues just as I had. I could see the tender finger of God leading them through this life preparing them for his kingdom.

"The perspective of looking back through the stream of time and reliving their triumphs and disasters with them revealed the nature and compassion of God better than a photograph of him. My heart was touched to depths I never thought possible. I had come out of the dark tunnel into a beautiful valley. I recognized this as a moment uniquely fashioned by God.

"I am not a member of the Mormon Church in Salt Lake City, nor of the church headquartered in Independence, Missouri, but I have used this book ever since because I find in it a clear image of The God of the Bible.

"My personal experience is not related here to provide a testimony of the Book of Mormon; it is intended to reveal how I was lead into the happiest of all stages of life: hungering and thirsting for knowledge of God. God used the record of these ancient people to rekindle my yearning to draw near to him. It was the catalyst for bridging the gap between my tentative desire to know God and a full faith. He was welcoming the prodigal son back.

"Other people return to an accord with God through different vehicles. We have seen individuals leap over the chasm when they get all the people, and the chronological order, and the history of the Bible sorted out so they can see God working through a planned process throughout time. During our retreats, people transcend the gulf by a directed, deep, spiritual experience which brings them into a yearning to come to God. There are other ways of making this leap; the results are the same.

"It was so meaningful to me that eventually Lilli and I began the Keys classes and retreats. We have seen it help others so dramatically that now we are putting it into a book.

"It is our fervent prayer that our book will be a vehicle for many others to make the transition."

"I can't speak for others, but it has made a dramatic change in our lives," Jan said.

"We have almost been able to see the kingdom as we have studied," Don added.

Sandy and Fran nodded agreement.

Ted and Paul had been listening intently with a growing excitement as though they were making an important discovery.

"When we were hiking Mexico," Paul said, "We saw the cities those people built. The ruins of those cities are being dug up everywhere. We climbed up one of the finest and largest pyramids in the world. It's called the Pyramid of The Sun and not far from it is a smaller one called The Pyramid of The Moon. We also saw an astronomical observatory they built."

"They had a very accurate calendar," Ted quickly moved in on the story. "They were very advanced for their time. They knew the earth moved around the sun and they knew precisely how long it took. They also knew the orbits of other planets. They knew that Venus was both the morning and evening star and that it took 583.92 days to complete one cycle. They apparently did some kind of surgery. There have been skulls found which have holes in them and plates fastened over the holes. The operations must have been successful because the bone had been growing back to fill the holes."

"We walked part of a highway they built which is over a thousand years old and a thousand miles long," Paul said.

"Places where earthquakes and forests have not destroyed it much of it is still good road."

"We went to the museum in Mexico City. They have fantastic things there from the civilization those people built. They had beautiful fine linen and jewelry," Ted related. "We took a lot of pictures, I wish we had them here to show you."

"The ruins from that civilization are all over the countries down there, especially Mexico and Peru.

"They told us of others farther South, but we didn't get to them," Paul explained.

Ted added, "In the museum we saw thin sheets of gold those people had used to write on. Apparently for things they wanted preserved. Many words and names and legends, such as the story of creation, are very much like those from the Hebrews in Jerusalem. The ancients worshipped a God they called Quetzalcoatl who they believed to have been the creator God, a God of Peace, who was born of a virgin, and had been crucified on a cross. He descended to them on a cloud, and when he left he promised someday to return."

Paul and Ted talked about the ancient civilization and the knowledge of physics, science and agriculture used by these people whom God had led away from Jerusalem so long ago. The study group was a spellbound audience listening to these adventures until the embers of the campfire turned black and brilliant stars filled the sky.

## FAREWELL TO TED AND PAUL

The sun was high and warming the tent when Art and Fran woke up. The night before, the stars had been brilliant for hours as the group sat around the campfire and listened to Ted and Paul tell of the ancients of Mexico and countries in the south.

Lilli came out of the camper and called to Art, "Where's the other tent?"

Ted and Paul were gone. They had left a note written on a flattened paper sack weighted down by a rock on the picnic table. "Thanks for your hospitality. We enjoyed camping with you, but we like to get on the trail early. Hope we meet again someday. Paul and Ted."

**BLANK**

# CHAPTER 18

## STAGE NUMBER FIVE
## HUNGERING AND THIRSTING FOR
## KNOWLEDGE OF GOD

"Paul and Ted touched our lives very briefly, but in a special way. They would have made a fine addition to our group," John noted as he sat on a log by the fire with a plate of bacon and eggs and pancakes.

"That's the way so many of life's contacts are. They touch you for a moment and then they are only a memory,"Lilli added. "But they make an impact on you."

"I was fascinated by what they told of the ruins of the ancient civilizations in Mexico and farther south. I had read about them in the National Geographic Magazine not long ago," Bob said, "But I never felt any kind of link with those people from the past. Now I feel that there is some kind of a bond between them and me. Does that make sense?"

Art set his coffee down on a stump. "They made me want to go down there and see it sometime."

"Not without me," Fran chirped. "Remember I'm the one who speaks Spanish."

While others talked on about a trip to Mexico, John wrote each of their names on slips of paper and put them in Bob's 49ers cap. "I want each of you to draw a name from this hat."

"To see who does the dishes?" Sandy grinned.

"No, not for that. Now don't tell whose name you draw

and if you get your own or your spouse's put it back and draw again."

After the drawing John explained, "Think about the name you have drawn. Tomorrow afternoon before we leave here each of us will give a present to the person whose name we have drawn."

"But there's no store within fifty miles of here," Fran objected.

"That's the idea. We don't want you to go buy a present. Just give some personal item which has meaning to you. The monetary value is not important, something you have made would be fine, the value is in the feeling that accompanies it," John explained.

"We do this at our retreats and it's best if it is not something you have bought or paid a lot for. At one retreat someone painted a funny shaped rock with her fingernail polish because she didn't have paint with her. I still have it," Lilli said. "John has two sheets of paper, like a scroll with psalms handwritten on them that were given to him. I'm sure we can find something suitable."

## LUNCH

Appetites seemed to be as high as the sun which was at the peak of its run, and the campers were straggling into the circle. Bob and Art beached the boat and Don called to them, "How's fishing?" Bob answered, "Art is the champ. He caught four, I only got three."

Art held up his string of fish, "Look at these beauties. This one is nearly eleven inches, that one is ten, and the others are about nine."

"Where are Jan and Sandy?" Bob asked.

Lilli, who was cleaning her paint brushes, pointed down

the lake shore and replied "They took their poles and went down there to fish along the bank. Here they come now— way down there." She pointed at the two figures emerging from the willows.

"I doubt if they could do much good from the bank," Art commented. "You can't get your line far enough out into the lake."

Fran began setting out sandwich supplies for the campers to prepare their own, "Art, your hands smell like fish eggs. I don't want my sandwich to taste like them. There's the soap."

"Hey look what they have," Don called as Sandy and Jan walked into camp and held up a string of five fish each. "Where did you catch those?" Art exclaimed. "What were you using?"

"Down there along the bank from that big rock," Jan said as she held up a fourteen-inch trout for display.

"My largest one is only thirteen inches, but isn't it a beauty?" Sandy displayed hers.

"But what did you catch them on?" Art had to know.

"We were using flies. Mine was a Royal Coachman," Jan answered. Then pausing in front of Lilli's easel she exclaimed, "Lilli, that painting is beautiful. Just look at that sky and the reflections in the water." After studying it a moment she added, "I don't know what it is, but it really does something to me. It makes makes me feel so—I know what it is. You have not only captured the scene, you have somehow put the feeling or spirit of our group into it. I Love it!"

# HUNGERING AND THIRSTING FOR KNOWLEDGE OF GOD

The group had drifted to the shade of some tall Ponderosa pines. Jan said to John, "Last night you mentioned hungering and thirsting for a knowledge of God as the happiest stage of all. Would you tell us what you meant?"

"I like to talk about that stage," John replied, "because it is such a joyous time. It is a natural outgrowth of the tentative reaching out we studied last and I think it is the stage this group is entering just now, so you should know about it and enioy it to the fullest.

"Our tentative outreach creates a growing faith in God which in turn creates within us an openness to God which we had not known. As this openness matures we reach a point at which we suddenly want to know God as intimately as possible. We read everything we can. We pray to God for light and understanding, we listen to other people's experiences and savor anything that draws us nearer to God. Our entire life begins to change. We may not change our work, but our attitude toward our work changes. The temporal things of life take on more beauty for us but we no longer grasp for temporal things as though our eternal lives depend upon how much we can accumulate."

"You are describing just the way I feel," Don said. "I seem to have an aching desire inside of me to speak with God, or to know I am acceptable to him. It might best be described as falling in love, but how can you fall in love with someone you have never seen and don't know?"

"I think you have a good hold on what this stage is all about," John said.

Lilli reached across Don's shoulder and gave him a quick hug. "You cannot withold love and worship when you are deluged by the overwhelming love you receive from God when you become receptive to it. He has waited a long time for you to open to him in this way. You are beginning to see God more than you realize."

"The awareness that you are of special loving concern to the infinite creator of the universe exceeds the mind's ability to grasp it." John agreed.

The parable of the prodigal Son tells of a great celebration when the son returned, and so it is when we come home to God. It goes beyond festivities. A hunger to know all about God and the way of eternal life grips you. Answers to questions which have perplexed you perhaps for years suddenly fall into place and a broad mural of God's works through the ages is painted across the wall of your mind. You pray, you read, and meditate upon the things revealed to you. Although you may have been baptized previously, you experience a true personal baptismal experience, and the Holy Spirit begins his work of leading you into all truth.

Jan's eyes were blurry moist. "That must be where I am. I feel so full and yet I have so many questions I feel starved."

## GOD HAS BEEN WAITING

John continued. "What actually happens is that your Eternal Father has been anxiously waiting all your life to bestow his blessings on you—his child. Now that you have granted him the opportunity, you are surrounded, almost submerged, as gifts are bestowed upon you.

"Your life is changing. Worldly things that you aspired to a short time ago become meaningless. You begin uprooting and getting them out of your life. Some things you aspired to yesterday you are repenting of today. You are being molded into the likeness of God. True worship has caused your pride to cave in and love and generosity drowns selfishness and greed. Trust in our eternal Heavenly Father bleaches out every spot of fear. A new person is emerging.

"We sense the heights of the worship of David the shepherd boy and David the King of Israel as he stood under Palestinian skies and looked to the heavens. In this kind of experience, he exclaimed:

I will extol thee my God O King; and I will
bless thy name for ever and ever.  Every
day will I bless thee; and I will praise thy
name for ever and ever. Great is the Lord,
and greatly to be praised; and his great-
ness is unsearchable. One generation shall
praise thy works to another, and shall
declare thy mighty acts. I will speak of thy
glorious honor of thy majesty, and of thy
wonderous works. Psalms 145"

"Amen," Bob said quietly. Sandy reached out her hand
and gave Bob an understanding touch.

"This is a sublime moment." John was looking at the coals
in the campfire. We are hushed by the awareness that we truly are
loved by God. And we are spellbound by the assurance in John
6:47, "He that believeth on me hath life everlasting." When we
come into this stage in our spiritual growth, who can help but
hunger and thirst for the knowledge of God?

"I would like for you to do something special this afternoon," John said. "Take a couple of hours and go off by yourself,
and have a quiet time of meditation. Perhaps you can reread
some of the things we have studied. Have individual prayers,
read the scriptures, but most of all, just meditate.

"Consider such scriptual promises as these:

John 8:12, I am the light of the world, He that followeth me
shall not walk in darkness, but shall have the light of life.

John 8:32 Ye shall know the truth and the truth shall make
you free.

John 14:7, If ye had known me ye should have known the
father also and from henceforth ye know him and have seen
him."

# CHAPTER 19

## STAGE SIX
## IN THE HAND OF GOD WITHOUT
## RESERVATION

## SATURDAY EVENING CAMPFIRE

Art, normally somewhat brash, was subdued and meditative. He had been this way all through dinner. Something had certainly affected him. In fact, the entire group was quiet and lost in private thoughts except Don and Jan, who were excitedly talking of their experiences of the afternoon.

"I knew the Lord was there and as I spoke to him the answers came back by clear thoughts planted in my mind so I could not misunderstand," Jan was saying.

Don agreed and added, "I found myself voluntarily making dedications I would never have considered making just a couple of weeks ago."

The group now gathered around the campfire faced the lake so they could watch the reflection of the setting sun on the water. Bob was preparing his gasoline lantern for use later.

John put more wood on the fire, then said, "Let's offer our opening prayer and invite the Spirit of God to direct our thoughts tonight." Lilli stood close to John. Bob set down the lantern and put his arm around Jan. Don and Sandy sitting in their campchairs reached out to clasp hands. Fran and Art stood together and held hands as John began, "O God our creator, in whose hands are the lives and destinies of all thy children. We look up to thee tonight for thou art the God who walked and talked with Adam , and Enoch, and Abraham, and Moses, and today has walked and talked with us. We sense thy spirit has already descended upon this little congregation, for our hearts are full and we have difficulty expressing the unspeakable joy within us. We pray thy spirit to quicken our minds and inspire our thoughts as we seek thee through our studies and prayers and meditations. We pray that the mysteries of thy kingdom would open to us as we walk hand in hand on the narrow path that leads us to that sacred setting. We come to thee in the name of Thy Son who promised, 'I am come that they might have life, and have it more abundantly,' We thank thee for the large measure of that abundant life which we have received today."

Moving his camp chair so he could face the circle better, John sat down and began, "I am aware that something special has happened to you today. For some it is difficult to talk about it until it has had time to be distilled by your meditations for a few days and the lump in your throat has time to subside. Others may want to share while it is fresh in your mind."

Jan was first to respond. "I didn't know just how to start my prayer and meditation so I simply asked God for help and that my life would be acceptable to him. I can't tell you how I know, but I do know the Lord was with me. It seemed like he was all around me, like I was in the middle of him like being in the middle of a glowing light. It brought a wonderful feeling of peace, of being loved more that I've ever felt. I never wanted it to end."

Art said, "I didn't plan to talk about this. I was afraid no one would understand or believe me, but now I want to tell you." "I sat by that big pine at the edge of the lake and when I closed my eyes and began to think of the master keys and others we have studied it seemed that I opened my eyes and saw a beam of light right at my feet. It went out over the lake and on up into the sky. I had an assurance that I could walk on it and when I reached the other end I would be standing in the Kingdom of God. It was so attractive to me that there was nothing in the world I could think of that would tempt me back. I stood up to go but as I lifted my foot to begin walking on the beam of light a voice said, 'Not now,' and the beam disappeared. But that beam was the most real thing I've ever seen. Before this I never could understand how Jesus walked on water, but now I can, because I know that I could have walked on that beam of light if the time had been right for me to go."

Don wanted to share his experience. "I took some of our papers and went to the top of that hill overlooking the lake and as I meditated it was like I was reliving past experiences but this time from a different perspective. Like I had lived them once before, but never realized the Lord was, with me. This time I knew he was so I began to write. Now, I'm not a poet. I've never done this before, and it may not be in proper form for poetry, but I felt a sense of poetry as I wrote."

## I KNEW THAT GOD WAS THERE

I looked down from the mountain top
Saw the vapors lifted from the ocean
To fall upon the forested hills and verdant valleys
so life might be
I knew that God was there

I walked along the seashore
Felt the tremendous power of the continuously moving waters
Was touched by the majesty, beauty and depth

# KEYS TO THE HIDDEN MYSTERIES

beyond my ability to understand
I knew that God was there

I walked the crowded city streets
Watched the grim faces of the harried crowds
Soften into smiles as distant church bells chimed
I knew that God was there

I stood beside a newborn baby's crib
And cupped a tiny perfect hand in mine
was awed by the potential of newly created life
I knew that God was there

I stood beside the casket of a loved one passed beyond
Was reassured by the eternal promise
"They that love and serve the Lord shall never die
but have everlasting life"
I knew that God was there

I sat in deep contemplation of the solemnities of eternity
My mortal life's pilgrimage
The Lord's care of me through every day
My calling to serve until one day he places his arm
upon my shoulder and walks me to his home
I knew that God was there

I lifted my eyes to the sunset
Saw the magnificent panorama of light and color
spread across the sky
My day closed with wonder, awe and peace
and I knew that God was there

"And just now," Don continued," I want to add another line."

> I felt the spirit pull me to this campfire
> I came into the sanctuary of our circle
> Felt the bond of friendship flow between us
> Heard the soft strains of Sandy's humming
> I know that God is here

John looked at the faces around the campfire and smiled. "The smoke must be getting in our eyes," he said.

Lilli addressed the group. "I want to share with you my experience at one of our first retreats. I had been somewhat down and discouraged but I went out to a secluded spot beside a stream of clear mountain water. I closed my eyes to pray to God. I felt a touch on my shoulder so I opened my eyes but there was nobody there that I could see, still I knew there was a presence just beyond the visible world which I could almost reach out and touch. As Jan related a moment ago, I felt that I was surrounded by a presence, and it seemed that a pure white cloak was placed on my shoulders and wrapped around me filling me with a joy and an assurance of God's acceptance of me. That cloak has never been taken away and in moments of discouragement I can sit down and close my eyes and feel that presence and seem to hear the words, 'I will never leave you nor forsake you.' It has truly been an abiding comforter to me."

There was silence in the group for a time, then John said, "I will tell you of an experience I had because it made me aware of certain principles which are applicable to each of us ."

The following is John's experience.

## STAGE SIX OF LIFE

I had been in the ministry for nine years and I thought I was as dedicated as it was possible to be. In my prayers I often used the phrase, "Thy will be done," reverently believing this to be my true desire, but subconciously I had reservations, such as, "Don't ask me to serve through blindness, don't ask me to serve through poverty, don't send me to Russia to preach at the Kremlin, etc." I had never put these into words; I had just hoped God would not require such of me. It had never occurred to me that "Thy will be done" could be a dangerous prayer.

The fall of 1964 I attended a weekend retreat for ministers near Battleground, Washington. Sunday afternoon, at the conclusion of the meetings, I was deeply moved by the spirit which attended this group of dedicated men, and I went alone into the nearby forest and knelt in prayer. What happened then took me several weeks to understand, and my life has never been the same. I was conveyed into a sharp awareness of Christ as never before.

## PRAYER OF DEDICATION

I began to open my inner heart in a prayer of worship and dedication. Then for the first time in my life and from the depths of my heart, with real intent and fully understanding the implications of what I was saying, I prayed, "thy will be done." I had no reservations. I was dedicated to the thought that whatever God might bring to pass in my life was what I wanted. I willingly offered myself to any sort of service he asked of me, thankful for the opportunity to make any sacrifice.

I was perplexed by what happened. I had expected a heavy responsibility to be laid upon me. Instead, every burden of care I bore was wafted away and I sensed a freedom such as I could not have imagined. There came to me a peacefulness as though all the world's time and motion were standing still and I was cradled in the everlasting, protective arms of God. In this sublime moment an indescribable happiness totally filled me. The wonder of that hallowed moment distilled in my heart compelling me to exclaim, "My God how wonderful thou art."

I recognized that this was a moment uniquely fashioned by God. Although it seemed I was under this endowment of the Spirit for only a moment, it proved to be over an hour; and the spirit that penetrated my soul that day lingered for days creating within me a deep meditation.

What happened? I wondered. Why was the experience so different from anything I could have expected? And how could I have such joy and freedom through telling God I was ready to accept anything he might bring to pass in my life? Lilli gave me the first clue as I recounted the experience to her. She said, "When you say, 'Thy will be done,' the load is transferred from you to the Lord. He carries the burden." It was immediately obvious that this was true. I no longer carried that load, but what about the peace and joy I felt?

## ENLIGHTENMENT COMES

I began to understand that I had put myself into the hand of God without reservation. So what could possibly come to me other than what God ordained? And what he willed was only that which was for my eternal good. Nothing else could come. There was nothing to fear, no reason for worry, no competition to reach for something greater, just a wonderful peace. In time, I began to see that I had fulfilled the first great commandment, to love the Lord thy God with all thy heart, and with all thy soul, and with all thy mind. I was totally submissive to his will, and the

191

promised divine influence flowed into me, bringing the leaven of healing, hope and joy, opening those insights and understandings which have been the heritage of the Enochs and Moses and Davids who have walked with the Lord.

# THE MOMENT OF ENTRANCE TO STAGE SIX

It is a portentous moment in your life when the finger of the Lord has been placed upon you, opening your heart to receive the revelation that "This is life eternal, that they may know thee the only true God, and Jesus Christ whom he has sent."

This is not the last stage of our lives, and it is never true that once the powers of heaven have converged upon you, you have fulfilled your life's mission and can joyfully await the Lord to call you home. You are still surrounded by the world and its influences. Satan is using every force he commands to snare you. The commitments of time pull at you, so the struggle to remain totally submissive to God continues, but now you have a new strength instilled within you which is the promised well of living water that never runs dry. And you receive, "The peace that passeth all understanding."

# A NEW VISION AND QUEST FOR THE KINGDOM

After you have fulfilled the first great commandment and have given your life unreservedly to God your whole perspective on life changes. You are secure in the knowledge that God is in control. You have no need to fear or worry because nothing can come to you except those things that God permits, and it is his work to bring to pass your immortality and eternal life. Only those things that further that objective can reach you. The passion to achieve great acclaim in this world no longer drives you, because the riches of the Celestial Kingdom await you. You lean on the promise of D.C. 10:3, "Seek not for riches, but for wisdom, and, behold the mysteries of God shall be unfolded to you, and then shall you be made rich; behold, he that hath eternal life is rich." With these concerns behind you your concerned attention is diverted to the problems of other people.

When your attention is diverted from personal concerns to compassionate ministry for others you fulfill the second great commandment, to love others as yourself. You are busy with your concerns for others. Your drive to attain the kingdom for yourself fades to oblivion.

You reach out your hand to lift another and with the other hand you point to the heaven above. As together you look up, you discover the clouds folding back to reveal Christ in all his glory, for he is our glimpse into the eternal world, and you sense a fulfillment of the promise (85:12) of the flow of the life of God into your soul.

# CHAPTER 20

## SUNDAY MORNING AT BIG DIPPER LAKE

### STAGE OF LIFE NUMBER SEVEN
### TESTING AND SPIRITUAL GROWTH

Lilli breathed the fresh mountain air. It was a mixture of morning dew on Ponderosa pines, fresh coffee, and bacon frying. She shook John, "Wake up! We went to Paradise! Just smell that!"

The sun had risen above the eastern hills and was shining full onto the white face of Mt. Achoon. The song of a killdeer running along the lake shore sliced the air. John turned to Lilli, "It looks like Paradise too."

Don had built up the campfire and had gone to a log at the edge of the lake to watch the changing reflections of the mountain on the water. Bob was at the picnic table looking up some references in his papers. Jan and Sandy were cooking the bacon, pancakes and coffee in the motorhome while Art and Fran fried the eggs and hashbrowns on the campstove. As John and Lilli emerged from the camper, Art called, "Now we have to believe in the resurrection of the dead."

After breakfast Lilli and Fran prepared for a worship by singing 'There's An Old Path'. Jan called from the motorhome where she and Sandy were doing dishes, "Wait for us."

"We are just singing until you get here" Fran
returned. The chosen text, Alma, 9:15-20

It is given unto many to know the mysteries of God—he that
will not harden his heart, to him is given the greater portion
of the word, until they know them in full; and they that will
harden their hearts, to them is given the lesser portion of the
word, until they know nothing concerning his mysteries;
and then they are taken captive by the devil and led by his
will down to destruction...

After the closing hymn, 'In Heavenly Love Abiding, No
Change My Heart Shall Fear,' and the closing prayer, Bob turned
to John, "That's one thing I no longer have to fear."

"What is?" John asked.

"After the experience of this weekend I will no longer fear
being taken captive by the devil, I've gotten so much insight and
strength from the experiences here that I know I'll never follow
Satan."

"Oh don't say that!" Lilli exclaimed. "That is the most
dangerous thought you can have."

"Why?" Don was surprised, "Last night John said that
once we had put ourselves into God's hand nothing could come
to us except what God permitted, and I've certainly dedicated my
life to God."

"There is one dangerous threat," Lilli warned. "You still
have your agency."

"I don't understand."

"This is what we planned to study this morning, and your
comment demonstrates the reason it is so important." John said.

"I just I don't understand what could be so dangerous
while I am in God's hand." Bob said.

John continued, "The danger is from wrong choices.

Satan cannot tear you away but he has means of quietly luring you out, and other more violent ways. Let's begin. You will see what we mean. Do you want to read first, Bob?"

# STAGE SEVEN
# SPIRITUAL GROWING AND TESTING TIME

There is a fantasy abroad that once you have accepted Christ as your savior your part is done; you can relax and wait for him to come for you. So it is a severe shock to those who have been lulled into this concept to discover that they are not immune to problems and temptations with which the rest of the world struggles. Some are shaken to the roots of their faith. Some fall away. Very many do not proceed.

Important principles are at work here, so we need to return to our master keys. (1) My work and my glory is to bring to pass the immortality and eternal life of man; (2) Let us make man in our image and likeness.

We have to keep focused on these keys, They set our course. You recall that this was the purpose of God from before the creation, and he will not be deterred from his objective.

The stages we have been through to this point led us to place our lives in God's hands, finally giving him permission to work within us. No matter what our age, when we give God permission, the work of molding us into the likeness of God is only beginning.

The powers of opposition attack us as they did Jesus in the wilderness when he was at the beginning of his earthly ministry. He was not immune to these attacks, nor are we.

Returning again to the plans for creation, we recall that man was to be released in the mortal life laboratory earth. Man had a royal heritage written in the millenniums of time, but

Lucifer was going to meet him here and use every scheme he could devise to rob man of his inheritance and bind him for delivery to hell.

God will not bind Satan to protect us from him because it is important that we meet Satan and render him powerless in our life as Jesus did by not succumbing to him. He offers us the directions for living the kind of life which can overcome the beckoning powers of darkness, but we must choose to apply the directions and live by them. It is like the relationship of a boxer and his coach. The coach gives him instructions which will make his fight successful, but then the coach must stay outside the ring while the boxer locks in battle with the opponent.

Don had been quietly sipping his coffee. "Now I can see the reason you call being obedient to Gods commandments a matter of following God's directions. It seems your greatest protection is to follow those directions so closely that they are an ingrained part of your life which you refuse to deviate from no matter what happens."

"This is one of the greatest of all the stages in life," Lilli affirmed. "This is the only way we can be tried and proven, and the results of these temptations are the tests by which we will be judged at the final day."

There has to be a screening of those who lean, even imperceptibly, towards Satan. So Satan is granted access to us just as God has. We meet Satan head-on as he spreads his tempting wares before us. We cannot be spared the temptation. We have to meet the devil in experience after experience for the rest of our mortal lives and learn always to win over him by choosing and obeying God. This is our strength. Although Satan cannot tear us away from God by force he is adept at planting thoughts in our minds that cause us to step out from the shelter of God's everlasting arm. This could, for example, come by way of a comment he plants through someone else which causes you anger, or jealousy. Before we realize that we have been duped, there is a deep rift between us and the other person; even worse, it creates a rift between us and God. Satan can allow us to see an opportunity for more money or honor if we will spend just a little of the time you have been giving to serving others to working for some worldly cause, and we are assured, by Satan, that "after all we deserve it." We can be induced by Satan to do an act that is damaging to us. We lash out physically, or go to court to get even, and hate wells up within us by the time we realize the dark powers that caused the trouble, we may be so deeply involved it seems impossible to return to God. But that is our only hope and strength.

Meeting the guile of Satan is a dangerous but necessary experience. It is through learning to overcome the devil and be true to God that we are proven worthy and acceptable. It is encouraging to know that if we defeat Satan in this life we will never meet him again. In Paradise and beyond he will not exist.

Sandy reads:

# A DANGEROUS TIME

At this point you have learned and received enough to convict you at the judgment if you fall away. You are positive that you will never fall. You think you are so sufficient now in your own strength that nothing could tear you away. The moment you tell yourself that you are strong enough to face Satan alone, you are at your weakest and most vulnerable. Because by determining to go alone, you place God on the sideline where he can only watch.

"Let's stop a minute and look at that," John said. "I can recall a time when I thought I had so many wonderful spiritual experiences with God that I would never fall. I felt secure. Almost immediately, Satan moved in an insidious way that I did not recognize until too late, and found myself in serious trouble. This has happened to us so many times that we have learned we don't have the power to stand before Satan without God's help."

"You and Lilli fell?" Sandy exclaimed "I find that hard to believe."

"Yes, Sandy," John answered. "We had never been warned about this process, so we were caught thinking we were at a level where we would have no problems. Since we were unprepared, we were vulnerable. By the time we discovered we were being manipulated by evil we were in trouble.

"We have learned that we need to lean on God for help every day of our lives. We were led into trouble without our realizing it, but we always turned back to God and asked for forgiveness. It was never an easy path back, but once we made the return we were stronger because we knew more. Now a part of our prayers everyday is for God to stand between us and Satan. There is another important lesson for you in this. Never, ever, put such faith in any person that when they fall it causes you to fall. That's true even if he has a title of prophet, apostle, bishop, or pastor. Holy robes and pretentious titles have never been a shield against sin. Under the robe and title there is a human being the devil is trying to win."

"There is another lesson in this as well," Lilli pointed out, "When a good person does fail you can understand what has happened, and instead of condemnation you can offer understanding and compassion. Your friendship may help the fallen to be restored."

"You are suggesting then," Bob asked, "That only God can protect you against Satan, and you have to continually be aware of your need for his support?"

"Exactly!" John said. "It is as important to understand our weakness and how subject we are to falling when we try to go it on our own as it is to have experiences with God in the beginning."

"We were unprepared for this kind of experience," Lilli added, "Now we always emphasize it to all our groups so they can prepare for it."

"When you lay it out that way, it is so obvious I wonder why I never realized these things happen," Bob said.

"Do you understand why I was so alarmed?" Lilli asked.

"Yes," Bob replied, "I hope I never try to go it alone."

"If we are to move forward toward the kingdom, our credentials must declare we that are free of the bonds of Satan. However, we will never be free of his attempts to get us into bondage to him during the rest of our mortal lives, so we will continue to pass through the fire of temptation. We must be certain we can safely pass through without succumbing to him.

"You can take comfort in the fact that temptations do lose their power when you concentrate your concerns on the Lord and build your aspirations on those things he opens to you rather than aspiring to things of the world, such as glory, or power.

"One of the most important things to learn is that Satan's power and guile is greater than we can withstand by ourselves; we must rely upon God and call for help daily."

Fran begins reading:

## SATAN CAN BE DEFEATED

We will always be confronted by the devil during this life, however, he can be defeated. We need not be discouraged. Jesus, who came to show us the way, met all the temptations the devil could offer. They were addressed to, 1) lusts of the flesh,

2) ambition for worldly power, and 3) hunger for glory and acclaim from the world. Jesus' response was: "Get thee hence Satan; for it is written thou shalt worship the Lord thy God, and him only thou shalt serve." D.C. tells of an experience recorded by Moses. At a time when Moses was caught up into an exceeding high mountain, and he saw God face to face, and he talked with him, and the glory of God was upon Moses; therefore Moses could endure his presence... After a marvelous revelation to Moses,

> "...the presence of God withdrew from Moses, that his glory was not upon Moses; and Moses was left unto himself..." Then, "...It came to pass ...Satan came tempting him, saying Moses, son of man, worship me. And it came to pass that Moses looked upon Satan, and said, Who art thou, for behold I am a son of God, in the similitude of his Only Begotten; and where is thy glory, that I should worship thee? For behold, I could not look upon God except his glory should come upon me, and I were transfigured before him. But I can look upon thee in the natural man...wherefore I can judge between him and thee...." Then Satan cried with a loud voice, and went upon the earth, and commanded, saying, "I am the Only Begotten, worship me." And it came to pass that Moses began to fear exceedingly; and as he began to fear he saw the bitterness of hell; nevertheless, calling upon God he received strength and he commanded, saying, "Get thee hence Satan; for this one God only will I worship which is the God of Glory..."

The contending powers are spiritual powers of the universe. Many very intelligent people have fallen to Satan when he has tempted them with pride, money, sex, jealousy, etc. We need to train ourselves to immediately call for God's help the moment we feel a first tinge of temptation.

John said, "We need a Celestial 911 number to call and we need to use it immediately, not waiting for something to actually happen. However, and please remember this, if you do find yourself in trouble, never be too proud to turn to God and admit you made a mistake and ask for help. It is your only source of strength and he will be there for you."

Fran continues reading.

D.C. offers thoughtful insight:

"He who is not able to abide the law of a celestial kingdom, can not abide a Celestial glory..." Vs. 6 continues: "Ye who are quickened by a portion of the celestial glory shall then receive of the same, even a fullness."

Therefore it is imperative that in this life we learn to live by the laws of the Celestial Kingdom.

"I see what you mean," Bob agreed, "but why haven't we run into this before?"

Lilli responded to Bob's question. "Until now you were going pretty much the way of the world, right? Well the devil didn't have too much to be concerned about did he? You probably considered your lifestyle to be good enough and had nothing to be concerned about, but now that you have learned the truth and have dedicated your life to God, the struggle has begun and it will continue."

# TIME OF OPPORTUNITY

There is danger of drifting from God and following in the pursuit of evil, but there is also the opportunity to be proven and lifted up to greater levels. Two examples: Helaman 3:15-124: Nephi had been speaking to the people in the street at a risk to his life. They rejected and ridiculed him. Detected he left that town and was on the path through the wilderness to his home, concerned by their wickedness.

"And it came to pass as he was thus pondering in his heart, behold a voice came to him, saying, Blessed art thou, Nephi, for those things which thou hast done; for I have beheld how thou hast with unweariness declared the word which I have given unto thee, unto this people. And thou hast not feared them and hast not sought thine own life, but have sought my will, and to keep my commandments. And now because thou hast done this with such unweariness, behold, I will bless thee forever; and I will make thee mighty in word and in deed, in faith and in works; yea even that all things shall be done unto thee according to thy word, *for thou shalt not ask that which is contrary to my will.* Behold thou art Nephi and I am God. I declare it unto thee in the presence of mine angels..."

God gave Nephi a contract witnessed by the courts of heaven that whatever he ordered would take place just as though it had been commanded by God. God could make this contract with Nephi only because he knew Nephi was so in accord with God that he would not call for anything which God himself would not have asked. This is the condition he would like for each of us.

"I had never considered such a thing as a contract with God." Don said. "Does he do that with other people?"

"Yes, he will make a contract with you, but we will look at that later. The main thing to remember is that it is best to let God make the contract because if you make the terms you may find you get more responsibility than you want, and you are bound by it."

Art begins reading.

It is ironic that the power, granted by God, to command whatsoever you may and have the command obeyed by the powers of heaven is the greatest power any man can ever have; he has the power to command as God does, but when a man can be trusted with such power, he himself will restrict its use by an inward consciousness which keeps the great power controlled. Nephi never used that power until he did everything he possibly could first. Knowing he could call down fire from heaven and destroy the people gave him an added incentive to work harder to save them.

> "Now it came to pass that when the Lord had spoken these words unto Nephi, he did not stop, and did not go to his own house, but did return unto the multitudes who were scattered about upon the face of the land, and began to declare unto them the word of the Lord which had been spoken unto them concerning their destruction...."Helaman 3:125

When Nephi's efforts proved futile and the people were about to destroy themselves in wars, Nephi still did not arbitrarily use the power. Helaman Chapter.4:

> Nephi did cry unto the Lord saying, 0 Lord, do not suffer that this people shall be destroyed by the sword; but O Lord, rather let there be a famine in the land to stir them up in remembrance of the Lord their God...and so it was done according to the words of Nephi.

Another example was the time Moses was carried up to a high mountain in the previously mentioned experience and Moses met Satan and refused to worship him. After the departure of Satan Moses again beheld the glory of God, and God said:

> Blessed art thou Moses, for I, the Almighty, have chosen thee, and thou shalt be made stronger than many waters; for they shall obey thy command even as if thou wert God.

There are other examples of God giving an individual great power, such as Joshua when the water of the Jordan River was backed up so the Israelites could cross. But, it has always been given to someone who has been proven worthy of God's trust. It is the wish of God for every one of us to achieve that level of trust.

## THE MOST COMMON FAILURE

God does not place a limit on how high you can climb in spiritual growth. People limit themselves. The most common failure occurs when you discover you have learned as much as those respected people around you. When this happens, you may feel at ease and settle into a circle of comfortable people and quit growing. You lose the marvelous excitement which has lifted you to this position. In short, you reach a level of comfort and stop climbing. This is terrible, because there is so much more God would have led you to. This happens because you have taken your eyes off of Christ and have begun comparing yourself with other people. It does not have to be that way. There is no place in God's plan for you to level off.

## SUMMARY

Spiritual growth and testing time is the major part of mortal life, but some people do not begin to grow spiritually until late in life.

Many people are dismayed to discover being a "saved Christian" does not lead to a life of tranquillity.

We will all be subject to encounters with Satan throughout our lives. We must face him to be proven, and we must win over him to be worthy of the Celestial Kingdom.

# GIFT EXCHANGE

Lunch was completed and everyone was reluctantly taking a last look at Big Dipper Lake before packing to go home. John and Lilli called them together, "There is one final thing we have on the agenda John said. It is time to exchange gifts."

I drew Sandy's name. "Sandy you have seen me prowling around shooting Polaroid pictures. This little album is to help you remember our experience here."

"For me? I could never forget this experience ever, now I can see it too. Thank you so much. I'll enjoy it forever.

"I drew Bob's name and I had a hard time trying to decide what to give him. I wanted it to be special, but I didn't bring anything camping so I went down to the willow trees and got some willow then picked up some pebbles along the shore. I borrowed some glue from your wife and put together this picture frame. I hope you like it," She handed it to Bob.

"Like it? I appreciate it very much. I'm impressed by how much trouble you went through to make it for me. That is what really makes it a special treasure."

"I hope you like the incense of willow because you will have it for a long time." Sandy added.

"I really like it. It reminds me of when I was a kid and played along the river. Now it will remind me of this weekend."

"I guess that makes it my turn. I drew John's name. I had no idea what gift to give until I saw John squinting in the sun to see across the lake last night. Here John, it's my 49ers baseball cap. I hope you are a 49ers fan."

"My favorite team, along with the Seahawks and Broncos and a couple of others," John laughed. "Maybe we should have had this exchange yesterday so I could have used it earlier."

"I drew Fran's name," Don announced, "So I made her a willow-whistle. See the end of it slides in and out like a trombone so you can change the tone when you use it to call Art to dinner."

As everyone laughed, Fran said "I was real happy to get Lilli's name because I wanted to give her something special anyway." She unfastened a large gold with porcelain brooch from her dress and stepped over and pinned it on Lilli's blouse. "This was given to me by my mother. It had been her mother's."

"Oh Fran," tears were on Lilli's cheeks, "you shouldn't give me that. It's part of your heritage and this was supposed to be just a little gift exchange."

"But I want you to have it. I think so much of you. I want someday to be like you."

Lilli hugged Fran with tears in both of their eyes.

John whispered, "Lilli you are next."

Wiping her eyes and trying to regain her composure Lilli said, "I drew Jan's name. She has been watching me make her gift all weekend. It's here on my easel."

"No!" Jan cried, "Not that. You shouldn't, it's too beautiful!"

"Jan you don't know how much pleasure I got from painting it knowing it was going to be yours."

"Look at what is camouflaged in those bushes in the lower right corner." Lilli instructed.

Jan found the hidden message and read slowly, "Jan's Big Dipper Cabin Home—L.H." "Oh I love it. I have just the place for it on the wall above my dining room table where we have our classes."

Jan turned to Art, "I don't have anything like an oil painting for you but I hope you will like this." She took a small plastic box with a fishing fly in it from her pocket and handed it to him. "It's a Royal Coachman."

"Wow, I'm going to stay here and fish this afternoon," Art exclaimed.

"No you are going to pack us up and take us home," was Fran's exaggerated order.

"I guess I'm last," Art said looking at Don. "The first day here I found this white quartz on the shore of the lake. It reminded me of Mt. Achoon, and the flat side could make it a good paperweight. I hope you enjoy it Don."

"I'll always remember Mt. Achoon and Big Dipper whenever I see it."

## FAREWELL TO BIG DIPPER

John and Lilli moved slowly in getting their things packed in the camper, then they strolled to the shore of Big Dipper Lake and stood with their arms around each other as they shared a parting look and Mt. Achoon.

"It has been a wonderful weekend" Lilli said, "and there will be another beautiful sunset again this evening."

"Yes," John drew her closer as they looked over the water.

"Sunsets like these remind me of beautiful lives. The most beautiful lives are those that have had a lot of clouds scattered around in them for the light from above to reflect from."

When the last of the campers had waved farewell, John slowly lead Lilli to their own car. "I still think we woke up in Paradise," Lilli commented. John smiled, thoughtfully and started the engine.

# CHAPTER 21

# MEETING GOD, STAGE EIGHT

Tuesday evening at Bob's andJan's

Art and Fran were the last arrivals at Bob's and Jan's home. As they entered, Art commented, "Well, it looks like you are all settled from the campout."

"Yes," Jan said, pointing to the wall behind the dining table. "Bob already got my picture up. Isn't it perfect for that spot? I knew it would be."

"Jan's Big Dipper Cabin Home," Art said as he cast an imaginary flyrod. "I can see myself out there flipping that Royal Coachman on the water by that big rock."

"We should have gotten a can of the campfire smoke. We could sit here and look at the painting and smell the campfire. It would take us right back to Big Dipper," Don joked.

"Oh! You are not going to free any campfire smoke in here with Jan's beautiful curtains," Sandy exclaimed.

Fran, always eager to learn the topic of the study sessions, took her place at the table and asked, "What's on for tonight?"

As John distributed the papers around the table, he answered, "Tonight we will talk about being in the presence of God."

"You mean we are going to study what happens after we die?" Art asked, "How can you know anything about that?"

"We are headed toward that subject," John said. "But tonight we will consider being in the presence of God in this life." John thought about how forthright Art's direct thinking always was, and wondered if this was an indication of honesty and lack of guile.

Lilli turned to Art and said, "There is a lot we do know about after death and what we know about that has a big influence on what we know about the purpose of life now. We will be studying that three or four sessions from now."

"You mean we can actually come into God's presence like Moses on the mountain?" Jan asked incredulously. "That sounds scary."

"To put this into perspective, let's review some of the ground we have covered," John suggested.

## REVIEW

"Reminisce for a moment," John began. "Remember, God's purpose was, and is, to prepare us in his likeness for his eternal kingdom. This is a lofty goal. When we consider the power that man will have to be given when in God's likeness it should be obvious that extensive preparation and training is required before being given freedom to use it. You just do not turn the driving of an eighteen-wheeler truck over to a ten-year-old kid and send him out in traffic, nor do you turn your armament over to your enemy for safekeeping. And God cannot trust power to anyone who is unprepared or disloyal.

"There are those," John continued, "who believe that by the time we leave this life we will be in the likeness of God. But I'm quite sure the major thrust of this life is to prove our loyalty either to Lucifer, or to God. This means the real work of our being formed into the likeness of God must be done in the life that follows this. And, John added thoughtfully, "it also means that throughout this life you will be faced with circumstances designed to tempt and test your decisions of loyalty to God. Until this is firmly established, you cannot be trusted with the endowment he is prepared to bestow upon you."

"Lilli would you begin reading for us tonight?"

# CHOOSING

The Spirit of God calls you upward to him, but Lucifer is granted access to you to tempt you to follow him. It is left to you to weigh the offerings and choose to follow one or the other.

"Who would be stupid enough to choose the devil?" Don broke in. "I can't imagine such a thing."

"I don't think it is ever presented to us as a black and white decision of either following God and go the heaven, or following the devil and go to hell," Bob proposed. "If it were nobody would choose the devil. But it is not presented that way. I see Lucifer like a smooth conman. First he tries to conceal the blessings that accrue to those who follow God in mortal life. Then he tries to make Christian living appear to require a spartan existence of sacrifice which is embraced only by the mentally impaired and the downtrodden. Next he tries to cast doubts in our minds about the reality of God and the promise of the kingdom. For those who won't give up their faith in God he suggests that God is simple and easily hoodwinked. He implies that it is okay, and we can get away with it, if we sin a little. But that's just to open the door and get us started. He wants us to believe we can enjoy the evils of this life and still go to the kingdom because God forgives. Then, he paints the life of sin as a life of freedom and pleasure and satisfaction.

"Finally, he tries to convince us that there is no devil, and there is no hell, that it's all in our minds, so we should forget those foolish traditions and enjoy life. Don't worry, take all you can get for your pleasure while you are here. Have a good time and let others worry about themselves."

"That's quite a speech for you." Jan looked at her husband.

"But Bob is right," Lilli said. "It's all a big lie. A wanton life is not the happy satisfying life of freedom. Besides that the followers of Christ sacrifice those things which are destructive to their eternal life, and caring for others brings happiness to everyone. It brings healing, which leaves us free of personal concerns so we can love others. Faith in God brings freedom which evil can never offer. It only offers bondage. I really get upset about Lucifer's lies and deception. If he told the truth he wouldn't have any followers."

Lilli returned to reading:

At times a person may find himself in a situation where he feels forced to follow Satan. But it is not true. Satan is not permitted to force you; the force comes from your following him into a situation which seems irreversible. You may have done evil which, in order to turn back, you would have to tell the world things which may cause you to lose respect and be scorned. So your pride will not let you. Perhaps confession would cause you to lose your freedom and send you to prison. Perhaps it would even cost your mortal life, but this is preferable to following Satan to an eternal condemnation. This life is short, and we need to be sure we are God's when we leave it.

God is so great, so powerful that he brings worlds into being and obliterates others, yet he has told us to choose him.

Gen 7:39-40 They are the workmanship of mine own hands, and I give unto them their intelligence in the day that I created them. And in the Garden of Eden gave I unto man his agency;...and also gave commandment that they... should choose me their Father.

God who is all powerful and who created us still gives us the freedom to reject him and choose Lucifer. Isn't that amazing? He rules us with the gentle persuasion even though we go through very difficult and trying experiences when we wander away from him. And we are put through some severe tests of our faith and loyalty even when we are trying to follow him.

"My that is incredible" Jan marveled. "When I try to grasp the tremendous meaning of this I get a new and enormously enlarged concept of how gracious God is."

"Yes," Lilli agreed, "he is so powerful that he could force us into submission yet he allows us to choose. It makes the difference between joy or misery for us. Because, without the freedom to make such choices, it would be like we were incarcerated in a mental prison. The joy comes when we choose God and learn of his ways as we are doing here. We get the blessings which he promises to those who are his. The misery comes when we make the other choice, and reap the rewards it holds for us."

"I have a question," Sandy said. "I always thought that when you weren't good, I mean when you didn't obey God, that he made awful things happen to you to punish you. Isn't that true?"

Bob lifted his hand slightly and said, "The thing that is coming through to me in this, is that we are constantly being sustained and blessed by the Lord, but when we turn from him we also turn from the blessings and reap the kind of life the world without God would offer. This would certainly seem like severe

**215**

punishment. It is just like following the devil. God does not send us to hell as punishment, we bring it upon ourselves, but that would be our destination and it certainly would be punishment."

John agreed: "It is amazing, and the signs all point in one direction, 'submission'. The ultimate conquest of yourself, which assures that your destination will be God's kingdom, is when you control your agency. This is when you deliberately choose to give yourself to Christ and accept whatever he brings into you life. His love for you was so great that he was willing to be executed in your stead, so your eternal salvation lies with him, but you must choose to be his. Then he will continue to lead you to the kingdom, otherwise, his dying for you would prove futile. Christ is the gift by which man is promised eternal life."

Bob's voice was strained, "A short time ago I thought I was my own man, but now I belong to him—if he wants me."

Don agreed: "I'm not sure I know all about this but I've learned enough that my choice is for Christ." Sandy placed her hand on Don's, indicating this was her choice too and the moist eyes of Jan and Fran spoke of their commitment.

"I think we have all made the same choice" Art said. "What can we do now?"

"Then it is time for you to meet God," John announced.

"What!" Art sat up straight. "Are you going to bring God right into this room?"

"God has already been with us in this room. You will meet him as you become aware of his presence." John said. "When Martha questioned Jesus about Lazarus' death, Jesus reminded her:"

> Jesus saith unto her, Said I not unto thee, that, if thou wouldest believe, thou shouldest see the glory of God? (John 11:40)

"This is a great moment which we have been working toward." Lilli said, "Still the initiative is on his side. He may enter your visible world, right in this room, if he chooses, or quietly into your heart. But by the power of his aura his presence will be known, and when his will becomes our will his will becomes our peace."

"I don't know if I can stand this." Sandy said.

To ease the nervous tension John said, "His love comes like soft rays of sunshine from which you cannot be shaded. He is behind the outer visible world and has been with you from your beginning. He has not changed, or come closer; you have changed and become aware of his presence."

The Apostle John (17:3) records the words of Jesus:

*This is life eternal, that they might know thee the only true God and Jesus Christ whom thou hast sent.*

It is time to enter the stage in which you might know the only true God, and Jesus Christ whom he has sent, that you may inherit eternal life. The son of God invites us to be like him and become sons of God."

"God in our house?" Jan wondered.

"More than that," Lilli responded, "it is God in your life."

"There are a few things we need to look at," John said. "The first is faith. Faith in God is the great key, which unlocks the mysteries of the kingdom. I know by now you all have the faith to believe in God and Christ; by this I mean you believe what you have heard about him. The faith you need goes farther. This faith is like a seed; you hold a seed in your fingers and examine it. It has not been proven to be fertile but you don't wait until it has been planted and produces before you believe in it. To the contrary, it is because you believe in the seed that you go ahead and prepare the ground and plant. The produce is the result of your faith. If you had not moved in faith, it would never have been planted and could not have born fruit."

"You need to have the same kind of faith in God," John emphasized. "A faith by which you live according to all the word of God without waiting to see if it will produce fruit in your life. Without that kind of faith you can never have the fruitful life."

# SHADRACH, MESHACH AND ABED-NEGO

"A good example of this kind of faith was given us by Shadrach, Meshach, and Abed-Nego, three young Israelites who were threatened with being thrown into the furnace and burned if they would not bow down and worship the statue of the king. They responded:

> *O Nebuchadnezzar, we are not careful to answer thee in this matter. If it so be our God whom we serve is able (or chooses) to deliver us from the fiery furnace, and he will deliver us out of thine hand O King, but if not be it known unto thee O King that we will not serve thy gods, nor worship the image which thou has set up,*

"God has told us to trust him. We cannot wait to see if God will be there. Our decision must always be made in faith before there is concrete evidence that he will surround us with protection. We have to move in faith, not waiting for a sign from heaven. We must adopt the attitude of Esther when she was going to the king to plead for her people. She had written to her uncle Mordecai, saying,

*I will go in unto the king, which is not according to the law; and if I perish, I perish.*

# MEETING GOD

"You have each been evaluating the stages you are in by your response to the call of the Holy spirit." John pointed out. "You have planted your seed of faith. Now you find yourself surrounded by his love. You wonder how you could have been blind to it for so long. Everywhere you look you see evidence of his presence. You are beginning to see yourself differently than ever before. You don't see yourself as the important individual you used to be, but as an integral part of God's creation. Like Jan's picture of Big Dipper up there. Whereas you would have thought of yourself as the picture, now you see yourself as one of those little light beams sparkling on the water. But even so you have a greater appreciation of the picture than when you felt you were the whole of it. As the revelation of our creator's whole picture opens we see that individually you are a minor speck in it, but the vast beauty of the great picture is so moving that you are filled with its wonders and you are happy to be only one of the tiny specks by which such beauty was created. And in seeing creation this way you begin to have great appreciation for all the tiny specks which make the picture possible and beautiful."

"I feel transparent, like you can see right through me," Don said, "because that is just the way I feel and think."

"When God comes to us, as he has here," Lilli confided, "we all feel that way. Our deeper self is in all people and they in us. The Holy Spirit begins tugging at our hearts and causing us to yearn for the fulfillment of dreams and to reach beyond ourselves like a flower seeking the sunlight. We look to the mountain top and see God is beckoning us to come higher. As we climb mountain toward its peak, people who were widely separated at the base of the mountain draw together and we can look back at the world from a new level and a new perspective because we are beginning to draw nearer and nearer to God."

The Spirit of God reaches down as though his hand is tugging at our hearts and it creates the desire within us to pass beyond the limits of ordinary consciousness and we long to reach the Celestial Kingdom, or to have it opened to us."

"You have been where I am now," Fran told Lilli.

Lilli put her arm on Fran's shoulders, "We will climb the Mountain together and support each other."

"We have come to the level where we completely reverse the infant and rebellion stages in which our only concern was ourselves," John continued. "We begin to establish a rhythm with all nature and feel at one with the heart of the universe; we open ourselves to the overwhelming love which God spreads abroad through all his creations, and as our spirits are transported to the presence of God, we are filled with a joy surpassing all others in life."

"I feel this, and I want it to be just that way." Art was almost pleading, "But I don't feel good enough to receive it. I feel like I've come to a banquet table in my dirty work clothes."

"Art," John said thoughtfully, "revelation is always much larger than our ability to comprehend it. God leaves us room to stretch and, over time, you grow beyond today's limitations. Already you have received a transcendent experience which enables you to see a kingdom beyond the veil that blinded you a short time ago. This event has changed your life. You can never go back. You are not the same as you were. To change our lives, we prepare the soil so it is receptive to the seeds which the Lord plants and cultivate."

"How do we prepare the soil?" Bob asked.

"At Big Dipper Lake, Don said he felt the experience was like falling in love. So, court God: look for ways to please him, be open and receptive to him. David (ps 26) felt as you do. He prayed, *'examine me O Lord, and prove me'* Allow God to test you and try you and mold you. Peter said, 'The trial of your faith is precious' (I Peter 1: 7). And Paul said 'we glory in tribulation.' So whatever comes to you after you have turned your life over to him is for your eternal good, so be receptive to whatever he brings into your life. Don't resent hardships or problems but look for the lesson God is teaching you through them.

"From this new perspective you can see beyond the trials of mortal life and join with the heirs of Abraham in 'looking for a city which hath foundations whose builder and maker is God'." (Heb 11:10)

"Could there possibly be any stage above this?" Sandy wondered aloud.

"There is another stage which in God's mind is most vital for us to go through, but we will get to that later," John said, then continued, "Jan before our closing prayer, would you turn to Alma 14:97 and read it to us as a closing thought?"

Jan read: "Behold, who can say too much of his great power, and of his mercy, and of his long suffering toward the children of men: Behold I say unto you, I cannot say the smallest part of that which I feel."

Jan closed the book, placed both hands on it and closed her eyes, but a tear slipped out anyway.

# CHAPTER 22

## STAGE NINE
## LOVE ONE ANOTHER

"Listen, it's beautiful," Jan said motioning John and Lilli to a seat.

Art had shown Bob how to hook his new compact disc player into his stereo system and the study group was listening to the flawless sound of 'Amazing Grace' when John and Lilli arrived.

The next hymn was 'How Great Thou Art', and Lilli leaned back with her eyes closed. "Sounds like the angelic choir. I could listen to this all night."

"Oh no," Sandy urged, "you will have to put the angels on hold. We have waited all week to learn what stage could possibly be greater than the last one. I can't imagine how anything could exceed last week's. We want to get started," and she began moving toward the dining table. "Come on everyone."

As Bob shut off the music, John commented, "The last verse of that song sums up our topic for tonight."

"What did that line say?" Fran asked. "When I think that God, his Son not sparing, sent him to die, I scarce can take it in," John quoted.

"It must have been very, very important," Fran replied, "to have Jesus actually die for it."

"It was," Lilli said as she slipped into her place at the table. "Besides that, do you know what is so important to God that he has pleaded with us for it from the time of Adam until now?"

"I'm ashamed to admit it," Bob said thoughtfully, "but I've never thought of what God might want. I guess I have only thought of what I wanted from God."

"I'm sure that is the case with most people," John replied, "but you can never really understand God, or the process of mortal life until you know the answer to that question, and until you make it a part of your life you cannot enter the higher stage which we will be talking of tonight."

"What is it?" Fran was impatient to learn.

"The second great commandment," John said *Thou shalt love thy neighbor as thyself.* (Matt: 22:38) In other words be as concerned for your neighbors welfare as for your own. Lift him from wherever he is to where he can obtain the Celestial Kingdom and work to relieve his distress in mortal life."

"That's a pretty big order isn't it?" Art asked.

"Recall that in the previous stage we submitted ourselves to God, and promised to go wherever he sent us and do whatever he asked of us. He has thousands upon thousands of people who will never find their way to the kingdom without help. So it is logical to expect he would lead you directly into serving others who are precious to him. When we see the magnitude of God's love for every individual on earth we are jolted into awareness that God's commandment, in fact his plea to Adam and every succeeding generation, has been the second great commandment.

We are important to God individually of course but too often we feel we are most important. Realize his love also encircles everyone; his deep concern for others tugs at his heart. But no matter how much God loves others, it does not diminish his love for you. Since we know the God who loves us cares so much for different people it should cause us to have greater esteem for all people. Unfortunately we are often like the brother of the prodigal son. He jealously resented his father's love, and the attention given to the lost son who had returned. If he had true love for his brother his joy would have negated the resentment, but instead of love he carried a self-righteous, superior attitude because he had not made the errors his brother made. The error of his attitude, however, was a sin as grievous as that of his brother.

In our desire to have a special place in God's heart we overlook the fact that God's love for us is so great it cannot be enlarged, but he loves every other person equally with us. When we judge ourselves better we diminish ourselves. "God has wonderful compassion for the alienated people who tread the forlorn and lonely roads of 1ife. His heart reaches out to those who are lost or discarded along the way, and to those who are locked in servitude to Satan as well. Because of his love, he yearns to bring them home. Therefore he has the highest esteem for any person who has mercy and concern for them and brings them to him. There is no greater stage in this life than to love God with all your heart, and have a compassionate concern that others also find refuge in his kingdom. I John 4:21

This command we have from him, that he who loveth God, love his brother also.

"I guess that when we learn of something extremely important to God we should be quick to please him," Fran remarked, "But I had just never thought God cared as much for the Chinese or Arabs or other non-Christians as he does for us."

"Last week we studied how each individual makes up a speck of color in God's great painting. No one alone can make the picture beautiful."

Jan said, "I've been thinking since we started these studies, about how many beautiful people there must be in the world.

They are so much a part of me and I'm a part of the same picture."

"Lock onto that concept, Jan." Lilli commented, "our lives are so intrinsically interwoven with others that we must lift them to lift ourselves. You cannot be in the likeness of God until you have the passion for souls God has."

John said, "People have not given enough consideration to this, but to God it's a vital concern. We can never achieve his ultimate purpose for us until we are united in mutual concern and care."

"Let's turn to the text now. Don would you begin reading for us," John asked.

## FIRST AND SECOND GREAT COMMANDMENTS

It is the will and plan of God for all people to live in peace and harmony. In his plan for us we would have equality.

> Matt 22:36-39 Jesus said unto him, Thou shalt love the Lord thy God. with all thy hearts and with all thy soul, and with all thy mind. This is the first and great commandment. And the second is like unto it; Thou shalt love thy neighbor as thyself. On these two commandments hang all the law and the prophets.

It is surprising that most people do not realize that to every generation from the time of Adam, God has commanded observance of these two commandments. They have been repeated over and over in different ways, because of his vital concern for every one of his creation.

> Gen 7:40 tells us: In the Garden of Eden I gave unto man his agency; and unto thy brethren have I said and also gave commandment that they should love one another and that

they should choose me their father.

This is only a different wording for the two great commandments: The first, Love God—Choose me their father, and the second, Love thy neighbor—Love one another.

It is evident that Jesus too, esteemed obedience to the second great commandment, to love thy neighbor as thyself, to be of supreme importance, transcending all other commandments except to love God with all our faculties. Dying was no easier for Jesus than for us. He asked The Father, "That this cup be taken from me." At a different time he said, "greater love hath no man than this, that a man lay down his life for his friends." But still he was willing to lay down his life for us.

This underscores Jesus' concern for all people, and he has a special spiritual endowment for those whose compassionate concern for others propels them to a dedication of service to their fellow beings. In the Garden of Gethsemane he prayed for those who followed him "That they may be one" In addition to this his last ministry before he was crucified was the Lord's Supper in which he instructed them to always remember him and to forgive one another. He insisted that his followers be united so people would be drawn together under his name. In later scripture he instructed us, "Be one or ye are not mine.."D.C. 38:6

Gen. 4:14 records that God told Adam to teach these things to his children, but Satan came among his children and they loved Satan more than God and chose him. God does not have spite nor does he act for revenge, and he had no joy in knowing of the suffering to come to those who chose to follow Satan. His heart hurts for them. In every way possible he wanted to reach out and draw them back to him. It makes no difference under what national banner they identify themselves; God said he had made of one blood all nations and his love is extended to all. For this reason if you will work to redeem even one of his lost children he will endow you with special insights and reward in his kingdom. Jesus promised that if you will just give a cup of water you will not lose your reward.

God spoke to Enoch (Gen. 7:43):

> Among all the workmanship of my hands there has not been so great wickedness as among thy brethren; but behold their sins shall be upon the heads of their fathers; Satan shall be their father and misery shall be their doom; and the whole heavens shall weep over them ...wherefore should not the heavens weep seeing these shall suffer?

God could see the path they had chosen would lead them to misery and doom and suffering so he was already agonizing for them.

# DEVELOPMENT OF DIFFERENT FUTURES

God's people spread throughout the earth from the Tower of Babel and in later expeditions. Because of different climates, different geography, different foods, raw materials, languages, and clothing they forged different cultures, dictated by the needs of their separate situations. These differences have caused people to erect walls between themselves and others, walls of fear, distrust, self-interest, pride, and religions. Their self-interest and competition with each other has separated them from the love of one another, but the mandate from Christ is to serve one another. To God they are still his one people, people of one blood.

"Now that these things are pointed out I can see them clearly," Art said, "but it had never occurred to me to think of others like that."

"I'm embarrassed to think of my attitude toward other people, especially those who never seemed to accomplish anything in life," Bob admitted.

"It seems that this is a common way that people look at other people," John observed. It is unfortunate that we have such a heritage, but suspicion seems ingrained in us until it is a natural instinct we must work to overcome."

The response of many of Adam's descendants down to our time is, "I am most important so I should be most favored by God." This is expanded into, "My family and friends are the best people and should receive special attention from God," then, "My church is the favored church," and finally "My country is a special country above all others, God protect us from those heathen, ungodly people of other lands."

But the Lord repeats, "I have made of one blood all nations...Go ye into all nations...care for them, preach, teach, baptize." God has never indicated greater love for one people or one nation than for another.

He knew that the temptation of Satan's appeal to the weaker senses of men and women so they would follow Satan. God prepared a nation to reveal to the world the blessings to those who hold fast to the ways of God, and also to demonstrate the appalling destruction and tribulations that comes upon them when they turn from him and follow Satan. The Israelites were the people chosen. They were chosen to display to the world both the goodness and devastation, depending upon whom they chose to follow.

God told Abraham, "In Thee shall all the families of the earth he blessed" Gen 12:2. The Israelites were not chosen because God loved them more. They were chosen to minister to all nations. Chapter 19 of Exodus deals with the priesthood call of the Israelites as a nation. They were to be a kingdom of priests to the nations. They would be highly blessed; God would uphold and protect them and cause them to prosper as they kept the covenant, not because the Lord loved them more, but that through their ministry all the world would learn there is one God, and he is true. And through them the world would learn of the love and benevolence of God to those who were his and were obedient to him.

The world was never separated by God into gentiles to be hated and Israelites to be loved. He saw a sinful world at large to be redeemed and the people of Israel were chosen to bear the burden of ministry to them. It was because Israel broke their covenant and joined the world that they received the wrath of God who had blessed them so richly. Despite man's choosing to follow Satan and his rejection of God, God still sent his own son to purchase their freedom, and Jesus bought the lives, not just of the Israelites, but of all people.

He paid as much for the life of a gentile as for a Jew. He paid as much for the soul of humble people as for kings, apostles, prophets or martyrs. His concern was lavished upon all people, and each person.

John said, "Fran said a moment ago that it must have been very important to God. We are seeing it was more important than we can imagine. We don't have the capacity to love like God loves."

# RIGHTEOUS LIVING DEMONSTRATED IN ZION

Enoch's people of the City Zion became so dedicated and righteous that they climbed to the spiritual level from which Adam had fallen and the veil parted so they passed over without death. They were translated, taken up from earth to be returned in the last days.

The city of Zion existed for three hundred and sixty five years; it became a powerful influence in the world of their day.

God had protected it from all invaders so it was said of Zion it was "terrible," as it must have been to their enemies. There are many things about Zion we would like to know. It is significant that of all that could have been told of Zion, the thing which was of primary importance to God and was recorded was: "They were of one heart and one mind and there were no poor among them."

## TEMPORAL THINGS OF EARTH

The management of temporal things of earth as designed by God provided an abundance. All the citizens of the city had plenty neither were there any poor. All became rich, for there was an abundance for all. Brotherhood, peace, and love for one another prevailed.

When Satan enters the hearts of men he produces pride, greed and lusts which cause division. Some to try to rise above their neighbors in positions and in the abundance of worldly possessions they obtain for themselves. Nobody gains from following Satan. In Zion, those who needed anything would have freely had all they needed without hoarding. There was no need for a ruling class. There was equality and everyone worked for the common good. Supposed benefits of class distinction is a mirage. The entire community would be more prosperous and peaceful if everyone received the education and training to develop their potential for contributions to the whole.

## SALEM

Melchizedek was a high priest who became king of the city of Salem, (later Jerusalem) at a time when wickedness was rampant. He ministered to his people and taught repentance until he obtained peace in Salem and was called the King of

Peace. The scriptures tell us, "his people wrought righteousness and obtained heaven and sought for the city of Enoch which God had before taken." This was a dramatic conversion of a city like Sodom into a city like Zion, righteous enough to be translated to heaven.

The method by which this happens has never changed. It is dependent only upon following the directions of the Lord and becoming righteous as a group. In Salem, as in Zion, there were no poor among them and through the principle of all working and depositing the results of their work in a storehouse for all people to use according to their needs, they were a happier people.

When working or learning is done in competition for money or grades it becomes drudgery, but when done voluntarily it is a pleasure. In Zion and Salem, work was never drudgery. In such circumstances there would never be conflict over wages because people worked for the common good, not for wages.

# CHAPTER 23

## REPENTANCE

H.S.: Jesus, I have a question that's bothering me.

JESUS: What is it, Holy Spirit? Maybe I can help.

H.S.: Do you remember when we were planning man's creation how worried we were about his use of agency?

JESUS: I certainly do. I'll never forget that problem.

H.S.: That problem is still bothering me. Remember God said we would put man in the lab and let him try things, you know, experiment, make mistakes, and get himself in trouble? Then God said we would recycle him and get him cleaned up and fit for the kingdom.

JESUS: That's right, Holy Spirit, in the middle of time I'll go down and show them how to live a kingdom life, and I'll take away the keys of death and hell from Lucifer so the way will be open for them to come back.

LUCIFER: Hi there, did I hear someone mention my name?

H.S.: Lucifer? What are you doing here? You don't work here anymore. We gave your job to Michael. He's Archangel now.

LUCIFER:    Oh, I don't worry about that; I'm working on something much bigger than that.

H.S.:    Really, what could be more important than being Archangel?

LUCIFER:    I'm God now. I've got all those people you are so worried about right under my thumb.

JESUS:    Beat it Lucifer! You're still the same old liar. There is no way you will ever be God.

LUCIFER:    Don't be too sure. Take a look down there. See what they are doing? They don't look very godly, do they?

JESUS:    That is because we have not yet enrolled them in the salvation plan.

LUCIFER:    Salvation plan! Ha! That's a joke, your salvation plan just touches their spirits. They can't even see or feel or touch what you offer them. I have all kinds of things they really go for. I've got things they can eat and all kinds of other gratifications for their bodies that they can feel and see. I've got all I need to make them mine. I'll give them things to make them proud and jealous and hate each other. Soon they won't even know they have a spiritual being. I'll even——

JESUS:    Lucifer, if you don't get out of here, I'll not wait until the millennial time to lock you up; I'll do it now.

LUCIFER: Okay, okay! I'll go; I've got lots of work to do anyway.

H.S.: I'm glad he's gone, but what he said is what's been worrying me. How do we recycle them?

JESUS: Before Lucifer interrupted us, I was explaining. I'll go down and open the way for them to come and I'll lead them back.

H.S.: I know, but what if they don't follow you? What if they want what the devil offers them and just stay there? Can't we bring some kind of pressure on them?

God:(enters) I know how you feel, Holy Spirit, but what I just heard you say is the one thing we won't do. That would spoil the whole plan and impose our will upon man so he could not choose. He will have to make up his mind for himself.

H.S.: This is a dangerous situation.

God: Yes, it is very dangerous; but it has to be this way, man has to learn in the lab and voluntarily choose to come back.

JESUS: That's right. If he is forced to come back, he will be worse off than he was before he went into mortal life.

# KEYS TO THE HIDDEN MYSTERIES

H.S.:            I'm really concerned about this. What are we going to do?

GOD:             I know you are concerned, so I am sending you to work with people. Work with them in every way you can to get them to see the truth. Cause them to understand the terrible end that Lucifer has planned for them. open their eyes to an understanding of the glory of the Celestial Kingdom we have planned for them. The only means I forbid you to use is force. You can coax, encourage, even frighten, but you are not to force.

H.S.:            I can see this job is going to take a long time.

JESUS:           Yes, you will have to work with each person a little at a time so they will understand and move toward the kingdom one step at a time.

H.S.:            It will be like watching a Redwood grow. I guess that's what it is, a process of spiritual growth. Since we will be reclaiming people from Lucifer and preparing them for Celestial Glory, I guess it truly is a recycling process.

God:             Yes, but let's not call it that. Let's call the process repentance.

# REPENTANCE

Art laid down his play script and said, "I think these plays make God, Christ, and The Holy Spirit look like boobs."

"That may be," Fran responded, "but the plays sure help me to understand things better."

Lilli smiled and said, "You are both right. By putting God, Christ and The Holy Spirit in a human-type situation and giving them human dialogue they don't seem very sacred and we must apologize to them for that.

"We hope you understand the plays are only fantasies, but they carry a message that helps to understand God's purposes."

"I don't have any problem with the plays," Bob said. "I appreciate how simple it makes it to get the points across in an understandable way. I also remember them much better."

As she opened her notebook Jan asked, "Is repentance our study tonight?"

"Repentance," John responded.

"Oh no," Fran moaned, "Everytime I hear that word I see a shrill-voiced preacher pointing his finger at me and shouting, 'Repent ye sinner, repent."

Don laughed, "I always think of the refrain from that old song that goes: 'Don't do this, and don't do that, Repent! Repent! Repent!'"

"Really you two, you make it sound so negative," Sandy laughed.

"I already repented three years ago, before I was baptized," Art stated.

John chuckled, "You are speaking in vain about one of my favorite subjects. You'll find this especially interesting. It's a message that should be well received by repentance enthusiasts everywhere."

"Okay, we will see. I'll start reading," Bob said.

## REPENTANCE AND THE FALL

When man fell from grace, he listened to Satan and became "carnal, sensual, and devilish" (Gen 4:13). The illustration below attempts to describe the situation we find ourselves in at birth. It is a sort of neutral Zone halfway between God's level and Lucifer's level. When Adam fell he did not go all the way to that of the devil, but he was below the level he had with God in the Garden of Eden.

This is substantiated by the fact the devil is constantly trying to pull us down to his strata. It is as though both God and Satan have big elastic cords on us. There are pulls to lift us up to God and there are opposite tugs trying to drag us down to Satan. The direction we go is determined by which pull we choose to respond to.

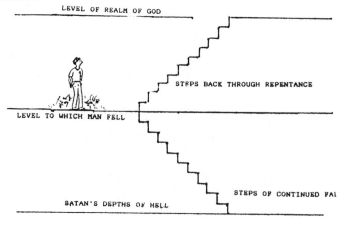

You can reach the point of depravity where God has given you every inducement to turn to him. If you spurn his final efforts, you snap the cord that would lift you to Paradise and you go beyond the reach of any influence he might exert to help you. By your choice you belong to Lucifer.

John interrupted, "This is the point where a person commits the unforgivable sin. We will study that later, but this helps to see how it works."

"The thought of being dragged all the way to the devil's level is horrible." Jan exclaimed.

"Yes," Lilli responded, "But the scriptures support it.

Gen 8:5, My Spirit shall not always strive with man. Also Romans 1:24 ...wherefore God also gave them up to uncleanness, through the lusts of their own hearts...

"You see they are not actually being dragged. Lust, or desire for the temptations Satan offers, causes them to go by choice. Of course, the end result is the same. They may feel guilty and look over their shoulders as they respond to Satan, but still it is a willing response."

Bob continues reading:

The other side is our response to the pull of God. When we yield to him, we begin our climb up the stairway of repentance. The higher we climb, the weaker the cord in the hands of Satan becomes because we are increasingly influenced by God.

Like climbing stairs to an attic, you reach a point where you can see into the attic. On the stairway of repentance, you can reach a point where you can see into the level from which Adam fell. When this occurs the cord Satan has on you snaps because once you can actually see the wonders and glory that lies above, there is no temptation on earth that can draw you back. Until you reach this point, however, no one is immune to the temptations that can cause you to fall, no matter how high you go on the steps.

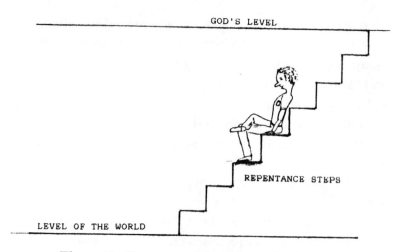

Theoretically you could continue climbing and pass over into that kingdom without going through death. This is what happened to Enoch and his people of Zion. There is a touch of irony here, however, because an individual can easily fall into Satan's hell by himself, but achieving the last step into God's level is nearly impossible by an individual. The reason is revealed by the second great commandment: "Love thy neighbor as thyself." You may climb up the ladder of repentance but you cannot reach the perfection which allows you to pass over into the kingdom without having compassion for others which causes you to reach out and lift them with you. It is a code written into the eternal nature of things that you will strive as hard to get others into the kingdom as you will for yourself.

Bob paused, "You mean I can work all my life to become perfect but I still can't cross over because other people are not right?"

John answered, "To become perfect you need to be in the likeness of God, and his concern is getting everyone there, so you won't be perfect until this is your concern too."

"Right here, I think we see one of the most important

attributes of God's nature and likeness, being revealed." Lilli spoke feelingly. "It is a demonstration of how truly he loves every individual, and when we don't have concern for others we can't be right with God."

"Lilli is right," John affirmed, "It becomes apparent how deeply God's concern is about this when we study the second great commandment."

Jan had been thumbing through the pages of her bible. She said, "I have a question. Is that what happened to Elijah? In II Kings 2:11 it says:

> And it came to pass, as they still went on, and talked, that behold, there appeared a chariot of fire, and horses of fire, and parted them both asunder; and Elijah went up by a whirlwind into heaven."

"It sounds like God sent for him to be taken up doesn't it," John said.

"The whirlwind and fire sounds to me like a jet-powered helicopter was sent for him," Art said.

"Oh, Art!, be real," Fran said, and began reading.

## ZION

The sixth and seventh chapters of Genesis in the inspired version tell of Enoch and the city Zion which he and his followers built. They had entered a spiritual growth period (repentance climb) of three hundred and sixty-five years, then, *"It came to pass that Zion was not for God received it up into his own bosom."* This was the culmination of spiritual growth through repentance by the entire community.

It was written of Zion, *"They were of one heart and one mind, and dwelt in righteousness; and there were no poor among them."*

A note of interest is that although the people of Zion were

translated without passing through the doorway of death they will return at the beginning of the millennial period and pass through that doorway in the twinkling of an eye.

The promise has never been withdrawn for others to be translated the same way; but when it requires a group of people to reach that level together, the difficulty is multiplied many times over.

"Great," Art exclaimed, "why don't we start working together toward perfection? Maybe in three hundred and sixty five years we can be translated to heaven."

"It would probably take longer for us," Sandy said. "In fact, with conditions the way they are today, I don't see how it could ever be done."

"Or maybe less," Lilli suggested, "if we all supported each other and grew together."

"Going through death is probably easier," Art decided and began reading.

## REPENTANCE IS NOT FORCED

God does not force man to climb back up, and Satan is not permitted to force man to continue to fall, although some of the situations people get into can seem to them that they have no choice. No matter how tantalizing the temptations may be, there is always a way out, but we make a choice. It is the same for us today as for Adam and Eve in the Garden.

From "F. Henery Edwards book *FUNDAMENTALS*, rebellion against God indicates one thing clearly...We have the power to rebel, hence we have some freedom. We believe that God has given us this freedom in an attempt to make us responsible men. As every parent knows there are times when children must be permitted to make decisions for themselves, and must be allowed to bear the cost of these decisions. They may be advised, but they must not be coerced. Sometimes they must be free to choose, and to suffer, and to grow. This is the very nature of things.

# DIRECTIONS MAYBE REVERSED

It should be noted that God's love is so great that he will continue to tug at us to redeem us from the bonds of Satan right up to the moment we leave this life in the custody of the devil. Even then he loves us and wants us back, but we have deliberately chosen to turn our back on him and walk away.

The reverse is also true. A person never rises so high on the repentance ladder that he is immune to the attempts of Satan to pull him down. In our study of the stages of life, we considered the dangerous period when people have risen high enough that they feel secure in their own strength; then they trip and fall. Many have risen to great heights as they followed the Lord, only to trip and fall to the depths.

Lilli observed, "You have been especially quiet Sandy, what are you thinking?"

"This sounds like we have to be struggling with the devil all of our lives."

"True," Lilli answered, "but if you let him, God will always be right there to help you."

Art asked, "Does that mean I have to repent again? I didn't plan to ever go through that again."

"A promising note to this is that, even if one finds he has made a grievous error and fallen from the heights, if he will turn back to God again, he can once more begin to climb the stairs as before, and God will still welcome him back," John stated, then turning to Art with a chuckle added, "Yes Art, it means your repentance must continue. It is not something you do once and get it behind you; it has to become a way of life, like climbing a hill; you keep trudging upward until you reach the top. This time the top of the hill is in God's domain."

Sandy takes over reading:

# THE STAIRWAY OF REPENTANCE

1. Each step up puts us farther from Satan and nearer to God, causing the influence of Satan to diminish and the influence of God to increase.

2. No step makes it impossible to fall until a person has passed into the level from which Adam fell.

3. The higher you climb the more eager you become to take the remaining steps. If you, and those with you live long enough and diligently continue climbing, you can reach the level from which Adam fell.

4. If you die before reaching the top, while ardently working to achieve the kingdom you have no reason to fear death; you will be carried over and judged as though you had made it all the way and are perfect. This is the meaning of "saved by grace." The reason this can be is because you are living up to all the direction God has given to you, and you will not be judged for that which was not known to you.

5. A person may stop at any level he chooses, but in doing so he has chosen his level for eternity. (fig 3)

HE HAS CLIMBED HIGH ENOUGH
TO SEE INTO GOD'S LEVEL

NO POSSIBLE TEMPTATION CAN
LURE HIM DOWN NOW SO HE
PASSES ON INTO GOD'S KINGDOM
(HE IS TRANSLATED)

"Does that mean that if I only know one thing God tells me, like don't steal, and I obey that, I can get to heaven?" Jan asked.

"That's what it says. That doesn't sound too difficult," Don mused.

"You must keep in mind, however, that although God does not overwhelm you with all of his commandments at one time, but he still keeps enough before you that you continue to grow. You always know more than you are living up to. It is doubtful that any adult only knows of just one commandment. So you see it is not likely you will ever be in a situation in which you have only known of one commandment which you have satisfied," John said.

"How could the grace of Christ save anyone so wicked he only made it up a few steps before he died?" Art asked.

"How would any of us be saved if we had to be so perfect we made it all the way to the top?" Fran returned. "Maybe Enoch made it. I don't think I, or you, ever will. Even if we are working hard for it and I don't think we will live long enough to learn and obey all of it. So without the grace of Christ we would all be lost."

"But I always thought all you have to do is believe in Christ," Art persisted.

"Yes," Fran was quick to answer, "but remember that

believe is a verb. If you believe in Christ you do. You do those things he tells you so you are climbing the stairs."

"Okay." Art said, "but how do I repent?"

"Here is a list of scriptures that might answer your question," John said as he passed a paper to each one.

Isaiah 1:16-17, Wash ye, Make you clean; put away the evil of your doings from before mine eyes; cease to do evil; learn to do well...

Isaiah 55:7, Let the wicked forsake his way, and the unrighteous man his thoughts; and let him return unto the Lord, and he will have mercy upon him

Jer. 26:13, Therefore now, amend your ways, and your do-ings, and obey the voice of the Lord your God, and repent, and the Lord will turn away the evil he has pronounced against you.

II Cor 7:9-10 Now I rejoice that ye were made sorry after a godly manner...for godly sorrow worketh repentance to salvation not to be repented of but the sorrow of the world worketh death.

Erekial 18:30-31 I will judge you, O house of Israel, everyone according to his ways, saith the Lord God. Repent, and turn yourselves from all your transgressions; so iniquity shall not be your ruin. Cast away from you all your transgressions...and make you a new heart and a new spirit; for why will ye die...

Gen. 5:1-2 I.V., The lord God called upon men, by the Holy Ghost, everywhere, and commanded them that they should repent; and as many as believed in the Son, and repented of their sins, should be saved. And as many as believed not should be damned. And the words went forth out of the mouth of God, in a firm decree, wherefore they must be fulfilled.

James 4:8 Draw nigh unto God and he will draw nigh to you. Cleanse your hands ye sinners and purify your hearts, ye double minded.

Matt. 3:35 Repent therefore, and bring forth fruits meet for repentance.

Bob pointed out, "None of these scriptures say anything about going through a suffering, or sorrowing process to repent. It sounds like you learn a better way to live and do it. If you are smart you do that anyway."

# DIFFERENCE BETWEEN SORROW AND REPENTANCE

A person convicted of a felony may be sorry but not repentant. He is sorry he got caught, not that he did wrong. He is sorry restraints are placed on him so he can't repeat his act, but he is not convinced the act was wrong, or that he should not repeat it if he had the opportunity.

The repentant person would consider his act wrong and whether or not the courts restrained him, he would determine never to do so again.

Repentance is more than one moment of exquisite sorrow for sins. It does not require rolling on the floor howling words of penance. Repentance is spiritual growth. It is way of life. It involves thousand of decisions and thousands of rejections of temptations to do wrong or to be disobedient to God. It involves removing from your life the traits which are barriers between you and God. It requires us to adopt godly virtues, those characteristics we see to be of God, so we begin to become godlike.

## DIFFERENCE BETWEEN OBEDIENCE AND REPENTANCE

Repentance comes from a desire to understand God and to live according to his instructions. We want to be acceptable to God and draw nearer to him.

Obedience is a willingness to do, whether or not we understand. You can be obedient without understanding the reason for the instructions. Adam offered sacrifices of burnt offerings in obedience to God's instructions because after his experience in the garden he was not going to make the same mistake. It was good that he was obedient, but this was not repentance.

# CHAPTER 24

## BAPTISMS

The study group was visiting at Bob's and Jan's while waiting for Bob to arrive from working late at the restaurant.

Bob came in carrying three pies and some ice cream.

"Oh," Jan pretended to moan for everyone's benefit. "Now you can see why I had to give up modeling and go into real estate. What kind of pies did you bring, Honey."

"Pecan and banana cream," Bob answered. "Which do you want?" he asked as a general question to everyone.

"You know, I'm going on a diet, next week," Don grinned, "So I'll have the pecan now."

"I'm on a diet too," Fran laughed, "I'll have the same thing with only two scoops of ice cream."

After the servings were completed the group enjoyed good natured banter as they ate.

As Jan was picking up the dishes Sandy asked, "Where are you taking us tonight?"

"We're taking you into baptism tonight." John smiled and began handing out papers.

"But I've already been there," Art protested.

# NOT JUST A CEREMONY

"We asked our pastor about being baptized and he told us it was just a pagan ceremony that is no longer necessary," Don and Sandy said, "He said that John the Baptist baptized with water, but it was just symbolic."

"Whoa, wait a minute," John exclaimed, "That is an area I had not planned to get into. There should be no need to, because it is such an overtly wrong concept. But what you are considering here is your eternal life, and words like those are so misleading that they amount to eternal murder.

"I know there are radio and TV preachers who tell people to just kneel in their living rooms at home and say, 'I accept Jesus as my Savior' I get very apprehensive for the spiritual lives of people misled by such teachings. The only reasons I can think of why they would teach such a thing is because they have a personal agenda, or they are totally ignorant of the significance of baptism. Let's stop right here and see what the greatest authority of all said about it."

> Mark 16:15 He (Jesus) said unto them, Go ye into all the world, and preach the gospel to every creature. He that believeth and is baptized, shall be saved; but he that believeth not is damned.

John the Baptist acknowledged Jesus to be far greater than himself for Jesus was the lawgiver, the one whose shoe latchet John was unworthy to fasten. The instruction given in the scripture above was after the death of John the Baptist so John could not have said it is done away with.

Matt. 28:18 Just before Jesus' ascension at the close of his earthly ministry he told the eleven apostles:

All Power is given unto me in heaven and in earth. Go ye therefore, and teach all nations, baptizing them in the name of the Father, and of the Son, and of the Holy Ghost; teaching them to observe all things whatsoever I have commanded you . . .

"Why would the pastor tell us baptism was eliminated? Was there later instruction given that rescinded Jesus' order" Don inquired.

"No," John answered, "there was nothing from the Lord to rescind baptism and remember that the apostles with Jesus practiced baptism continually. They even traveled many long miles to baptize people. The baptism they taught and practiced continued for five centuries, and the changing of that ordinance by men was a major factor which caused the downfall of the church, and brought on the great apostasy.

"When we study tonight you will understand why there must be baptism and why it is so vital, and also why I get so upset about people who teach it is not important. Either Jesus, or the people who take away vital things from the gospel, are not telling the truth. We know of the authority of Jesus, but from what possible source do the others get their authority?"

"The pastor is a REVEREND, and he has nine years of college and seminary," Sandy said.

"I think education is fine," John said, but we need always to remember, that no matter what a man's title is, Reverend, Bishop, Apostle, or Pope, he is still a man, and he can be wrong, regardless of the education. It is your eternal life which is at stake. That is much more important than your physical life, which is temporary; so you want to be sure. Don't just take someone's word for it. The best way to judge is to go to the source. Who said it? Then ask is it in agreement with what the Lord has previously

251

given to us? God's word does not change, so when someone tells you something disjunctive to that previously given, they are in error. New revelation, for instance, may enlarge on truth and expand your understanding, but the moment it takes a different direction, it is wrong.

As we study baptism I think you will see clearly the reason it must be," John concluded.

## MOST IMPORTANT MOMENT OF LIFE

"You know, most of us have been baptized, so why are we going to spend a whole evening on the subject?" Bob asked.

"What do you consider to be the most important moment of your lives?" John asked, "graduation? promotion?"

"I expect it was our wedding day." Bob replied and others nodded agreement.

"I think that after tonight, and our next study, all of you will agree that the confirmation of your baptism was far and away the most important event of your lives." John affirmed.

"What could make it that important?" Jan asked. "our wedding day was a great day. We took off for Hawaii on our honeymoon"

"Have you ever walked up the plank of a teeter-totter?" John asked. "Remember how, when you got to the center, the plank tipped so you walked down to the other end? Your baptism is the pivot point in your lives; everything leads up to it, then your life suddenly makes a drastic change. If you didn't notice the change you missed a great event.

"Who wants to read?—Okay Sandy."

# BAPTISM OF WATER AND OF THE SPIRIT

No part of God's plan stands alone. Each point of doctrine is an intricately interwoven and interdependent part of the whole fabric. There is no separate doctrine of faith, another of agency, another of revelation; each is an integral part of the mosaic of God's great eternal plan. Each is as necessary as light and shadow, or the color and shape in an oil painting. Not one can be left out. Every key that we study in this text is involved in baptisms.

## BAPTISM A BEGINNING, NOT AN END

There is an idea abroad that once a person had been led to baptism, his journey to the kingdom is achieved and all that is required following that is a certain level of goodness until death. You did not, however, grant God the right to begin molding you until your baptism, so his work with you has just now begun. Baptism is the beginning, not the end.

Baptism is the doorway that lets you enter the mansions of glory and the green pastures of God's estate. It is the means of escape from the end that Lucifer has planned for you. It is your release from a miserable, mortal life. And even though baptism is not a release from the problems and trials of life, it can be a release from the trauma which accompanies the trials of a life without hope. It is a beautiful means provided by which we can signify that we have chosen to give ourselves to God, and that we have buried our old being and become a new person.

# BAPTISM A CONTRACT

Baptism is a contract you sign with God giving him permission to work in your life. In the stages of life study we pointed out that our natural tendency of progression is along the track of self-worship and self-importance because of the competition instilled in us. Until we are baptized, the Holy Spirit attempts to reveal our spiritual destitution to us. His work is to lead us to choosing baptism. If we do not reject the message, we begin a process of repentance in which we look for a richer life acceptable to God. As we follow the repentance process, we are led to desire to be right with God which, in turn, directs us to present ourselves to God through baptism. Then there is a distinct change in the work of the Spirit with us. Upon our confirmation, the work of the Spirit changes to *"leading you into all truth." This means* that for the remainder of our lives he will uncover one truth after another until we come face to face with Christ in a way that is an undeniable testimony to us that Jesus is the son of God. But until you make that decision, God maintains a hands-off attitude because of your agency.

When you are baptized you are saying to God, "Here I am. I have given myself to you. You are finally given my permission to work within me to prepare me for eternal life in glory." In effect, you are dropped like a newborn baby on his doorstep. This is the beginning of a new life for you.

"Now I understand what you mean about the pivot point in our lives. It is when we give God permission to work in us and he starts making things happen," Bob said. "Our lives take a different direction because we are God-directed instead of self-directed. That means we will be directed toward the Kingdom of God rather than toward trying to achieve glory for ourselves here."

"Or even worse," Jan injected, leaning over to Bob, "achieving a place in Hell."

"That's right," Lilli spoke quickly, and added, "Just see what happens now. It is like the sun coming out of the clouds and shining on you on a cold winter's day."

# BECOMING PRINCES AND PRINCESSES

The confirmation seals upon you that God has picked you up from his doorstep and holds you in his arms. He adopts you as a son or daughter. It is his signature on the contract that he will take the responsibility of preparing you for eternal life, in his kingdom of glory.

As a son or daughter of the eternal king, you are a prince, or princess, so the King sends his Holy Spirit, to teach you step by step the ways of the kingdom. The Holy Spirit will not drag you or push you, but he will lead you all the way to the Celestial Kingdom if you will continue with him. You may, however, choose to stop along the way. It could wrench God's heart to see his new-born child turn from him and go his own way again, but he will let you go. If you do go, and remain away, you have chosen your level for eternity.

# A MORE DETAILED LOOK AT BAPTISM

This has been only an overview of baptism. There is a lot of information we need to understand to appreciate its importance.

Following the making of a contract through baptism the Lord immediately begins the work of perfecting you for his kingdom. If you understand what is happening it is an exciting time; you not only see things happening in your life, you begin to eagerly anticipate events.

You have the assurance now that you are in the hand of God, so everything which happens to you is for your eternal good. The problems which arise in your life are to teach you. So you should understand that as you learn the lesson from one problem it will pass away. You can learn to skip over some problems by meditation and by prayer and being quick to yield to God's will. As you learn of any of his will for you, you adopt it, making it a part of your life. You will receive a peace you never knew because the Lord takes your burden of sin from you. Free of sin you begin a fresh new life. As long as you walk with the Lord he carries the load. He carries them for you to the final judgment, where they will be erased from the book of your life. However, if you choose to go your own way away from Christ, that bag of sins, which is yours is handed back to you. They become your burden again D.C. 81:2 explains it this way, "I the Lord, will not lay any sin to your charge; go your ways and sin no more; but unto that soul who sinneth shall the former sins return."

"Sometimes I wonder if I've filled another bag since my baptism," Jan mused.

"I don't remember all those things you say will happen after baptism taking place in my life," Bob said thoughtfully. "In that case I'm sure that if we sit down and trace what did happen you will find the problem is that you didn't fully understand what baptism was so you didn't truly give your life over to God," John said. "Then you resisted changes the Lord was bringing to pass in your life because you did not expect what was to happen, and some things that did happen you took to be new problems rather than blessings."

"I think that is exactly the way it was," Bob said.

"Now you can see these events take place as the spirit works with you. It will still be happening. I would not be surprised to find your participation in these studies was directed by the Holy Spirit in the course of his work of 'leading you into all truth,'" John affirmed.

## SPIRITUAL LIFE RESTORED

In stages of life study we pointed out that we need to go back to our innocence at the beginning of our mortal life and start anew on a different course, one of dedication to God and service to others. This is extremely important, but now we want to reveal an even greater meaning of Jesus' statement that "Ye must be born again."

Remember that Adam was told by God that on the day he transgressed he would "surely die?" Adam and Eve's death was more than just a separation from God, as many have supposed. They actually had a death of the spirit which God had breathed into Adam. The confirmation, or the baptism of the spirit, restored to Adam the spiritual life he had lost. We were born into mortal life after Adam's fall so we never had that special life and won't have it until the confirmation of our baptism. This is so important, and so exciting we will not study it further in this key, but reserve it for our next study which will be dedicated wholly to it.

The Apostle Paul wrote to the Ephesians

"I speak unto you...that ye put off the old man, which is corrupt according to deceitful lusts; and be renewed in the mind of the Spirit; and that ye put on the new man, which after God is created in righteousness and true holiness." (Eph 4:22-24).

With the confirmation comes the Joy and freedom and peace of being released from Satan's bonds. And the birth of a new spiritual life within us. You would expect joyful spiritual growth to result from your new beginning, because you are prepared to walk with God. Unfortunately it does not always happen this way, and you should know why. It is because people do not expect changes to come into their lives as a result of baptism. They think the only change to take place will be that which they initiate in their attempts to live up to their new covenant. So when God begins bringing events into their lives to mold them they think they have just run into a series of bad trouble. They don't recognize the hand of God at work so they struggle against the problems rather than learning from them.

"Hey, you mean I should be happy all the time when I see what a mess the world is in, and the kind of troubles Fran and I have trying to make a go of it with inflation the way it is?" Art said in disbelief as he exchanged looks with his wife.

"Art, when you see the role you are cast in, your joy will make the problems of life so small they will be meaningless," Lilli assured him. "You can learn from the problems of today, then move on."

"The point is," John added, "that when you see how God works in your life, many of those problems will be eliminated and you will see the others in an entirely different light so they don't create the worries for you that you have now."

"After seeing this, I don't understand how anyone could say baptism is not important," Sandy said. "I'm just glad we learned this now while we can still do something about it."

"Well, Bob," Fran smirked, "Do you feel we wasted a whole evening now?"

"No," Bob answered, "I had no idea there was so much involved in baptism. I would like to go back over it because there are a lot of implications I need to study more."

# CHAPTER 25

# BAPTISM AND SPIRITUAL LIFE

Don and Sandy, and Art and Fran arrived at Bob and Jan's home nearly half an hour early, as though getting there early would get the class started sooner.

"I've been thinking about last week's class. There is so much more involved in baptism than I realized that I'm wondering if I was ever really baptized," Jan was telling Fran.

"I understand," Fran replied. "I've thought a lot about it too."

Art said, "I told one of the fellows at work about the class and he said that if I hadn't spoken in tongues I wasn't baptized, because on the day of Pentecost they spoke in tongues."

"A friend told me that baptism isn't necessary, that it is just a ritual." Sandy joined in, "but after our study last week there is no way I would buy that."

"That's right," Fran added, "I might have accepted the idea that all you need to do is hold up your right hand and swear that you accept Jesus as your savior, but now that I know what baptism really is, I know it has to be just the way the Bible says." Noticing that Bob seemed to be in deep thought she asked, "What do you think, Bob?"

"I had never seen it in the light John and Lilli presented it, but I know it is true. However, I have been reading the Bible and I have a couple of questions I want to ask them tonight."

"Hey, here they are," Art said as John and Lilli came up the walk.

Jan opened the door and called, "Hello, we have been waiting for you."

John went directly to the table and began laying out papers so everyone began taking places.

"Coffee anyone?" Jan asked, already pouring the first cup

Not waiting for everyone to be seated, Bob said, "Your study last week stimulated considerable thinking, and a few questions as well."

"Good," Lilli answered as she reached for a cup of coffee. "That's what we like to hear."

"Maybe we should look at the questions before getting into the class," John suggested opening his book. "What would you like to discuss?"

"First of all," Bob began, "I looked in the scriptures to see why you used the term 'baptisms' rather than just baptism. I found that one is the baptism of water which you go into, and the other is the baptism of the spirit which is given to you by the laying on of hands. That part I understand, but the eighth chapter of Acts tells of people in Samaria who had been baptized with John's baptism but they had not received the Holy Ghost, so the Apostles went all the way from Jerusalem to lay hands on them so they could receive the Holy Ghost. Another time, at Corinth, Paul found people who said they were baptized with John's baptism but they had not received the Holy Ghost either, so Paul baptized them again and then laid his hands on them and they received the Holy Ghost. That story is in Acts 19. I understand that John the Baptist was a great prophet, so my question is what was wrong with his baptisms? What was going on?"

"You certainly have been studying," John said. "I had not intended to open that question until later, and we won't have time to go into it as thoroughly as I would like to now but those are good questions which deserve an answer tonight."

Your questions are based upon authority. You should know that not all the ministers who graduate from seminaries have authority to baptize and confer the Holy Ghost. They have legal authority granted by the corporate laws of the country, but many don't have divine authority from God, and that is what is required. It was the same in the days you are speaking of. John the Baptist preached, "I baptize with water, but there cometh one mightier than I, the latchet of whose shoes I am not worthy to unloose; he shall baptize you with the Holy Ghost and with fire." (Luke 4:23)

John the Baptist's ministry was the Levitical priesthood through the lineage of Aaron which had authority from God for the water baptism for repentance but not the higher authority for conferring the Holy spirit. The higher priesthood which was after the order of the son of God, and had the authority for the conferring of the Holy Ghost, had been taken from the earth when Moses died, leaving only the Levitical priesthood (Ex, 34:1 I.V.) Recall that when Jesus was baptized by John the confirmation, or the baptism of the Holy Ghost, did not come through John. It had to come down from above in the form of a dove sent from God because John lacked the authority for this baptism. Later Jesus ordained others to the higher priesthood with the authority for both water baptism and for conferring the Holy Ghost by the laying on of hands. Those at Samaria who John had baptized had to be confirmed by someone who had the higher authority. They sent the Apostles Peter and John who had been ordained by Jesus and granted this authority to confirm their baptisms. (Acts Ch 8)

You may remember also that the sorcerer Simon saw the results of their confirmation and offered money to buy the authority to lay on hands for the confirmation, but Peter made it clear the authority could not be purchased; it had to come from God.

Those at Corinth thought they had been baptized, but their baptism was done by men who had been baptized by John, These men then took it upon themselves to go out and baptize others. They did not even have the authority for water baptism for repentance so Paul baptized them in water and then confirmed them.

"I know this is a brief answer for now, but does it answer your question?" John asked.

"Yes, more than I had anticipated" Bob answered.

"I have a question," Art spoke up. "I was told that I had not been legitimately baptized because I did not speak in tongues. What do you think about it?"

Lilli looked at John and smiled knowing this too was a question which might well occupy the entire evening. But John began, "This is another good question which needs much more time to examine in detail. The scriptures cite instances in which people who received the Holy spirit spoke in tongues, so to many people this has become a test of whether or not the Spirit has come to an individual. Tongues, properly exercised, is definitely a gift from God. Individuals have testified to me of having been given this gift, some in a silent manner which was just for communing with God and though I have never had the experience, I do not doubt them, and certainly would not attempt to refute their testimony. They were sincere people. I would consider this to be a cherished gift.

"Your question is whether this determines your reception of the Holy Ghost. I say no, it is not, because of several reasons. First, Jesus received the Holy Ghost in the form of a dove at his baptism, but he did not speak in tongues. Second, there are a number of cases cited in the scriptures in which those who were baptized did not speak in tongues, but did receive the spirit. And third, it is pointed out in scriptures, such as I Corinthians chapter 12, that there is a diversity of gifts, and not everyone receives the same gift. In fact, no one receives all the gifts. We would not expect everyone to have the gift of tongues. And a fourth reason is that the gift of tongues is for communications with people of different languages. Jesus always resisted making a display of miracles just for a show, and if there is no need for communications, there should be no need for speaking in a foreign tongue.

"Does that answer your question?"

"Yes," Art replied, "but I have another. Have you ever spoken in tongues?"

" Yes," John said, "at least three times, but I did not realize I had spoken in tongues until more than fifteen years later, because I spoke in English. "

"How in the world could you speak in tongues in your native language?" Don asked in amazement.

Everyone leaned forward eagerly awaiting the answer as John began: "About thirty years ago I had a speaking engagement at a mission in a farming community. All through my sermon, I struggled for words I would normally have used, but they were not forthcoming. Then I began to use little grade school words which I felt were inadequate to express my message. It was a frustrating and humiliating experience. But after the service a man came to me and said, 'I sure got a lot from your sermon. You speak our language.' I realized immediately that God had used me in this way to bring them a message on their level. I learned later that the education level of most of the congregation was about the fourth grade.

"Not long after that experience I was assigned to speak at a mission in a logging town. I went there expecting to speak to a congregation of loggers, but when I arrived I found the congregation was nearly all children. I was flabbergasted, but as I spoke I realized that my language, and even my tone of voice was on a children's level. The anecdotes I had planned to use were replaced in my mind by illustrations which were easily understood by children. This time I realized what was happening and I did not try to fight it. It turned out to be a pleasant experience."

"What about the third time?" Jan was eager to know.

"That time I was speaking to a group composed largely of college students and instructors. I found I was easily speaking on a level which I would call my reading vocabulary, which is well above my normal speaking vocabulary. This time, too, I realized there was a good spirit with me."

"I understand. God must have been working with you," Bob said, "but why do you call this the gift of tongues?"

"That is a story in itself. Years after these experiences I have just spoken of I was reading in the book of Second Nephi. In chapter thirteen I read,

> Yea then cometh the baptism of fire and of the Holy
> Ghost; and then can ye speak with the tongue of angels, and
> shout praises unto the Holy One of Israel...and can speak
> with a new tongue, yea even with the tongue of angels.

Then in chapter fourteen it says,

> Why do ye ponder these things in your hearts? Do ye not
> remember that I said unto you, that after ye had received the
> Holy Ghost, ye could speak with the tongue of
> angels?...Angels speak by the power of the Holy Ghost;
> wherefore they speak the words of Christ.

"I knew I had received the Holy Ghost, but I felt I had never received the fulfillment of this promise, and couldn't understand why. For over a year I studied and restudied those scriptures and prayed nearly every night for help in understanding."

"You mean you would pray about something like this every night for a year? I would have given up after a week." Art declared.

"Yes," John continued, "it was very important to me.

"Finally, one night it was laid out to me in such a simple explanation I wondered how I had missed it."

"What happened?" Sandy pressed.

I read again,

*'Angels speak by the power of the Holy Ghost; therefore they speak the words of Christ '*

from chapter 14:3 then I turned back to 13:5

*'The Lord giveth light unto the understanding: for he speaketh unto men according to their language unto their understanding."*

I suddenly realized it was not the tongue which was important, it was the message conveyed. It must be presented in an understandable way, or it would be meaningless. If I had spoken in German, or Japanese, or any other language the message would not have been understood, and it was the message which was important not the tongue. It said the angels speak the words of Christ, and the words of Christ must be understandable to them, otherwise it is of no value. Therefore, if they were to receive light, or understanding from my sermons, I had to speak to them in the language they comprehended. That is what the spirit had led me to do, in fact forced me to do, in each situation, otherwise it would have only been a meaningless babble to them."

"That seems so simple, yet profound," Bob said.

"I guess if you were in China you would have spoken in Chinese," Don added.

"All this makes me question whether mine was a valid baptism," Jan said. "Maybe I need to be baptized again."

"Hey, I went through it once that should be enough," Art commented.

Lilli softly replied, "Art, baptism is so important to my eternal life, that if God required it I would gladly be baptized every month. I would never hold out just because I had been there once."

"Oh, well, I guess you're right" Art conceded.

"Those are questions we need to look into, but are you ready to get on with tonight's study?" John asked.

"Ready? We've waited all week for it," Sandy said and, Fran nodded agreement, adding, "I'll start reading."

# CHAPTER 26

# THE SILVER THREAD OF SPIRITUAL LIFE

We are approaching our study of life beyond mortal life, and to best understand it we wish to return to Adam and Eve and trace the silver thread of life by looking at some of the scriptures we previously studied, but this time from a different perspective.

## ALL THINGS CREATED SPIRITUALLY

Gen 1:22-26 I.V. God said let the waters bring forth abundantly, the moving creature that hath life, and foul which may fly above the earth... And I God, created great whales, and every living creature that moveth,... I, God, said, Let the earth bring forth the living creatures after his kind; cattle and creeping things, and beasts of the earth, after their kind; and it was so...

Gen 2:11 adds plant life. And out of the ground made I, the Lord God, to grow every tree naturally,... and it became also a living soul; for it was spiritual in the day that I created it; for it remaineth in the sphere in which I, God, created it...

The Lord reminds us that all were created spiritually before any were placed upon the earth. The stage was being set for the advent of man. It is also notable that the spirits of all men who were ever to come into this life were created before Adam came on earth.

Gen 2:5-6 I, the Lord God, created all things of which I have spoken, spiritually before they were naturally upon the face of the earth; for I, the Lord God, had not caused it to rain upon the face of the earth. And I, the Lord God, had created all the children of men, and not yet a man to till the ground...(verse 9 continues), Nevertheless, all things were before created, but spiritually were they created and made according to my word

Sandy paused in reading and said, "That says 'all the children of men were created before any man was placed on earth.' Right?"

"Yes, that's right." John responded.

Sandy continued, "Then that means we must have all been with God for a long time before we came into this life."

"See," Bob smiled at Jan, "I told you our marriage was made in heaven. You just didn't remember it."

"Nor do I remember anything else about heaven," Jan replied.

Lilli leaned forward and said, "In the book *LIFE AFTER LIFE* by Raymond Moody Jr. he tells of people who have died and gone to the next life, only to be sent back to finish their time in this life. Many of those who returned indicated they felt right at home on the other side because they recognized they had been there before. He also tells of the people reporting they had gotten a glimpse of a place in which they received 'all knowledge' whether past, present or future but they were not permitted to retain it when they returned, except for very brief traces which were only enough to remind them of what they had seen."

"Please continue reading, Sandy," John said, "We have only begun to uncover some amazing things."

# MAN'S CREATION DIFFERENT

Despite the fact that all living things, including the plants, were given a spiritual life, man was different. He was to be a special creation.

> Gen 1:27 I, God said, "Unto mine only begotten, which was with me from the beginning. Let us make man in our image, after our likeness; and it was so." Then in Gen 2:8 God states, "I, the Lord God, formed man from the dust of the ground, and breathed into his nostrils the breath of life; and man became a living soul..."

This was a different kind of life than any other. Man was to be made in the image and likeness of God. Everything except man was given either a plant or animal life, but man was to be special. He received his life directly from God, as a transference of the spirit of God into him.

However Adam was not to enjoy this privileged life for long, because God put him before the tree of knowledge of good and evil and told him he could choose whether or not to partake of it, but, God told man, *"In the day that thou eatest thereof thou shalt surely die."*

Death is not just a change of location, it is a loss of life. And Adam did die that day. Adam and Eve's death was more than just being forced out of the vicinity of God as many have supposed. They actually had a death of the spiritual life God had breathed into Adam. Adam and Eve had lost their spiritual lives and bodies. These were needed for them to be able to live in the Kingdom of God and for personal communion with God.

It is important for us to know what actually happened at Adam's death on that day. He was still a living being here in mortal life, so it is reasonable to ask what Adam's death meant.

269

Because we came into mortal life through Adam and Eve and inherited their new environment. Whatever he lost, has been lost to us, his descendants also.

# ADAM AND EVE'S DEATH IN THE GARDEN

In the Garden of Eden, Adam and Eve were able to commune directly with God, which indicates that they were in different bodies than we know here. Those bodies remained behind in their death from the Garden just as the physical body remains on earth at death here. In mortal life they found themselves in a physical body uniquely designed for living on earth.

The eternal body is much different than the physical body which we have in mortal life. We believe it is that perfect eternal body which was left on the other side which will be lifted up in the resurrection rather than this physical mortal body which is a vehicle for us in this life. This body is destined to return to the earth from which it was formed, but the eternal body will go on forever either to everlasting glory, or to everlasting condemnation.

Alma 19:90 tells us: The soul could never die, and the fall had brought upon mankind a spiritual death as well as a temporal...

"That line about spiritual and temporal death, sounds like Adam lost both his spirit and body," Don remarked.

"Read on and it will tell more about it." John said.

The difference between spiritual life and mortal life is demonstrated in a number of places. Good examples are the following: our physical bodies cannot survive the presence of

God. For example: Satan came to Moses soon after Moses had been in the presence of God and it is recorded:

> Moses looked upon Satan, and said, Who art thou, for behold, I am a son of God, in the similitude of his Only begotten; And where is thy glory, that I should worship thee? For behold, I could not look upon God except his glory should come upon me, and I were transfigured before him. But I can look upon thee in the natural man. Is it not so surely? (D.C. 22)

Even Jesus was transfigured from his earthly body so he could speak with Moses and Elias who came to him from beyond the veil.

> Matt. :1-2 Jesus taketh Peter, James, and John his brother, And bringeth them up into a high mountain, apart, and was transfigured before them; and his face did shine as the sun and his raiment was white as the light. And, behold, there appeared unto them Moses and Elias, talking with him...

When Adam and Eve found themselves in mortal life they were in a totally different situation. They were functioning as other physical beings, albeit they were especially gifted with greater mental and emotional capabilities than other animals. they were still potentially sons and daughters of God, but this was not to be automatically granted to them.

The new lives they had acquired which kept their bodies functioning was the physical life with which all animals were created. Man was given only his physical nature and life.

"This is obvious even today when we see so many animals in human bodies. Their brutish nature completely obviates any suggestion of godliness," Fran said.

The spiritual life God had breathed into Adam in Paradise was dead. Instead of being a son of God, Adam was only a especially endowed animal created by God. Instead of walking with God in the safety of Paradise he was under the threat of hell. Alma explains:

> Alma 19:60 behold, an awful death cometh upon the wicked; for they die as to things pertaining to righteousness; for they are unclean And no unclean thing can inherit the kingdom of God.

Adam lost the spiritual life of God that was breathed into him :

> Gen 4:4 Adam called upon the name of the Lord, and Eve also, his wife; and they heard the voice of the Lord from the way towards the Garden of Eden speaking unto them, and they saw him not; for they were shut out of his presence.

Adam lost his Father-child nearness in which there existed a two-way face to face conversational relationship. He lost the peace, the tranquillity and love which pervaded the atmosphere of the Garden. He had not yet learned to work with the tremendous power which must have been available to him as a child of God in God's Kingdom, and he lost the omniscience, the perfect and total knowledge which fills those in Paradise.

Even though he had lost the perfect knowledge, Adam was taught to pray by "the voice of God from the way toward the garden," and by the ministry of angels.

## SPIRITUAL LIFE MAY BE RESTORED

> Alma 19:60 Our first parents were cut off both temporally and spiritually from the presence of the Lord; and thus we see they became subjects to follow after their own will... Therefore it was expedient that mankind should

be reclaimed from this spiritual death;" GEN 4:9 adds to this thought,

As thou hast fallen, Thou mayest be redeemed, and all mankind, even as many as will.

# ADAM'S REBIRTH

Adam remembered enough about his disobedience in the Garden that he was determined never to disobey God again. So when he was commanded by God to offer sacrifices he didn't ask why, he just did as he was told.

Fran sipped on her coffee and commented, "Poor Adam, He must have really learned his lesson in the Garden."

"Because of Adam's willingness to obey, we are benefactors of an astounding message given to him." John said. Just look at Gen 4:6

Adam was obedient unto the commandments of the Lord. And after many days an angel of the Lord appeared unto Adam saying, why dost thou offer sacrifices unto the Lord. And Adam said unto him, I know not, save the Lord commanded me. Then the angel spake saying, This thing is a similitude of the sacrifice of the Only Begotten of the Father, which is full of grace and truth; Wherefore, thou shalt do all that thou doest, in the name of the Son. And thou shalt repent, and call upon God, in the name of the Son for evermore.

**BLANK**

# CHAPTER 27

# ADAM REBORN INTO SPIRITUAL LIFE
## ADAM'S BAPTISM

Sandy brushed her hair back and began reading.

Adam had learned the disastrous consequences of disobedience, and he determined not to make that mistake again. He began to implore God's direction, until finally God spoke to him as recorded in Gen. 6:52-54

> God hath made known unto our father Adam, by his own voice, saying, I am God; I made the world and men before they were in the flesh. And he also said unto him, If thou wilt turn unto me and hearken unto my voice, and believe, and repent of all thy transgressions, and be baptized, even in water, in the name of mine Only Begotten Son... Ye shall receive the gift of the Holy Ghost, asking all things in his name, and whatsoever ye shall ask it shall be given you.
>
> And our father Adam spake unto the Lord, and said, Why is it that men must repent, and be baptized in water?

## THE REASON EXPLAINED

"Adam's question was very important and God answered it, explaining the reasons for repentance and baptism (verses 57-67). This answer is one of the most profound passages of all scripture," John said. "Let's read it all to catch the full message before we discuss it."

And the Lord spake unto Adam saying Inasmuch as thy children are conceived in sin, even so, when they begin to grow up sin conceiveth in their hearts, and they taste the bitter, that they may know to prize the good. And it is given unto them to know good from evil; wherefore, they are agents unto themselves. And I have given unto you another law and commandment; wherefore teach it unto your children, that all men, everywhere, must repent, or they can in no wise inherit the kingdom of God. For no unclean thing can dwell there, or dwell in his presence; for, in the language of Adam, Man of Holiness is his name; and the name of his Only Begotten is the Son of Man, even Jesus Christ, a righteous judge, who shall come in the meridian of time.

Therefore I give unto you a commandment, to teach these things freely unto your children, saying, that by reason of transgression cometh the fall, which fall bringeth death; and in as much as ye were born into the world by water and blood, and the Spirit, which I have made, and so become of dust a living soul; even so ye must be born again, into the kingdom of heaven, of water, and of the Spirit, and be cleansed by the blood, even the blood of mine only begotten; that ye may be sanctified from all sin...And now, behold, I say unto you, this is the plan of salvation unto all men, through the blood of mine Only Begotten, who shall come in the meridian of time...

John looked up from his paper and said, "We should note in this scripture that Adam was told that his spiritual death was due to his transgression. Then he was made into a living physical being of dust (the elements of the earth). But the Lord made it plain that he must be born again with a spiritual rebirth or he may never live in the kingdom of God. This can only be accomplished through the sacrificial shedding of Jesus' blood."

"Oh, I have a question," Sandy said. "Does that part about children being conceived in sin mean that it is sinful to have children, or does it mean that they are sinful because of Adam and Eve's sin in the garden?"

Lilli turned to Sandy and said, "Actually, neither one, children are not responsible for the sin of their parents but, because Adam and Eve were banished from the garden, children are born into an environment subject to temptation and sin."

"Well, what about the next line which says that as they grow up sin conceiveth in their hearts?" Sandy asked.

"That seems to be the way our lives go," John answered, "As a child gets old enough to be accountable for his decisions, he, just like Adam and Eve, is faced with temptations and he makes wrong choices. Each will be responsible for his errors, or sins, and each must repent of them. You see, God makes each of us agents unto ourselves.

In other words we will not be responsible for the sins of Adam and Eve, but we will carry the responsibility for our own sins. Does that answer your question?"

"I see," Sandy responded, "and each must be forgiven by Christ before we can enter the kingdom of God."

"Wait a minute," Art said. "This is talking about Adam's time, so how can it be telling about Jesus who didn't come until centuries later?"

John answered, "You may recall that in our first key, the master key, Gen 1:27 I God, said unto mine Only Begotten, which was with me from the beginning...so Jesus was involved with us from the beginning. In fact," John continued, "in Genesis 1:2 I.V. God told Moses *I am the Beginning and the End; the Almighty God By mine only Begotten I created these things.* So Jesus was the director and the power behind the creation of the worlds. There is no time in man's history when Jesus has not been involved. Even in Hebrews 1:2 in the new testament, it tells that it was by Jesus 'by whom also he (God) made the worlds.' and it will be Christ who judges us at the Great Last Judgment. So Jesus is involved in all of man's history from the creation of the world through the final judgment, even though he didn't take upon himself the flesh and blood of man until he came in the meridian of time."

"I don't see how Adam could have been forgiven at that date though. Jesus hadn't even been crucified then," Art said.

"Do you recall in the fifth chapter of Luke the story of the healing of the man with palsy?" John asked. "This was also before the crucifixion, but Jesus said to him 'thy sins are forgiven thee.' The Scribes and Pharisees were incensed about it, but Jesus said 'that ye may know that the Son of Man hath power on earth to forgive sin, I said it.'

"So it is apparent that Jesus has always had the power to forgive sins. Revelation 13:8 calls Jesus 'The Lamb slain from the foundation of the world.' For all purposes the fact of Jesus' crucifixion was determined before men came upon the earth. There was never a time when Satan had power over Jesus. He could never prevent Jesus' forgiving or loving people. So as soon as the plan was made, it was as though the act had been completed.

"Even the sacrifices made before the coming of Christ on earth were symbolic of Jesus' sacrifice on the cross. Genesis 4:6-7 tells that an angel spoke to Adam and told him, "This thing (the sacrificial offering he was making) is a similitude of the sacrifice of the only Begotten of the Father..."

Lilli added, "In the nineteenth chapter of Alma he points out that even though Jesus could forgive, there would not be a resurrection of the dead at that time. He said (Alma 19:29-30):

I say unto you, that there is no resurrection...until after the coming of Christ. Behold, he bringeth to pass the resurrection of the dead. But behold,...the resurrection is not yet.

"Then," Lilli continued, "he pointed out that there was a time between death and the resurrection in which the souls of those who had died were consigned either to Paradise, or to hell, according to whether they had been righteous, or evil. They would remain there until their resurrection. And the first resurrection would not come until Jesus arose from the dead as the first fruit of the grave."

"That's what I wanted to know," Art said.

"Shall I continue reading?" Sandy asked.

Art nodded his assent.

"Let's read on to see what Adam did after God answered his question about baptism," Lilli said.

## ADAM'S RESPONSE

Adam had been repenting of those things which were a barrier between him and God, and he had learned obedience to God's commands. Now with an enlightened understanding of baptism, he was quick to respond.

Gen. 6:67: It came to pass when the Lord had spoken (explained baptism) unto Adam, our father, that Adam cried unto the Lord and he was caught away by the Spirit of the Lord and was carried down into the water, and was laid under the water, and was brought forth out of the water, and thus he was baptized, and the *Spirit of God descended upon him, (the confirmation of his baptism by the Holy Ghost) And thus he was born of the Spirit, and became quickened*

*(Made alive) in the inner man. And he heard a voice out of heaven, saying, Thou art baptized with fire and with the Holy Ghost; this is the record of the Father and the Son, from henceforth without beginning of days or end of years, from all eternity to all eternity. Verse 71 adds, "Behold thou art one in me, a son of God; and thus may all become my sons.*

# ADAM BORN AGAIN

With the confirmation and granting of the Holy Spirit following Adam's baptism, he was literally born again. The spiritual life he had lost in death in the Garden because of disobedience was restored to him in mortal life through repentance and baptism. God told him: (Gen. 6:62)

It is given to abide in you, the record of heaven, the comforter, the peaceable things of immortal glory. the truth of all things (Perfect knowledge) that which quickeneth all things, which maketh alive all things. That which knoweth all things, and hath all power according to wisdom, mercy, truth, justice, and judgment.

So to Adam was restored his spiritual life and all those things which he had lost by his fall. (The line, *Thou art after the order of him who was without beginning of days or end of years*...tells us that Adam was also ordained to the highest order of priesthood at the same time.)

There was, however, a major difference. He was not suddenly jerked back into Paradise with an endowment of all things being restored to him. He was still in a physical body and he was subject to the limitations of that body. He was still an earthbound mortal so he could not exercise all the gifts with which the spiritual body will be endowed.

He still had years to complete his days of probation in his mortal lifetime, so in verse 62 he is promised he will: enjoy the words of eternal life in this world, and eternal life in the world to come; even immortal glory.

The "words of eternal life" reveal that he received the understanding and promise of eternal life, and a vision of that life to come. He did again receive his spiritual life. This was truly being born again. Although he was limited by the body he was in while in mortal life, when he returned to Paradise, he would not have just the words of eternal life but he could partake of the tree of life and inherit the fullness of eternal life.

D.C. 85 explains this further in verse 6:d, Ye who are quickened by a portion of the celestial glory shall then receive of the same, even a fullness...

All this was made possible by the sacrifice of Christ to win our release from the devil.

## THE IMPORTANCE OF BAPTISM EMPHASIZED

The knowledge that the confirmation of our baptism restores to us the spiritual life which Adam had lost in the garden places a far greater importance upon baptism than we had previously known, because the promise is *"and thus may all become my sons."*

"That must include us," Jan said.

The restoration of Adam's spiritual life through his baptism and confirmation does not extend blanket coverage to his descendants. Each person is an agent unto himself, and shoulders his own responsibilities.

## EFFECT OF OBTAINING SPIRITUAL LIFE

John 1:12 continues the promise,

"As many as received him, to them he gave power to become the sons of God; only to them who believe on his name

Another promise is recorded in John 5:24, Jesus told the crowd at the temple,

Verily Verily I say unto you, He who heareth my words, and believeth on him who sent me, hath everlasting life, and shall not come into condemnation; but is passed from death into life."

John interrupted, "This is true because the spiritual life restored in the confirmation does not die at the end of mortal life, but goes on eternally."

John 3:36 "He who believeth on the Son hath everlasting life; and shall receive of his fullness—"

This brings us back to receiving again a fullness of those things the death of Adam took away.

## EFFECT UPON THOSE WHO DO NOT RECEIVE SPIRITUAL LIFE

An indication of what the loss of spiritual life means to those who have not regained it through baptism is shown by their inability to receive the Holy Spirit which would "guide them into all truth."

Abel, who was murdered by Cain, was a righteous man, as were Seth, Enos, and others, but a division occurred between those who believed and sought God and the kingdom, and those who followed Satan. Those who believed in God became known as the sons of God, and those who yielded to Satan became known as the sons of men. The sons of men became very numerous and evil even in Adam's time.

Referring back to Adam's loss of perfect knowledge and memory of much of the Garden events, we see why those people who do not have the Holy Spirit to guide them cannot understand what the followers of Christ know. At one time, Jesus had followed his custom of using parables to teach people who crowded around him. At the conclusion of his teaching he proclaimed, *He who hath ears, let him hear.* Later when the Apostles were alone with Jesus they asked why he taught in parables. Jesus responded, *unto you it is given to know the mysteries of the Kingdom of God, but to others in parables, that in seeing, they might not see, and in hearing they might not understand* (Luke 8:10).

The sons of men and the sons of God were being separated by this simple expedient, Those who were not the Lord's could not understand the message of the parables. Jesus made a statement to Nicodemous who came to him at night to learn the way of salvation, John 3:3. *"Jesus answered and said unto him, verily verily I say unto thee, Except a man be born again he cannot see the Kingdom of God."* There were two parts to this response. The first is that as a man, he would never see the kingdom, even if he were to be placed in the center of it, because he could not understand what he did see. The second was that unless a man comes to God through repentance and baptism, he will never receive the spiritual life which gives him access to the kingdom.

The group had earnestly listened without speaking. Now Bob said, "That must be the most interesting story ever to come from the scriptures. It says to me that I came here without a spiritual life, and with the potential of becoming a devil bound for destruction, but when I was baptized I was released from the devil by Christ and received eternal, spiritual life. I also became God's adopted son. When I return to him, I will receive glory beyond anything I could possibly have dreamed of."

"Yes," Lilli replied, "and our next study will be equally wonderful."

Don leaned forward with excitement glowing in his eyes, and said, "Bestowing spiritual life through baptisms makes it very clear why a person would have to be chosen and ordained to act as God's representative. He would truly have to be authorized by God."

Jan wiped a tear from the corners of her eyes and said, "I have to be baptized again." Art put his hand on hers and added, "Me too."

# CHAPTER 28

# LIFE BEYOND DEATH

Don and Sandy were swept by the delightsome odor of freshly baked cookies as they entered the home of Bob and Jan. The power of the cookies was causing John and Lilli to feel starved although they had just eaten a few minutes earlier.

Bob was showing Art some of the intricate operations of his new VCR and Fran was arranging a bouquet of pansys on the coffee table.

"It looks like the gang's all here," Bob said as he turned the TV off and everyone moved to the dining table.

"Cookies anyone?" Jan asked, placing a freshly baked tray of cookies on the table.

"Are you kidding?" Don teased as he took two, then added, "I'll bet you left the range fan off just to hold all that cookie smell in the house."

"I have been feeling tortured by them ever since we came in." Lilli contributed.

Slipping into her chair Sandy asked, "What are we studying tonight?"

"This is our big night," John responded. "Everything we have studied so far points directly to tonight's subject. We will look at death and beyond."

"That sounds morbid. I liked our happier studies," Jan said as she chose a cookie for herself.

"It really isn't" Lilli promised, "It is one of the most beautiful of all our studies and there is nothing happier than what God has planned for us. I think we learn more about God from this study than from any other."

"What's there to learn?" Art asked "You die and go to heaven or Hell, that's all there is to it," he said with assurance, then added, "Isn't it?"

"That's what I've always understood," Fran offered. "What more could there be?"

"A lot of people accept that idea," John said. "Even a lot of preachers who should know better. It's because they have not done their homework and haven't put all the scriptures together so they can see the whole picture. But before we get into the study, let's take a look at that thought?"

"It always seemed simple enough," Art said. "The Bible says to accept Christ as our savior and be saved. Doesn't that mean we go to heaven?"

"Yes the Bible tells us that but it also says to believe and be baptized to be saved," Lilli responded.

Don smiled and made his contribution, "I like the one I found in Lamentations 3:26. It says, It is good that a man should both hope and quietly wait for the salvation of the Lord."

"Pass the cookies this way please." Sandy said, "The one I thought was neat was Paul saying we are saved by the foolishness of preaching."

John looked around the group and said, "These are all true, but none of them stands alone. None is complete by itself, and each has a problem. Believe and be saved is necessary, but that is followed by repentance and baptism in acceptance of Jesus as our savior. Then we have to ask what to do with God's claim of being absolutely just and impartial? Millions of people have never had the opportunity to hear of Jesus, so how can they believe in him? How could God be just by accepting only those who have believed?

"Added to the problem of showing equality in glory, is the fact that some people have lived sacrificial lives of service to God, while others have resisted God until the end. Some have laid down their lives for their testimony of him, like the early Christians who were thrown to the lions. There is no question they have proven worthy of the highest of glories. But compare them to a criminal who never did a worthy thing in his life, who lived handsomely on the gains from defrauding innocent people, and was finally convicted of murder. After all appeals to the courts failed, he turned to God shortly before his execution and asked for forgiveness and he accepted the salvation of Jesus. With the 'Heaven, or Hell' concept he would be rewarded equally with those who lived dedicated lives. Does that seem like justice from God? Even our courts try to be more fair than that."

"If it works like that," Don laughed, "the trick would be to figure out when you are going to die and live it up until then, then accept salvation and have the best of both worlds."

"Oh," Lilli exclaimed, "they may have a lot of glamour and money and everything that goes with money, but there is no way they have the best of this life."

"I agree with that, but that is not the point." John said, "Belief in Jesus is not sufficient in itself. James 2:19 points out 'The devils also believe, and tremble.' Certainly their belief does not save them."

"While I was in high school," Sandy recalled, "I didn't believe because of some Christians I knew. I thought if that is Christianity I don't want it. If I hadn't learned that the way they lived was not like Christ it would have kept me from becoming Christian."

"That would be awful," Lilli agreed, "If because of their sin you were condemned, but God knows about these situations, so despite what they did to you he would have placed you into Terrestrial Glory even though you might have missed the Celestial Kingdom."

"Oh," Jan suddenly looked up, "I thought all of heaven was the same. I never heard of Terrestrial Glory. What is that?"

"These are the things we want to study tonight. The study is quite lengthy, so let's get started. Lilli, we'll ask you to begin the reading," John directed.

"Don't you think it would be wise to give some explanation before we get into all the scriptures involved," Lilli suggested. "It will make it so much easier to understand and see where we are going with this study."

## FASCINATING BUT COMPLEX

John begins, "The total story is complex and there are various paths that different people follow. To project the overall picture with a minimum of confusion, we will first present an overview without details and scriptures then we will return, presenting the close-up and scriptural support. It is a fascinating and exciting study. We call it photograph of God because we can see the likeness of God most clearly in what he has planned and prepared for us.

"At death our physical bodies are returned to the earth from which they came and our spiritual lives go directly to God for the separation Jesus spoke of in which the goats were sent to his left hand and the sheep to the right."

"I thought you told us in an earlier study that when you have given yourself to God in baptism you never die," Fran commented.

"He did," Bob said, "but remember the illustration of driving a big earth mover and parking it for the night. The driver steps out of the vehicle and it dies, but he goes home to his family."

"Unless the Devil's KGB is waiting to arrest him when he steps out. Then he and the vehicle both die," Don added.

Fran shivered, "Oh! What a terrible thought."

"Yes," John continued, "but although the vehicle dies the spirit goes directly to God to be judged. This is not the great and final judgment. The goats are never permitted to enter Paradise. They are sent directly to Hell, which is also termed in scripture as "The Pit" and more aptly "The Prison." The sheep are consigned to Paradise."

## PARADISE A PLACE OF LEARNING AND PREPARATION

Paradise is a place of learning. It is a staging area for preparing us for eternity. The universal knowledge of the ages will be available to its inhabitants. We will be filled with the knowledge of God and his everlasting plan. There is a training process to prepare us for the glorious splendor God has reserved for us

The process of Paradise could not have been done on earth in mortal life because we are in the throes of making our choice of complete loyalty to God or submission to Satan. On earth we work through the processes in which we are subject to temptations and evil. In Paradise, Satan will not exist, and the processes of temptation will be behind us. So with freedom from the influences of evil we can go on to things we can scarcely dream of in this life. It will be like a great university, or finishing school, but beyond anything your mind can now conceive.

When Christ returns to earth the spirits will come out of Paradise and be given their perfect new bodies. This is the first resurrection. They will live and reign on earth with Christ during the millennial period. Satan will not be free during this period, so there will be no temptation for evil. In addition to other blessings, those who have come through Paradise have been tried and found worthy, so they will never again need to worry about falling to Satan.

During the thousand years there will still be mortals on the earth who will live to "the age of man," and babies will be born and live a full life, then be changed from mortal to immortal beings "in the twinkling of an eye." They will not be tempted by the Devil, because he will be bound.

The millennial period will be followed by a short season when Satan will make one last great attempt to win souls to his side. He will gather a great army from the nations and surround the saints to destroy them. Any of the saints who are weak in their faith in God, may, if they wish, defect to Satan for it will appear that his forces are about to destroy the saints. But suddenly, like a bolt of lightning and a clap of thunder, time will end, and God will bring fire down from heaven and devour the forces of Satan. Then the Devil and his followers are cast out into the Lake of Fire and brimstone forever.

# HELL ALSO A PLACE OF LEARNING

During all the events related above, those who had been confined to the Prison are still locked up. People of various levels during their mortal lives are confined there. There are many who were basically good people, but were too busy with other things, like their businesses, to get around to seriously considering the call of Christ to them. Many of them likely attended church on

Sundays and let the words of the preacher soothe their feelings of guilt, but did nothing to change their lives and follow Christ.

There will be others in Hell's prison who represent unsaved people, down to the most vile forms of humanity to have walked the earth; even those who had been given a sure testimony of the divinity of Jesus in this life, but rejected it and followed Satan.

## THE PRISON TO BE OPENED

At the time fire comes down from heaven and destroys the armies of the devil and saves the saints, the doors of the prison shall swing open and all Prisoners who were incarcerated in it will come forth and receive their bodies. This is the second and final resurrection. They will not be released to go free, however, they will be brought before God for their final judgment.

## GREAT FINAL JUDGMENT

All people from the eons of time, and from all the earth will now be assembled before God for the great and final judgment of both the righteous and wicked. The time of judgment of all beings from the most righteous down to Lucifer, the most evil will have come.

There are four places of consignment from the Judgment:

1. Celestial Glory: for those most righteous and holy who have been made into the image and likeness of God.

2. Terrestrial Glory: for those who have been honorable men and women on earth but were blinded by the craftiness of men. They died without law and were kept in the prison. They were not valiant in testimony of Jesus.

3. Telestial Glory: who inherit this glory received (accepted) not the gospel of Christ nor the testimony of Jesus. However they do not deny the Holy Spirit. They were thrust down to hell, not to be redeemed from the devil until the last resurrection when Christ shall have finished his work.

4. Endless Punishment: these are the "Sons of Perdition" who deny the Son after the father has revealed him. They go into everlasting punishment with the Devil and his angels. This is the lake of fire and brimstone also called outer darkness. This is the second death.

After the great and final judgment, there will be no more mortal life, no more time, no hell, no Paradise, and the earth will have fled away. These have all served their purposes.

"Wait a minute!" Art suddenly spoke out, "I thought that hell was everlasting."

"And I thought Paradise was the eternal life we were all working toward," Sandy added.

"Many people have thought the way you do," John answered them, "but wait until we get into what the scriptures tell us about these places."

# END OF THE OVERVIEW

"The overview alone has been quite lengthy, but we feel it is important in order to follow through the maze of scripture which supports it. We will use scripture from The Bible, The Book of Mormon, and from D.C. Also we will refer to testimonies of people who died but were sent back.

"Before we go on to the detailed study let's look at the charts on the next pages. It will help to visualize what is taking place and the order in which things happen," John said as he turned to the next page.

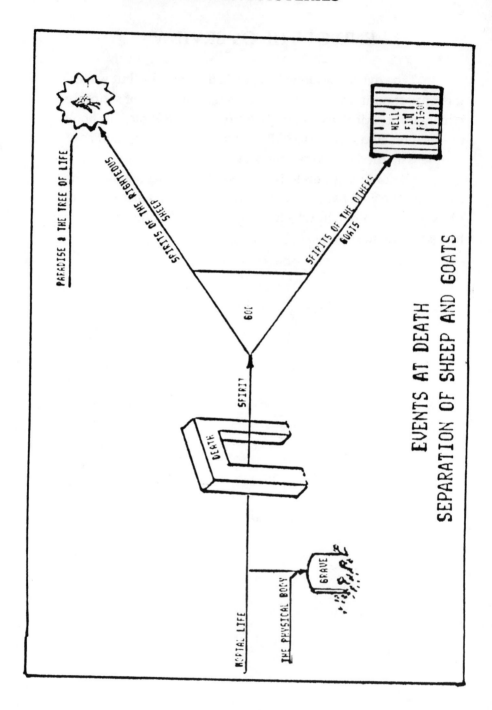

EVENTS AT DEATH
SEPARATION OF SHEEP AND GOATS

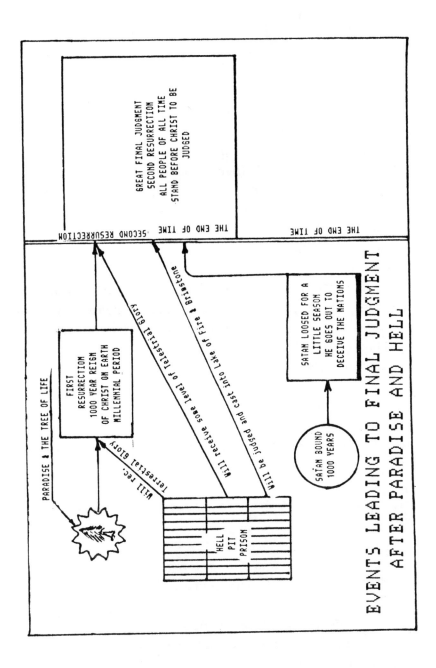

EVENTS LEADING TO FINAL JUDGMENT
AFTER PARADISE AND HELL

# IN THE MIDST OF ETERNITY A SCRIPTURAL STUDY OF LIFE AFTER DEATH

The study of life after death properly begins with a study of man's creation, because the plans for eternal life were made then. Everything related to our mortal life reaches a climax at the death of our bodies, so now it is well to take a quick review of the major keys we have studied.

D.C. 2:1 The works and the designs and the purposes of God cannot be frustrated, neither can they come to naught, for God does not walk in crooked paths: neither doth he turn to the right hand nor the left; for his paths are straight and his course is one eternal round.

The plans which are not to be frustrated are those which were made before time began. They are for the process which man was to be put through to prepare him for the Celestial Kingdom .

Gen. 1:27: And I God said...let us make man in our image and after our likeness...

D.C. 22:23b: This is my work and. my glory to bring to pass the immortality and eternal life of man.

Moses was shown everyone who ever lived and he saw God's plans in detail from before time began and was shown that they extended into eternity after time ends.

God began his work by creating every individual who was to come into this life. Each was created before Adam was given a physical body. The book *LIFE AFTER LIFE* by Raymond A. Moody Jr. is a book about the testimonies of people who have died and gone on into the experience of the after life. Many of them said knew they were home again. They knew they had been there before, and it was a happy reunion for them.

To mold man into God's image and likeness, a special laboratory was prepared. It was set in time and humans were locked into it by their mortal life bodies. As we study what has taken place and we see God's great plan unfold, we become keenly aware that mortal life is a very deliberate process which we are put through; it is not in any way happenstance. God had every detail planned.

> D.C.28:12 I say unto you, that I the Lord God, gave unto Adam and unto his seed, that they should not die as to the temporal death, until I, the Lord God, should send forth angels to declare unto them repentance and redemption...and thus did I appoint unto man his days of probation; that by his natural death he might be raised in immortality unto eternal life.

## SKIP OVER PROCESS OF LIFE

Skipping over God's process for our lives, which we have been studying, we pick up his plan for us at the doorway of death. Hebrews 9:27 states what seems obvious to us: *It is appointed unto men once to die, but after this the judgment.* There is a difference between the death of the wicked and the death of the righteous. At the time of our physical death our spirits go directly to God and there is an initial separation which was spoken of by Jesus (Matt. 25:32-33) when he said.

297

"He shall separate the one from another, as a shepherd divideth the sheep from the goats; the sheep on his right hand, and the goats on his left."

This is not the final judgment but it is the division of the righteous from the wicked. The righteous only experience a release from being locked into their bodies, their spirits live on and go to God.

Eccl. 12:7 Then shall the dust return to the earth as it was: and the spirit shall return unto God who gave it. John 5:24 adds to this, He who heareth my word, and believeth on him who sent me, hath everlasting life, and shall not come into condemnation; but is passed from death into life.

Prov.12:28 In the way of righteousness is life; and in the pathway thereof there is no death.

John 11:25-26: Jesus said unto her, I am the resurrection, and the life; he that believeth in me, though he were dead, yet shall he live; and whosoever believeth in me shall never die...

John 3:16 For God so loved the world, that he gave his Only Begotten Son, that whosoever believeth on him should not perish; but have everlasting life.

John 8:51 Verily I say unto you; if a man keep my saying he shall never see death.

John was not alone in seeing that men chosen for the kingdom do not die when the body quits functioning. D.C.42-12f states,

"It shall come to pass that those that die in me shall not taste of death, for it shall be sweet unto them;

Revelation 2:7 Promises, To him that overcometh will I give to eat of the tree of life which is in the midst of the Paradise of God.

This is the tree which Adam and Eve were prevented from partaking of before their mortal life. Those who do partake of it receive eternal life.

Those who die in Jesus are in Paradise. However this is not yet the resurrection; they have not yet received their bodies. Paul, in 2 Cor. 5:6-8, and Moroni in Moroni 10:31 explain.

> Paul: Whilst we are at home in the body, (here in mortal life) we are absent from the Lord...We are confident, I say and willing rather to be absent from the body, and to be present with the Lord.

> Moroni: And now I bid unto all, a farewell. I soon go to rest in the Paradise of God, until my spirit and body shall again reunite...

# THE RIGHTEOUS

We will first follow the path of the righteous. Jesus said to the thief on the cross... *Today thou shalt be with me in Paradise Luke 23:43*
Alma 19:44

> Behold, it has been made known unto me, by an angel, that the spirits of all men, as soon as they are departed from this mortal body; yea, the spirits of all men, whether they be good or evil, are taken home to that God who gave them life. And then shall it come to pass that the spirits of those who are righteous, are received into a state of happiness, which is called paradise; a state of rest; a state of peace, where they shall rest from all their troubles, and from all care and sorrow...

It is in Paradise that they partake of the tree of Life.

Nephi 2:48-52 tells of a vision which his father, Lehi was given of the Tree of Life:

> I beheld a tree who's fruit was desirable to make one happy. And it came to pass that I did go forth and partake of the fruit thereof; and I beheld that it was most sweet above all that I ever before tasted. Yea, and I Beheld that the fruit thereof was white, to exceed all the whiteness I had ever seen. And as I partook of the fruit thereof, it filled my soul with exceeding joy...

Nephi, the Son of Lehi, prayed that he too might see the tree of life. The ensuing experience gave even more light to Nephi than had been given to his father. Of the tree Nephi said,

> "...I looked and beheld a tree; and it was like unto the tree which my father had seen; and the beauty thereof was far beyond, yea, exceeding of all beauty; and the whiteness thereof did exceed the whiteness of driven snow. ...I said unto the Spirit, I behold thou hast shown unto me the tree which is precious above all.

# PARADISE IS A STAGING AND HOLDING AREA

John said, "I want to repeat that Paradise is not permanent. It is where the tree of life is and those righteous people who go there will partake of it. In addition to that they are retained there while awaiting the resurrection, and during their long wait they receive knowledge in preparation for eternal life in the Celestial Kingdom.

"Paradise will be emptied at the first resurrection when all of its inhabitants receive their bodies. This coincides with the beginning of the millennial period when Jesus comes and Satan is bound for a thousand years.

"Because Satan is bound and there will be no evil, those mortals still living in the presence of Christ during the millennium will be taught in an environment free of the influence of Satan. Therefore they can be prepared to be changed from mortal to immortal beings in the twinkling of an eye. There will no longer be a need for Paradise and it will be eliminated."

## CHRIST COMES AT THE FIRST RESURRECTION MILLENNIUM'S THOUSAND YEAR REIGN BEGINS

Rev. 20:4-5 I saw the souls of them that were beheaded for the witness of Jesus, and for the word of God, and which had not worshipped the beast, neither his image, neither had received his mark upon their foreheads, or in their hands; and they lived and reigned with Christ a thousand years, but the rest of the dead lived not until the thousand years were finished. This is the first resurrection."

Those who went to Paradise have remained there until Christ comes upon the earth for the millennial period of a thousand years. This is the time of the first resurrection when all the righteous come out of Paradise and receive their new bodies and live and reign on earth with Christ for a thousand years.

Rev 20:6 Blessed and holy are they who have part in the first resurrection; on such the second death hath no power, but they shall be priests of God and of Christ, and shall reign with him a thousand years.

II Nephi 6:31: 0 how great the plan of God!...the Paradise of God must deliver up the spirits of the righteous and the grave deliver up the body of the righteous.

He goes on to say in verse 33 "our knowledge shall be perfect." (Those in the Moody's book, *LIFE AFTER LIFE*, reported that they went to a place of perfect knowledge where all things were made known to them. This verifies what the scriptures say about this being a place of perfect knowledge.)

> D.C. 98:5c-i: And in that day whatsoever (question?) any man shall ask it shall be given unto him. And in that day Satan shall not have power to tempt any man. And there shall be no sorrow because there is no death. In that day an infant shall not die until he is old and his life shall be as the age of a tree, and when he dies he shall not sleep (that is to say in the earth) but shall be changed in the twinkling of an eye, and shall be caught up, and his rest shall be glorious. Yea verily I say unto you, in that day when the Lord shall come he shall reveal all things; things which have passed, and hidden things which no man knew; things of the earth by which it was made and the purpose and the end thereof; things most precious; things that are above, and things that are beneath; things that are in the earth and upon the earth and in heaven. And all who suffer persecution for my name, and endure in faith though they are called to lay down their lives for my sake, yet shall they partake of all this glory. Wherefore, fear not even unto death; for in this world your joy is not full, but in me your joy is full.

## SATAN SHALL BE BOUND

John the revelator tells us, in Rev. 20:1-2, of a great turning point in the affairs of men. "I saw an angel come down from heaven having the key of the bottomless pit and a great chain in his hand, and he laid hold on the dragon, that old serpent, which is the Devil and Satan, and bound him a thousand years."

# SUMMARY OF THE PATH OF THE RIGHTEOUS

1. At death the righteous are released from imprisonment in their physical bodies.
2. Their spirits go directly to God where they are separated from the wicked.
3. They are consigned to Paradise, a place of rest and joy, but also a place of preparation for eternal life. They will be free of evil influences and receive total knowledge.
4. They receive their perfect bodies at the first resurrection, which comes with the beginning of the millennial period, when Christ returns to earth and Satan is bound.
5. They remain with Christ through the millennium, and through the little season the devil is loosed.
6. At the sudden end of time, which is also the end of the little season, they, and all others, appear before Christ for judgment.
7. They go to their eternal reward.

# THE PATH OF THE WICKED?

We have followed the righteous through from death to judgment. Now we return to the separation of the goats from the sheep, which occurs just after death, and follow those who were not righteous enough to go to paradise " *They that die not in me, woe unto them, for their death is bitter"* D.C.42:16f

> Ps. 55:15 Let death seize upon them, And let them go down quick into hell for wickedness is in their dwellings an among them.
>
> Alma 19:45-47 And then shall it come to pass, that the spirits of the wicked, yea, who are evil; for behold, they have no part nor portion of the Spirit of the Lord: for behold they choose evil works, rather than good: therefore the spirit of the devil did enter into them, and take Possession of their house; and these shall be cast out into outer darkness; there shall be weeping, and wailing and gnashing of teeth; and this because of their own iniquity; being led captive by the will of the devil.
>
> Now this is the state of the souls of the wicked; yea, in darkness, and a state of awful, fearful, looking for, the fiery indignation of the wrath of God upon them; thus they remain in this state, as well as the righteous in paradise, until the time of their resurrection.

"Oh!," Jan crossed her arms and shuddered, "what a horrible thing to look forward to."

"Yes," Lilli agreed, "Hell seems to be as indescribably horrible as Paradise is indescribably wonderful. Just look at Doctrine and Covenants 76:4 g-k."

And this is the gospel, the glad tidings which the voice out of the heavens bore record to us, that he came into the world, even Jesus to be crucified for the world, and to bear the sins of the world, and to sanctify the world, and cleanse it from all unrighteousness; that through him all might be saved, whom the Father put into his power, and made by him; who glorifies the Father, and saves all the works of his hands, except those sons of perdition, who deny the Son after the Father has revealed him; wherefore he saves all except them; they shall go away into everlasting punishment, which is endless punishment, which is eternal punishment to reign with the Devil and his angels in eternity, where their worm dieth not and the fire is not quenched, which is their torment, and the end thereof, neither the place thereof, nor their torment, no man knows; neither was it revealed, neither is, neither will be revealed unto man, except to them who are made partakers thereof; nevertheless, I, the Lord, show it by vision unto many; but straightway shut it up again; wherefore the end, the width, the height, the depth, and the misery thereof, they understand not, neither any man except them who are ordained unto this condemnation.

"Brrr," Jan shivered again, "What a horrible end, I can't think of anything so terrible."

"It sounds like this is not the end for them," Bob said, "if their 'worm dieth not' and it is an endless, eternal punishment."

"Who are these people who go there? " Art asked, " I sure don't want to be one of them."

"A good place to find out is where we were just looking in D.C. Section 76:7," John said.

These are they who say they are some of one and some of another, some of Christ, and some of John, and some of Moses, and some of Elias; and some of Esaias, and some of Isaiah, and some of Enoch, but received not the gospel, neither the testimony of Jesus, neither the prophets; neither the everlasting covenant; Last of all, these all are they who will not be gathered with the saints, to be caught up unto the church of the Firstborn, and received into the cloud: These are they who are liars, and sorcerers, and adulterers, and whoremongers, and whosoever loves and makes a lie; These are they who suffer the wrath of God on earth; these are they who suffer the vengeance of eternal fire; these are they who are cast down to hell and suffer the wrath of Almighty God until the fullness of times, when Christ shall have subdued all enemies under his feet...

"The first part of that sounds like they are members, of various denominations, but, although they were members, they did not get to know Jesus," Bob observed. "In fact, some of them sound like people I know who are considered good people. Many people tell lies, and do the other things enumerated in that scripture."

"I wonder if they realize the seriousness of what they are doing," Don said.

"Of course there are sins which seem more serious such as murder, robbery, pride, covetousness and turning against Christ after knowing him to be the son of God," Lilli said.

Sandy added, "I always thought those in hell were those who joined with Lucifer in his wickedness and turned against God, and people like Hitler who killed thousands of innocent people." "And what about the *'angels which God spared not, but cast them down to hell, and delivered them into chains of darkness, to be reserved unto judgment,'* that I read about in

II Peter 2:4?" Fran asked.

"All of these are included in the residents of Hell," John said.

## THERE ARE DIFFERENT LEVELS OF HELL

"My, that's a wide spread of people and angels," Bob said. "Everything from people we know as friends who don't accept Christ, to the fallen angels and human monsters like Hitler. Will they all receive the same punishment for eternity?"

John replied "There are other scriptures we need to look at now to answer that question. For example, Isaiah says,

> *they shall be gathered together in the pit, and*
> *shall be shut up in the prison, and after many days*
> *shall they be visited."* (Is.24:22)

"Who in the world would visit them there?" Sandy asked, "the Devil?"

"No," Lilli chuckled. "It would be a much more distinguished visitor than that. Look at Isaiah 42:7. He is speaking of the ministry of Christ to the prison during the three days after his crucifixion."

## HELL TO BE OPENED

To open the blind eyes, to bring out the prisoners from the prison, and them that sit in darkness out of the prison house.

In Is.49:9 the prophet is still speaking of Christ's ministry and he says,

> *"That thou mayest say to the prisoners, go forth;*
> *to them that are in darkness, show yourselves."*

"But why did Jesus preach to the spirits in prison," Bob joined in, "It doesn't seem rational if they will be in hell for eternity. Why tell them about the kingdom? It's too late for them now, isn't it? Are you actually suggesting, that those who are in hell will be freed? I find it hard to believe."

"Hell will be opened by Jesus, but they will not all be freed," John said. "Lets look at scriptures which bear on this."

John said, "The first indication we are given that hell will be opened is from Isaiah as quoted above. Remember when we were tracing the path of the righteous. When Jesus returns at the first resurrection at the millennium, those in paradise will come forth and receive their new bodies. There will also be some in hell who learned of Christ through the ministry of Jesus and they accepted him there. Some from hell will also come forth at the first resurrection."

"Why," Don asked, "after they were in prison for such a long time would God allow them to come out."

"God's love is so great that he will save everyone he can, if they will only turn to him," Lilli said.

"The answer is found in the purpose of Jesus' mission to Hell at the time of his crucifixion and the three days before his resurrection," John said. "I Peter 3:18 Tells us,

> For Christ hath once suffered for sins, the just for the unjust,
> that he might bring us to God, being put to death in the flesh,
> but quickened by the spirit; by which he also went and
> preached unto the spirits in prison."

"What does all that mean?" Fran asked, "I got lost in the 'Just for the unjust' double talk."

"Okay," John answered, "it does sound confusing so let's take it one piece at a time. You remember that in Romans 3:23-24 Paul said, 'All have sinned and come short of the glory of God,'

Because we have all sinned we would be forever lost, and every time we sin, Satan gains a little stronger rope to bind us. We cannot release ourselves, nor could the prisoners be released from the prison.

"So Christ, who is 'just' suffered death on the cross for all of us who are 'unjust.' He was put to death in the flesh.

"In other words they killed his physical body but he was quickened (made alive) in the Spirit. His spiritual being lived on. He descended into the prison where he gained the keys of death and hell because Satan had no power over him.

"Jesus lived a faultless life. If he had yielded to just one of Satan's temptations, Satan would have had power over Jesus and he could not have gained the keys to Hell. Moreover, if Jesus had been unwilling to go through the trials. of life for us, and death on the cross, we would all be bound in Satan's prison for eternity."

"That leaves me with a question," Bob said. "We have been studying that those of us who have given ourselves to Christ do not endure a spiritual death. We will go to Paradise and won't be in the prison. So how can his going to hell and getting the keys over hell and power over Satan help us?"'

"The only reason that those who are Christ's will not be in the prison is because he holds the keys, so he has the power to forgive any who come to him, and he cuts Satan's ties on them." John explained. "And this is also the reason those who refuse to come to Christ go to the prison, He is the only way of escape."

"That explains something I've wondered about for as long as I can remember," Sandy broke in. "I've always questioned how Jesus' dying on the cross hundreds of years before I was even born can save me?"

"You are not alone in that question Sandy," Lilli said. "I used to wonder the same thing, because my sins didn't happen until so long after Jesus died. It all fits together and makes sense though, doesn't it."

"They will all come out of the prison, but they will not all be released," John said, "Lets look to the explanation in I Peter 4:6"

> "For this cause was the gospel preached also to them that are dead, that they might be judged according to men in the flesh, but live according to God in the Spirit.

"You see, there have been many people who for one reason or another never heard of Christ while they lived in the flesh, they must have their chance also. There will be some, perhaps like those Sandy mentioned, who didn't become Christian because of the acts of other people. There must be millions of souls who have been cheated this way. There is the gray area of people who very nearly achieved paradise, they too need a chance to be fairly judged. Christ took the message to those spirits in hell so they could be judged like those who had their opportunity while in the flesh.

"You see, God is absolutely just in every possible way."

"That makes me feel a lot better," Art commented, "because if I goof off in this life and go to Hell, I can work my way back up."

"Oh Art!" Lilli exclaimed. "That's not what John meant at all."

John said, "I hope I didn't give you the impression that you could do that. The scriptures say you cannot work from one glory to another. The part about God being absolutely fair and just means he is going to make certain that everyone has a chance, not a second chance. There will be a lot of souls in Hell who had their chance but belong to Lucifer forever. These will be cast into the lake of fire and brimstone for eternity. we will get back to this when we look at the Unforgivable Sin."

"Too bad," Art smiled, "I thought I had a good out for a minute."

John looked at Art seriously and quietly said, "Art, if you had ever had the kind of experience God gave to me when I was sixteen, you would never risk even a moment in Hell, because that moment would be the most indescribable eternity you could imagine. You would be screaming to come back here and have another chance. Don't ever, ever, flirt with Hell, or for that matter with Lucifer."

"Okay, sorry I said that about a second chance. Let's go on with the study."

The order of resurrections from hell is revealed in D.C. 85. Let me read an excerpt from it, beginning at verse 28. Another angel shall sound, which is the second trump; and then cometh the redemption of those who are Christ's at his coming; who have received their part in that prison which is prepared for them, that they might receive the gospel, and be judged according to men in the flesh. Vs 29 goes on, but speaks of other people.

> *another trump shall sound which is the third*
> *trump: and then cometh the spirits of men who are*
> *to be judged and are found under condemnation:*
> *and these are the rest of the dead, and they lived*
> *not again until the thousand years are ended,*
> *neither again until the end of the earth.*

These are the ones who will barely scrape by and miss the eternal lake of fire and brimstone; they are not saved until the last moment, and then only by the grace of Christ, and only because they do not deny the Holy spirit. "And there is even another group following these."

> *And another trump shall sound, which is the*
> *fourth trump, saying, These are found among*
> *those who are to remain until that great and last*
> *day, even the end, who shall remain filthy still.*

**311**

"That comment about those who remain filthy still refers to those who will never enter the kingdom of God because no unclean thing can enter there," Lilli said.

John pointed to the illustration and said, "Look at the diagram, and see that, except for those who are Christ's and come forth at the first resurrection, the rest of the dead, are confined in prison through all of time, including the millennial period, and the little season in which the devil is loosed again. They will stay there until the final judgment, but much will take place before that occurs."

## SATAN RELEASED FROM PRISON

An amazing thing happens at the end of the thousand year reign of Jesus on earth. Satan, who has been locked up will be released for a little season.

"Why in the world would they allow that?" Don questioned; "I would think that once they had him bottled up they would seal a cork so it could never be gotten out."

"With all the destruction and slaughter he has caused through the years, there should be some kind of capital punishment for him, a gas chamber or electric chair of some kind to get rid of him forever,'" Bob suggested.

"What we see here," John said, " is an extreme example of God's justice and fairness. Remember that during the thousand years Satan is bound people are living in peace and plenty with no temptation. As dreadful as it may seem they have the right to choose to follow Satan. They could never be judged without the opportunity to choose between God and Satan.

"Well," Jan affirmed, "After being with Jesus a thousand years, I doubt if many will choose the Devil"

"What's going to happen?" Sandy asked.

"Let's go back to the 20th chapter of Revelation again and see," John suggested. "Don would you read verses 7-10 for Us?

Rev:20:7-10 "And when the thousand years are expired, Satan shall be loosed out of his prison, and shall go out to deceive the nations which are in the four quarters of the earth, God and Magog, to gather them together to battle; the number of whom is as the sand of the sea. And they went up on the breadth of the earth and compassed the camp of the saints about, and the beloved city; and fire came down from God out of heaven and devoured them. And the devil that deceived them was cast into the lake of fire and brimstone, where the beast and the false prophet are and shall be tormented day and night forever."

"I don't believe it," Jan exclaimed. "How could he get that many to follow him right after the millennium? Talk about his power, it must be fantastic."

"What happens next," Sandy wondered aloud.

# SUMMARY OF PATH OF THE WICKED

1. At death the wicked are separated from the righteous and sent to the prison.
2. Despite their anguish in hell, they will be taught and have an opportunity to know of Jesus.
3. Those who had no previous opportunity, but now follow Jesus now will be released from hell and come forth in the first resurrection. They will then join the righteous who come from paradise.
4. The rest of the dead remain in hell through the millennium and through the little season when Satan is loosed. They will be brought out of the prison for the great final judgment.
5. Hell is now empty and its purpose fulfilled so it, along with the doorway of death, is cast into the lake of fire and brimstone and destroyed. (Rev. 20:14)

# ETERNAL JUDGMENT

"Immediately after Satan is cast into the lake of fire we will have the greatest reunion there has ever been," Lilli said. "Every one from all ages and all around the world who has ever lived will be there. This is where both the righteous and evil meet again, and each will 'know as he is known.' This will be the time of the great and final judgment. Nobody will have any secrets. "Let me read some of the scriptures about this."

> Rev. 20:12-13 I saw the dead, small and great stand before God; and the books were opened, and another book was opened which is the book of life, and the dead were judged out of those things which were written in the books, according to their works.
>
> The sea gave up the dead which were in it; and death and hell delivered up the dead which were in them; and they were judged, every man according to their works.
>
> II Nephi 6:36 It shall come to pass that when all men shall have passed from this first death (Death from mortal life) unto life, in so much as they have become immortal, they must appear before the judgment seat of the Holy One of Israel; and then cometh the judgment; and then must they be judged according to the holy judgment of God...They who are righteous shall be righteous still, and they who are filthy shall be filthy still.

"What are the books Revelation, speaks of in that scripture?" Fran anxiously asked.

"The first books are books of each individual's life. There is a record kept on your life and on mine too and on each of us. Everyone's life will be an open book.—no secrets," Lilli answered. "The other book, which is the great book of life, is a listing of everyone who will receive eternal life in any degree. Look at verse 15 in the same chapter:

*Whosoever was not found written in the Book of Life was cast into the lake of fire.*

"The record of your life will either send you to a glory or condemn you forever. Your name must appear in the Lord's Book of Life. If your name is not found in the Book of Life you are not Christ's and have no part in any glory, so you are automatically sent to the lake of fire and brimstone. This is the second death. If you have given yourself to him through baptism, however, and then were confirmed it will be there in bright and shining letters," Lilli's eyes sparkled and she smiled.

"Don would you read Mat. 16:30 for us. This refers to the coming of Jesus at this great and final judgment," John said.

Don reads: "The son of Man shall come in the glory of his Father, with his angels; and then shall reward every man according to his works."

"Jesus, who lived in mortal life showed us the way to the Celestial Kingdom. He will be our judge. He will be a righteous judge. He has been through all the kinds of experiences we have had. He will judge those who judged him and condemned him to die on the cross. He will also judge those who crucify him anew and put him to an open shame by their acts, and notice also, the importance of Works. See how often the phrase 'shall reward every man according to his works,' is used." John said. "That phrase will prove to be very important as we go on."

## THE REWARDS?

In II Cor. 12:2-4 Paul wrote:

"I knew a man in Christ above fourteen years ago...such a one caught up to the third heaven."

315

"Wait a minute John," Art suddenly spoke up, "I thought there was only supposed to be one heaven and one hell. Hell has already been destroyed, by being cast into the lake of fire and brimstone, and now you're talking about three heavens. How many heavens are there?"

"Why not let Paul answer that for you? Read I Cor. 15:41," John replied.

> There is one glory of the sun, and another glory of the moon, and another glory of the stars; for as one star differs from another in glory, so also is the resurrection of the dead."

"That's a new one to me," Art said and shook his head.

"For some reason a lot of people read over that and never seem to see it," Lilli remarked.

"Does Paul mean we will go to the sun, or the moon?" Don asked.

"No," John said with a laugh. "But I know what you are thinking. In one of our classes a lady insisted that she didn't want to go to any glory if that's where they were located.

"Paul is using the Sun, moon, and stars as metaphors to create some kind of comparison between the glories. He is saying the Celestial Glory is the most brilliant and wonderful of all. It is the brightest thing imaginable. It is above all. Next he compares Terrestrial Glory to the moon for quality and brightness and size; it is far less brilliant than the Sun, but to the people of his day it was still the most marvelous thing in the heavens next to the Sun. Then the stars! Go out on a clear night and see the thousands of stars, some are brilliant spots in the night sky, others are smaller and dimmer until they fade away. Paul is explaining the way the Telestial Kingdom will be. Those who inherit it will be as varied in their quality as the stars you see. These are the last ones to be brought from the prison in the resurrection of the unjust. Some just barely escaped being sent to the lake of fire, while others were nearly worthy of coming out at the first resurrection. The degree of reward and glory is varied to match the worthiness of those who go to them.

"God has had such compassion for us that he has worked through all the ages and all the processes to try to lift us to Celestial Glory, which is the Kingdom of God, the very highest. Anyone who would respond, in dedication and faith is lifted to the top, but those who don't have that kind of faith and response still have a special place prepared for them. In the end there is a glory for everyone except those who have committed the unforgivable sin.

"Don, please read these excerpts from D.C. 85: for us.

D.C.85:5b He who is not able to abide the law of a celestial kingdom, (in this life) cannot abide a celestial glory, and he who cannot abide the law of a terrestrial kingdom cannot abide a terrestrial glory; He who cannot abide the law of a telestial kingdom cannot abide a telestial glory: therefore he is not meet for a kingdom of glory. Therefore he must abide a kingdom which is not a kingdom of glory."

"Does that really mean that in this life we have to live like we would in the Celestial Kingdom?" Bob asked.

"I don't believe we will be able to live the same in this life because of the totally different environment, " Lilli answered. "But we must learn here to live by the law of the kingdom."

"What kind of law will that be?" Jan asked.

"It will be complete submission and dedication to God and to have love, charity, and respect for each other," Lilli replied. "It will have to be that way in the kingdom."

"We would be a lot better off if we lived that way now," Sandy said.

"You see," John explained, "at the judgment, the Lord does not point a finger at one and say, 'You have been good and I like you, so you go to the Celestial Kingdom,' and to another, 'I don't like you, so you are cast off forever,' our lives will be reflected from the perfect example Jesus lived. He will be the Yardstick by which we are measured. He has invited each to the highest glory of all, but we accept what we ourselves prove worthy of. We could never be happy on a higher level than we deserve".

"Do you remember when we were studying repentance and I pointed out that you can climb as high as you are willing to go, but if you reach a point where you stop, you have chosen your level for eternity? This shows how that works. Look at line 6g for a good example,

> They who remain (those who do not make it to any glory) shall also be quickened; nevertheless, they shall return again to their own place to enjoy that which they are willing to receive, because they were not willing to enjoy that which they might have received.

Bob said, "That puts it pretty squarely right on our own shoulders doesn't it?"

"Then those whose glory is compared to one of the weakest stars must be very close to being like they are in hell." Don observed.

"Again, we need to find the answer in the scriptures, would you turn to D.C. 76:7g.

> ...and thus we saw in the heavenly vision the glory of the telestial which surpasses all understanding, and no man knows it except him to whom God has revealed it."

John added, "apparently even the very least glory, which is found in the very lowest level of glories, is greater than anything we can comprehend. I think that is a wonderful display of God's love."

# QUALIFICATIONS

"I've been wondering," Art said, "about what the qualifications are to get into Telestial Glory, the lowest one."

"Practically no qualifications at all," John said, "You see God will save everyone he can and give to each person the best he can. In Telestial Glory are people who may never have done a worthy thing in their lives. They did not accept Jesus in life, nor in the prison, when he went there to minister to them. They have nothing to be rewarded for, but still God does not destroy them. Look at D.C. 76:7

> These are they who deny not the gospel of Christ, neither the testimony of Jesus; these are they who deny not the Holy Spirit; these are they who are thrust down to hell; these are they who shall not be redeemed from the Devil, until the last resurrection, until the Lord, even Christ the Lamb shall have finished his work...

"Although these are saved from the second death they will not receive the kingdom of God and will only receive of the presence of the Holy Ghost. God and Christ will not be here.

"You see, they never accepted or supported the gospel, in fact, they even resisted Christ and the Holy Spirit. The one thing that saved them was simply that they did not deny the Holy spirit or Christ. This does not mean denying the existence of the Holy spirit. It is the special work of the Holy spirit to lead us into all truth, and 'No man can say that Jesus is the Lord, but by the Holy Ghost' (I Cor. 12:3) so to deny the Holy Ghost is to deny the testimony of the divinity of Christ which has come to you through the work of the Holy Ghost.

"Even though the lives in Telestial Glory have nothing of note to be rewarded for, they did not commit the unforgivable sin of denying that testimony. Therefore they are salvaged from the Lake of Fire and Brimstone."

"That's not much qualification is it?"

"No, it certainly isn't," Jan agreed, but what are the requirements for Celestial Glory?"

"Strange as it may seem, they actually are not much more difficult," John responded. "The main difference is that they live lives dedicated to God rather that to themselves, which means they live totally reversed lives. They live by faith and have the assurance the Lord is with them. They seek the will of God. Other people may work just as hard in a frustrating attempt to satisfy, or glorify themselves.

Revelation 20:4 comments on this.

> I saw the thrones, and they that sat upon them; and I saw the souls of them that were beheaded for the witness of Jesus, and for the word of God, and which had not worshipped the beast, neither his image, neither had received his mark upon their foreheads, or in their hands: and they lived and reigned with Christ a thousand years

"Remember that God said *it is my work—to bring to pass the immortality and eternal life of man.* He will be working with you. So instead of resisting God, submit to him. He will not only make you into a person worthy of the Celestial Kingdom, you will also have a richer fuller life here and all along the process we go through."

"The qualifications may not be more difficult, but it makes a world of difference," Lilli exclaimed earnestly. "They have a richer life during their time here, then they go to Paradise and avoid the prison. Also they come forth at the first resurrection and go through the millennial period with Christ, and finally they receive the highest of all glories.

"It does not make sense for anyone to accept anything less."

"'Lilli is right," John affirmed, "Look at D.C. 76:5 again," John continued. Begin at 'Concerning them who come forth in the resurrection of the just'

> They are they who received the testimony of Jesus, and believed on his name, and were baptized after the manner of his burial, being buried in the water in his name...and receive the Holy Spirit by the laying on of hands of him who is ordained and sealed unto this power; and who overcome by faith, and are sealed by that Holy Spirit of promise, which the Father sheds forth upon all those who are just and true...

"Basically all God requires is for you to learn of Christ, and trust him. Don't try to be a self-made god, but surrender your sinful will to him and let him shape it. Follow his directions and endure to the end. He will lead you to his kingdom."

"Just look at the glory promised them in the next paragraph. (lines h-r)"

> Wherefore, as it is written, they are gods, even the sons of God; wherefore all things are theirs, whether life or death, or things present, or things to come, all are theirs, and they are Christ's and Christ is God's; and they shall overcome all things; wherefore let no man glory in man, but rather let him glory in God, who shall subdue all enemies under his feet; these shall dwell in the presence of God and his Christ for ever and ever: These are they whom he shall bring with him, when he shall come in the clouds of heaven, to reign on the earth over his people; these are they who shall have part in

the first resurrection; these are they who are come unto Mount Zion and unto the city of the living God, the heavenly place, the holiest of all...these are they whose bodies are celestial, whose glory is that of the sun, even the glory of God the highest of all; whose glory the sun of the firmament is written of as being typical.

Only those who receive this glory have fulfilled God's original purpose when he said 'Let us make man in our image and likeness.' This is the Kingdom of God. The presence of God, Christ and the Holy Ghost will be here.

"I remember Arthur Oakman's statement that 'All you can contribute to your own salvation is your sin,'" Lilli said.

"I think I can even do that" Art said.

"I know you can Art, you are already doing it," Lilli assured him. "You have been studying to learn of Christ and you believe in him. You are well on your way to the Celestial Kingdom."

"Do you really think so?"

"I'm sure of it."

"We've looked at the top and bottom glories, who are those in the middle—in Terrestrial Glory?" Sandy was anxious to know.

"Good question," John affirmed, "D.C.76 also answers it."

These are they who died without law; and also spirits of men kept in prison whom the Son visited, and preached the gospel unto them, that they might be judged according to men in the flesh, who receive not the testimony of Jesus in the flesh, but afterwards received it; these are they who are honorable men of the earth, who were blinded by the craftiness of men...these are they who are not valiant in the testimony of Jesus...

"This glory is not known as the Kingdom of God, and his presence will not be here. In this glory there will be the presence of Christ, and the Holy Ghost," John said.

Bob leaned back with a thoughtful expression on his face, "There are a lot of people like that who have never taken time to learn of Jesus, or to accept the gospel," he said. "They are basically good people, they just can't be bothered with religion."

"Yes," John agreed, "these are those who were in the prison, and finally turned to Christ there. They came out at the first resurrection, but they can never receive higher than Terrestrial Glory. They did not 'abide the law of a Celestial Kingdom' on earth, so they cannot 'abide a Celestial Glory' in eternity. Still they were not mean or vicious people. They probably even attended church; they just didn't let it direct their lives. They were likely well respected and even affluent but didn't take the time to turn their lives to Christ. Note the comment, 'these are not valiant in the testimony of Jesus.' Their failure to attain the Celestial Kingdom seems to be largely a problem of neglect. They were too busy with other things."

"There is, however, one important promise in their favor," John began.

"Just getting out of hell would seem to be benefit enough," Don interrupted, "what more could they ask for?"

"Let's read Revelation 20:6," John replied.

Blessed and holy are they who have part in the first
resurrection; on such the second death hath no power...

"Those who come forth in the first resurrection will never need to fear the lake of fire and brimstone," John continued.

"There is one other group" Don commented, "those who are cast out with the devil. Who are they?"

John responded, "First let me say this, God does not find pleasure in the condemnation, or suffering of any of his creations. He does not want to lose a single person. He tries until he has saved all who will be saved, but there are those to whom he has shown the truth by the Holy spirit, in ways they cannot dispute, that Jesus is the Christ, the son of God. They still turned their backs on God and followed the devil. This is the unforgivable sin. It is not because God would not have them back, but they have rejected God's every inducement to return until that bolt of lightning and clap of thunder that marks the end of time, and they are lost."

"It sounds like they are playing eternal musical chairs and they were left standing." Don mused. "That must be the ultimate disaster in the use of agency."

"Yes," John agreed, "They are bound for the second death in the lake of fire and brimstone. They have turned their backs upon the rewards God would have given to them, and this is the reward they receive for their allegiance to the devil."

## THE UNFORGIVABLE SIN

"You promised to tell us more about the unforgivable sin and God's justice" Jan remembered.

"Yes," John recalled. "The work of the Holy Spirit is to bear testimony of the divinity of Jesus Christ as the son of God. Remember the scriptures tell you that the Holy Spirit will lead you into all truth? This is not just to tell you that Jesus is the Son of God, but to make it known to you in a way which goes beyond just faith in Christ. It will be a certain knowledge.

"Jesus came as our example and our savior. He displayed for us the way of life. He gave us the law of the kingdom. He allowed himself to be murdered by the forces of evil to prove that those who follow him can arise victorious over death. He is the way to the Celestial Kingdom. Now he is going to be our judge.

"To be absolutely certain that all who appear before him have had an opportunity to know him, every individual will meet him in an experience in which they can have no question about who he is and his supreme divinity. No one at judgment will be able to say, 'I didn't know.

"Some will receive this testimony during their mortal lives, others will receive it either in Paradise, or in Hell, but by the time we face judgment, every individual who comes before Christ will know absolutely who Christ is. No one can use ignorance as an excuse for rejecting him or for the way they have lived. To reject him after receiving it by the Holy spirit is the unforgivable sin which will cause them to be cast into the lake of fire and brimstone.

"To blaspheme against the Holy Ghost, is to have received this testimony through the work of the Holy Ghost, and then turn your back on it and follow the devil." John said, as he turned to Alma 19:8 and read: Behold, if ye deny the Holy Ghost when it once has had place in you, and ye know that ye deny it; behold, this is a sin which is unpardonable.

Sandy asked, "Why don't they teach this so people will know that it is more than one heaven or one hell, saved or lost."

"Camouflage," Lilli stated.

"What do you mean by camouflage," Don asked.

Lilli answered, "When something is hidden by camouflage you can look right at it and not see it, but once you do spot it, it seems to stand out so clearly you can't miss it. I think that is the way it has been with these scriptures. You have read them many times and didn't see what they were saying, but now you will never fail to see the whole story."

"That is certainly true," Sandy agreed. "It seems so clear I wonder how I ever missed it.

"What is next?"

"That is all for tonight. But I have a riddle for you to think about until our next session," John smiled.

"You may have noted that every place the scriptures told you what you are judged and rewarded by they always say you are judged by your works. For example, Rev. 20:12 says, *'The dead were judged out of those things which were written in the books according to their works.'* Verse 13 restates the same thing, and it is this way throughout scripture. So it is vital to understand the works of eternal judgment.

"Your riddle for the week is, what is meant by 'works'?"

## SUMMARY

1. The end will come suddenly. There will be no chance for change or repentance at that moment.

2. Every person who ever lived will stand before Christ for judgment at this point.

3. There are three levels of glory. Celestial Glory, (known as the Kingdom of God), Terrestrial Glory, and Telestial Glory.

4. There will be some place in these glories for each person who has not committed the unforgivable sin.

5. The Lake of Fire and Brimstone is a very real and severe punishment. Those who have rejected the testimony, which comes through the Holy Ghost, have no place in any glory. They are not Christ's, so by default the are consigned to the second death.

   Although their spirits never die, they will pass into oblivion as far as those in the glories know. They will never be known again.

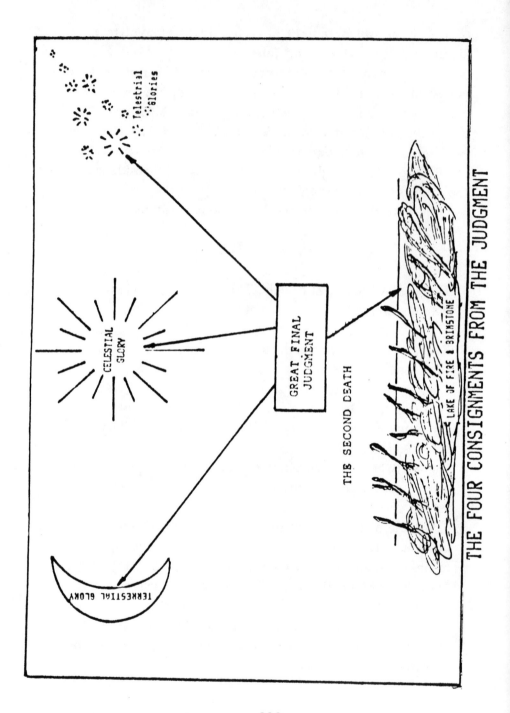

THE FOUR CONSIGNMENTS FROM THE JUDGMENT

# CHAPTER 29

# THE WORKS OF ETERNAL JUDGMENT

Lilli and John were met at the door of Bob's and Jan's home by Sandy. She grabbed John's upper arm to hurry him to the table. "I've been anxiously waiting all week for tonight to find out what the works of eternal judgment are. If it is not going out to help people, or to carry the gospel to them then I can't imagine what they would be."

Jan came out of the kitchen with a pot of coffee; "I think it was a sneaky trick to leave us guessing all week," she said.

"Look," Fran displayed her tablet, "I've made a list of things it might be, but I'm not going to show it to you. I'll just wait and see if it's on my list."

"I've been more concerned with the study of life after death which we had last week." Don remarked as he and Fran eased toward the table. "It's the most exciting story I've ever heard. I've never had the scriptures explained that way.

"To tell the truth I really didn't think it was in the scriptures that way so I checked every scripture and it was just the way you said, even in the King James version," Bob admitted to the group as he laid his previous week's papers on the table with the margins filled with notes.

"It's a beautiful plan isn't it?" Lilli finally had a chance to speak. "You can see why I said it is a photograph of God. You can see more of God's nature in what he has planned for us than in anything else I know."

"Now, is everyone ready to discover what the scriptures mean by works?" John was handing out the papers.

"Yes," Fran was quick to reply, "And I'll start reading."

# THE WORKS OF ETERNAL JUDGMENT

Our look at Life After Death revealed some wonderful, and also some awful, destinies beyond mortal life for human beings. But what determines who goes to which one? The scriptures tell of about twenty-one ways by which we may be saved. II Nephi 7:42 says, "It is only in and through the grace of God that ye are saved." Other scriptures tell you to enter through hope, baptism, repentance, Apostle Paul even says you are saved "by the foolishness of preaching." I Cor 1:21. In the end, of course, it is the sacrifice of Jesus on the cross that made salvation possible. However, none of these tell you to which of the destinies you go.

For people who considered only heaven and hell to lie beyond the doorway of death, there was no question; you either made it over the line into Heaven or you perished in Hell. Now that you see God has prepared many glories so we can be exactly fitted in where we are best suited, it becomes pressing for you to understand what determines your ultimate fate.

Although there are several avenues leading to salvation, in the end they all lead to Jesus as the way. There is also only one way by which you are judged, and by which your ultimate fate is determined. This is "works." Works is the key word whenever judgment, or eternal glories are mentioned because this is what the outcome of your final judgment is based upon.

Revelation, Chapter 20 is the best example.

> I saw the great white throne and him that sit upon it...I saw the dead, small and great stand before God...The dead were judged out of those things which were written in the books, according to their works...And death and hell delivered up the dead which were in them, and they were .judged. every man according to their works.

John leaned back from the table and interrupted, "obviously 'works' is one of the most important words in the scriptures but it isn't defined. What can it mean?"

Fran waved her hand and said, "I know what you are going to say, read on and find out. Right?"

In view of the importance of works in your final judgment and eternal life, it is of utmost importance that you understand what the scriptures mean by works.

## CELESTIAL GLORY IS NOT A REWARD FOR DOING GOOD DEEDS

Through an inspired experience, I was given to understand that God loves all people, and he loves each one equally. This is true, regardless of how righteous or depraved one may become. God loves even those who fight against him as well as he loves those who have given many years of dedicated service. Rewards and ultimate glories will be different, but God's love is extended to each one equally. There is no way you can elevate yourself to obtain a greater share of God's love than is given to another. There is no way God can love you more than he does. God is love and he extends himself fully to all of his creations. It is like the Sun which shines equally on both the righteous and the sinners.

God's love continues to be showered upon all people regardless of problems they have, the mistakes they make, or the sin they bear. His love is so expansive, so great and abundant, his concern and compassion cannot be constrained, so it is spread abroad for everyone. The invitation to enter the Celestial Kingdom is extended to all; the key to being able to enter is <u>works.</u> The Celestial Kingdom is not given as a reward; it is a result.

# WHAT KIND OF WORKS?

Who knows what works he can do which are best and most acceptable to God? What one person considers to be a good and worthy work is often deemed a disgraceful act by another. For example, a man who feels sure he knows the true gospel calls it his duty to make sure his neighbors have the benefit of his knowledge. The neighbor may consider the man an obnoxious nuisance and a religious nut.

Another example is the person who contributes so freely to his church that he deprives his family so they suffer. He feels this to be a good work; many consider him foolish.

Some live to the standards and morals of their average countrymen and attend to church duties, but the morals of the average church member are measured by the imperfect standard of what they consider to be good. This is insufficient to prepare us to face eternal judgment.

The opinion of some is that you must be absolutely honest and always truthful; others say it is more charitable and loving to sometimes tell a 'little white lie' than to hurt another's feelings with the brutal truth.

It is often suggested that you do good Samaritan type works, but others claim that this merely leads people to dependency.

What are the works which lead us to the Celestial King-dom? You don't even know what the kingdom is like or what kind of beings inhabit it. How can you by works, mold yourself into becoming something that you do not comprehend?

D.C. 76:8 Highlights the difficulty:

> Great and marvelous are the works of the Lord and the mysteries of his kingdom which he showed unto us, which surpasses all understanding in glory, and in might, and in dominion, which he commanded us we should not write, while we were yet in the Spirit, and are not lawful for man to utter, neither is man capable to make them known, for they are only to be seen and understood by the power of the Holy Spirit, which God bestows on those who love him and purify themselves before him; to whom he grants this privilege of seeing and knowing for themselves.

## COUNTERFEIT WORKS

Works may be counterfeited. Men hide inner beings of jealousy, hatred, greed, and other secret sins by presenting an exterior person who smiles, does not drink or smoke, rob or kill. You cannot be certain in your judgment of others. Ministers throughout the ages have served under the banner of Christ and claimed to be doing good works, but how many TV evangelists have you known to fall in recent years? We cringe when we see a newspaper headline about something a minister has done or has said, because it is often so ridiculous it suggests he is not in touch with the real world and does not understand the rudimen-tary purposes of God.

"This has told us a lot of things which aren't the works of eternal life," Sandy was getting impatient. She flipped the pages to look at what the story was going to reveal. "Are you sure it is going to tell us what is?"

Lilli laughed and put a reassuring hand on Sandy's shoulder, "Read on. We'll get there, I'm positive," Lilli assured her. Jesus met the same kind of ministry in his day, see Matt. 7:31-32:

> The day soon cometh that men shall come before me to be judged according to their works. And many will say unto me in that day, Lord, Lord, have we not prophesied in thy name; and in thy name cast out devils; and in thy name done many wonderful works? And then will I say, ye never knew me; depart from me ye that work iniquity.

Many other people who do works they consider good will be judged the same way.

God loves you regardless of your condition, and there is no way you can earn his love or salvation, or grace. If even works which you do in his name may be subject to rejection, how can you present a work worthy of eternal judgment? The traditional concept has been that "If it takes good works to receive a great reward in glory, I'm going to win a good place there by working. I'll become a missionary and tell the story to the world, or I'll take care of the sick, or the poor; I'll work—work—work." As fine as these works are, they are not the works which lead you to the Celestial Kingdom. Still, there is a way, and it is imperative for you to apprehend it.

"At last we have gotten to the moment we have been waiting for; anyone want to take a break," John smiled.

Several voices: "No!" and their heads were shaking.

# THE WORKS WHICH LEAD TO GLORY

For the moment, set aside the thought of what you can do to produce worthy works, and try to determine what is really being said in the scriptures. Look at Matt 22:35-39

> Jesus said unto him, Thou shalt love the Lord thy God with all thy heart and with all thy soul, and with all thy mind. This is the first commandment, and the second is like unto it; Thou shalt love thy neighbor as thyself. On these two hang all the law and the prophets.

You should find your answer here if all the law hangs on these, so look at them one at a time. Look at the first great commandment to love God with all your being; this is reminiscent of baptism. You came to God through wanting to give yourself totally to him, because you did love him with all your being. After you presented yourself to him through the ordinance of the water, it was confirmed upon you that God would accept the responsibility of leading you all the way to the highest kingdom if you would continue to walk with him. God promised that the Holy Spirit would be there to lead you all the way.

Let's go back to the master keys again. God said "It is _my_ _work_ and _my glory_ to bring to pass the immortality and eternal life of man." In both instances, the Lord is saying he is responsible for this; it is his work, and he will do it. Add to this the other master key. "Let _us_ make man in our image." It becomes clear that it is not the work you do which leads you to that glory, but the work you allow God to do within you. There is no work you can do to perfect yourself to become worthy of God's realm. Isaiah had discovered this when he exclaimed, "O Lord, Thou art our Father; We are the clay, and thou our potter; and we all are the work of thy hand."

Bob set down his coffee cup, "Do you actually mean that for something as important to us as our own salvation, we can't even contribute works to it?" he asked, surprised.

"Yes and no," John replied, "God does the work, but we have to yield to him and allow those works to take place in us. Our lives change as God works in us. God leads us but we must follow. We will follow to the point at which in total submission we exclaim, 'Thy will be done.'"

"You mean God wants us enough that he will do all that just for us?" Art was awed.

"Yes, Art," Lilli answered. "He did even more. He sent his only child, Jesus, to save us. And he knew beforehand that Jesus would be murdered, but there was no other way so he sent him anyway." Then she added, "Arthur Oakman once said, 'The only thing you can contribute to your own salvation is your sin.' In other words, you can contribute by giving up those sins which separate you from him."

Once you see this as the work of God you see it written into all the scriptural environment. Eph. 2:8:

> By grace are ye saved through faith; and that not of your-
> selves; but it is the gift of God; Not of works, lest any man
> should boast."

John, who understood Jesus' mission and work better than any of the other apostles, records, *Jesus answered and said unto them, This is the work of God, that ye believe on him whom he hath sent, John 6: 8*

Alma wrote to his wayward son, Alma.

> Do not endeavor to excuse yourself in the least point, because
> of your sins, by denying the justice of God, but do let the
> justice of God, and his mercy, and his long-suffering, have
> full sway in your heart. Alma 19:114

Bob begins reading:

# LET GOD DO HIS WORKS OF PERFECTION WITHIN US

To be molded into perfection by the hand of the eternal potter, you continue to yield yourself to him. God has never taken your agency from you. Your job is to continue to cooperate with him as he forms you. This must be done voluntarily. You will never be forced, but you will eventually be judged by how much freedom you gave the Lord to work with you, and how well you have followed the directions he has given to you.

Jesus left an example for you. John the revelator was shown how Jesus was always perfect even though he changed as he grew physically and in understanding. He came to show you the way. It would have been a futile effort unless he took a path which you could follow.

The way that Jesus took is the way to be judged perfect.

D.C. 90: John (the apostle) tells us,..."I, John, bear record that I beheld his glory, as the glory of the Only Begotten of the Father, full of grace and truth; even the Spirit of truth which came and dwelt in the flesh, and dwelt among us. And I, John, saw that he received not of the fullness at the first, but received grace for grace, and he received not of the fullness at first, but continued from grace to grace until he received a fullness; and thus he was called the Son of God, because he received not of the fullness at first."

Jesus came as an infant, lived as a child, and grew into manhood with the human limitations we have. He was inspired by the Holy Spirit to know God's commandments. As he learned each commandment he was immediately obedient to the will of his Heavenly Father and through prayer looked for more truth. As additional truth was given to him, he made it his life. By

337

always following God's teachings he could always be judged perfect. He went from grace to grace, or truth to truth. This is the way to continue spiritual growth and become perfect.

As new truth is revealed to you, and you become aware of a step God would have you take, you must make it a part of your life. You cannot take steps which lie beyond the hill if you don't take the steps which carry you over the hill. This means a constant study for understanding and always changing your life as your understanding matures.

The third requirement is to "endure to the end." (Matt 10:19). There is no place in this life where you can say, "It's all done now. I can quit working at it."

# HOW GOD DOES THE WORKS OF ETERNAL LIFE

The more you allow God to work in you, the greater his works can be. D.C. 76:2 discloses the way:

> Thus saith the Lord, I, the Lord am merciful and gracious unto those who fear me, and delight to honor those who serve me in righteousness, and in truth unto the end; great shall be their reward, and eternal shall be their glory; and to them will I reveal all mysteries; yea all the hidden mysteries of my kingdom from days of old; and for ages to come will I make known unto them the good pleasure of my will concerning all things pertaining to my kingdom; yea even the wonders of eternity shall they know, and things to come will I show them, even the things of many generations; their wisdom shall be great, and their understanding reach to heaven; and before them the wisdom of the wise shall perish, and the understanding of the prudent shall come to nought;

for by my Spirit will I enlighten them and by my power will
I make known unto them the secrets of my will; yea even
those things which eye has not seen, nor ear heard, nor yet
entered into the heart of man.

Alma 19:108 adds a closing thought to this:

"Thus God bringeth about his great and eternal purposes,
which were prepared from the foundation of the world."

Don looked at John and asked, "What about those other
works that were listed like carrying the gospel to other people, or
the good Samaritan works, or taking care of the sick or poor? Are
you suggesting there is no value in these?"

"Oh no!" John said. "Jesus promised us our reward
would never be taken from us if we just gave a thirsty person a
cup of cold water. But remember the master key? God said to
Christ, 'Let us make man in our image, and likeness' now that
you have turned your will over to God he begins making you into
his image and likeness. Then as you grow more and more like
him you begin to see other people as God sees them so you have
compassion for them. Because of this you will do whatever you
can to alleviate their suffering, or needs, and to assist them in
finding the way to the kingdom.

"The difference is that now you are not doing these works
to qualify for salvation, but you are doing them from the wellspring of God-like love. And in doing this you are fulfilling the
second great commandment."

## SUMMARY

The works which lead you to be judged worthy of eternal life in Celestial Glory are works which you cannot do. They are done within you by God, but with your active cooperation, and willingness to learn and accept what God is showing you, followed by the willingness to put what you've learned into your being and life.

Bob stood up and thoughtfully paced for a moment. Then stopping behind his wife's chair he placed his hands on Jan's shoulders and said, "I feel this must be a special time meticulously engineered by God."

# CHAPTER 30

# FASTING AND SPIRITUAL POWER

Art leaned back in his chair patted his stomach and grinned, "I got rid of all the wrinkles."

"You probably put in a few stretch marks," Fran joked.

"That was a great dinner Bob; you have excellent cooks," Don said.

The study group had chosen to meet together in the private dining room at Bob's restaurant for Saturday evening dinner and fellowship.

WE ARE BOTH PHYSICAL AND SPIRITUAL BEINGS IN ONE BODY. ONE BEING WILL DOMINATE THE OTHER.

Bob motioned for the waitress to clear their table, then looking at John, said, "I've looked up all the scriptures from our study on works, and was fascinated by what we learned. But I ran into a number of references about fasting which I don't understand. What is the purpose of fasting? What possible spiritual significance could there be in going without food?"

"Bob, how can you think about fasting when we have just had a dinner like this?" Lilli teased.

"I've been thinking of it for several days. It sounds like a person who is destitute and has no food to eat would be closer to God than the affluent."

John smiled, but before he spoke, Jan joined in, "Maybe that would be the motivation I need to stay on my diet."

"I have wondered about fasting a lot of times too," Fran said. "What good could it do to abstain from food?"

"The doorway to spiritual power, and authority, wisdom and gifts of the spirit is through fasting and prayer." John began. "Fasting opens the channel between God and man. However, the value of fasting is negated by blindly abstaining from food without understanding the purpose of fasting. There is a big difference between dieting and fasting, even though the action may be similar. The reason goes back to the dual nature of man."

"Is that something like a split personality?" Sandy asked. "I read about a woman who had four personalities in her."

"I suppose in a way, it is like that," John said. "But this is more basic, we all have two beings in us. Let me explain," John continued.

## MAN'S DUAL NATURE

Genesis 2:5-6 informs us, I the Lord God created all things of which I have spoken spiritually before they were naturally upon the free of the earth...and I the Lord God, had created all the children of men and not yet a man to till the ground, for in heaven created I them, and there was not yet flesh upon the earth.

Taking a paper napkin, John drew a vertical line on it, let this line represent our spiritual being which God created. Now turn again to the second chapter of Genesis, verse 8,

I the Lord God, formed man from the dust of the ground...and man became a living soul; the first flesh upon the earth...

John then drew another line parallel to the first and said, "Let this represent the physical being of man which God formed from the dust of the ground. Now, in the same verse in Genesis, God says he breathed life into the man he had formed from the ground. D.C. 85:4a adds to this: *The spirit and the body is the soul of man,* so in mortal life we are both a spiritual and a physical being, each in competition with the other. We are spiritual beings trapped in a physical body subject to survival on a material earth but given a spiritual law to obey in order to inherit a Celestial Kingdom."

John drew a spiral line around both vertical lines and said. "One body bound together."

"Now that's what I call a real split personality," Sandy commented.

## DOMINION OVER ALL THINGS

"God instructed us to have dominion over the earth and subdue it and all living things," John said. "Most of all we need to subdue our own brutish nature, exercising dominion over ourselves. Jesus pointed out that man cannot serve two masters. This is especially true if the two are within him. Therefore, the God-seeking spiritual man must take charge, firmly controlling the direction of his life, or his greedy gluttonous physical being will rule him."

"I know just what it means," Art said, patting his stomach again.

Lilli nodded to Art and said, "Apostle Paul pointed directly at our dual nature:

> Romans 8:5-8: They that are after the flesh do mind the things
> of the flesh; but they that are after the spirit, the things of the
> spirit. For to be carnally minded is death, but to be spiritually
> minded is life and peace, the carnal mind is enmity against
> God; for it is not subject to the law of God, neither indeed can
> it be. So they that are after the flesh cannot please God.

"That's right" John continued. "if we allow our physical beings to control our lives, they will feed all the appetites and

343

lusts of our carnal beings. Soon our debauchery would lead us completely outside the effect of any spiritual law and then, ignoring the commandments of God, we would become lawless entities.

# TUG OF WAR

The tug-of-war between the physical and spiritual is present in all of God's scheme for man. Man can go so far to the carnal side of his nature that he quenches the spiritual light by which God is leading him, thereby severing his lifeline and hope. He then rejects all heavenly law, and because he has gone completely outside the law, he is no longer subject to it; so he is ruled only by his carnal, sensual, and devilish desires."

"Our physical being must be awful," Sandy said thoughtfully.

"I don't think so," Lilli responded. "I believe we are wonderfully created with marvelous bodies, but when the lusts and appetites of the body take over, we become like brute animals, so our finer beings must maintain control."

# THE SPIRITUAL PERSON SEEKS GOD

John continued: "The spiritual side of our nature seeks the spiritual attributes of our creator. As one's spirit reaches out to God with a thirst for eternal truths he drinks of the 'living waters' of God's spirit. This person finds beauty in the physical things of the world for he sees in them the testimony of God's creativity. He thinks of the world with awe and appreciation, and yields himself to the molding hand of his maker. He becomes considerate, concerned and loving toward other people. He finds joy in living and, as he uses the natural things of the world they become a catalyst in his worship experience because they testify of God. Although he loves the world and its beauty, he becomes less possessive and grasping. He perceives God's ownership and finds joy in freely sharing the wonders God has prepared for us.

## MAN'S PHYSICAL BEING SEEKS GRATIFICATIONS

"Man's physical being demands satisfaction of needs, such as food, water and air. It also cries out for gratification that bring pleasure such as sweet food, sex, praise, and other indulgences. To the extent that these are actual needs, we should provide them, the control of them, however, must be delegated to the wisdom of our spiritual being, and never released to the gluttonous physical being to satisfy its wants.

Some people indulge in emotional adventures of the mind feeding their minds on pride, fear, hate, pornography, and other trash. A person completely given to the physical side of his nature is selfish, drawing to himself all the physical pleasures he can reach. He becomes insensitive to the beauty of the world but he displays a compulsion to grasp as much of it as he can, as though his eternal security is found in his accumulation of temporal things."

John opened his scriptures and said, "This condition is well described in

Genesis 4:13 'And man began from that time forth to be carnal, sensual, and devilish'.

## WE MAY CHOOSE

Such a person gradually loses his ability to love deeply, and eventually becomes miserable. He is a physical glutton.

"Agency, our right to choose our way despite God's wishes for us is so important that God will allow us to turn ourselves over fully to our carnal beings. "Finally," John added, "As we pursue this course, we become our own Gods and reach a point where God will give us up:

> Romans 1:21-25 "Because that when they knew God they glorified him not as God, neither were they thankful, but became vain in their foolish imaginations and their foolish hearts were darkened professing themselves to be wise, they became fools and changed the glory of the incorruptible God into an image made like to corruptible man, and the birds and four-footed beasts and creeping things. Wherefore God also gave them up to uncleanness through the lusts of their selves; who changed the truth of God to a lie and worshipped and served the creature more than the creator, who is blessed forever, Amen."

Percy Farrow (Saints Herald, Oct., 1977) wrote: "Our response must be one of trust and obedience. We must be willing to risk our lives in the hand of God. In so doing, we must subordinate our wills to the will of God, for our self-willness is at the very heart of our sinning."

"Apostle Paul told of his struggles with the two forces within him, each trying to dominate his life.:

> Romans 7:25-27 "and now I see another law, even the commandment of Christ, and it is imprinted in my mind. But my members are warring against the law of my mind, and bringing me into captivity to the law of sin which is in my members and if I subdue not the sin which is in me, but with the flesh serve the law of sin; O wretched man that I am! who shall deliver me from the body of this death? I thank God through Jesus Christ our Lord, then, that so with the mind I myself serve the law of God."

"The spiritual man maintains dominion over his animal being through fasting," John continued. "He forces his physical being to submit to the rigors of a discipline which he consciously imposes upon it and enforces by the strength of his will. In doing so he keeps his carnal nature subject to its spiritual master. He has in this way freed himself to reach up to God with all his faculties and to fully dedicate himself, having an eye single to the glory of God."

Bob asked, "You are saying that if I cannot control the demands of my body, I don't own myself, so I cannot give myself to God? That makes sense."

"Yes," John said. "If a person is addicted to coffee or cigarettes, drugs, or anything which forces him to submit to the physical part of his being, he has lost control of the brute of his being and is no longer free to give himself to God in the fullest sense. He does not own himself. I point to my experience of drinking coffee for many years. This left me so addicted to it that whenever I did not have it by mid-morning I would have a throbbing headache. This would drive me to find relief through a strong cup of coffee. In this condition I could not fast without great suffering, so the coffee became my master. It required two weeks of headaches to free myself from that master before I could give myself totally to God."

## FOOD FOR SUSTENANCE

"What about food for sustenance," Sandy asked. "We have to have food to live."

"This question is answered in several places in scripture," John explained:

D.C. 85:21 also I give unto you a commandment that you shall continue in prayer and fasting from this time forth.

"Obviously this did not mean they were to be on their knees in prayer continually from that time forth, nor did it mean they were to continue without food or water. The intent of the scripture is for the spiritual person to maintain a close communication relationship with God. In doing this he will enforce discipline over his body, giving it only what is needed."

"Are there any kind of guidelines on this in the scripture," Sandy asked.

"Oh yes," Lilli declared. D.C. 86 gives a very good guide. This was long before the modern nutritionists began telling us what foods are best for us and those which we should avoid. It also warned about evil men in the last days who for profit would sell adulterated food which is not good for human consumption.

"In addition to this, when we do not understand how to follow God's instructions, we need to study the lives of those who lived in close harmony with God, who did apply God's directions," John pointed out.

"The prophet Daniel was such a person, and concerning a period of fasting he said, '*I ate no pleasant food neither came flesh nor wine to my mouth,*' ' Dan. 10:3 Since this period of fasting continued twenty four days, it is reasonable to expect that he did eat and drink enough food and water to maintain his body.

"Daniel and three other young Hebrews who were taken to Babylon were offered fine food by the king. This included a daily provision of the king's meat and of the wine which he (the king) drank. They refused the king's fine food and asked for pulse and water to drink. To Daniel and the three who forsook the king's food and maintained this fasting regimen,

> "God gave them knowledge and skill in all learning and wisdom; and Daniel had understanding in all dreams and visions." (Dan. 1:17)

The point is, that although they did eat well enough to be in better health than all who ate of the king's food, their eating was under their control. They did not permit a gluttonous appetite to rule them. The way in which we 'Fast Always' is not through starvation but by a proper self-controlled healthy diet, without excess, and coupled with a close prayer relationship with God."

"Is it okay if the diet tastes good," Jan asked

"Certainly," Lilli laughed, "If you have healthy food, and are not eating just for the pleasure of eating."

John said, "There are many examples of how the combination of fasting and prayer is the doorway to spiritual gifts and power and knowledge. One example is given in the twelfth chapter of Alma:

> And now it came to pass that as Alma was journeying...to his astonishment he met the sons of Mosiah...What added more to his joy, they were still his brethren in the Lord; yea and they had waxed strong in the knowledge of the truth; for they were men of sound understanding, and they had searched the scriptures diligently, that they might know the word of God. But this is not all: They had given themselves to much prayer and fasting, therefore they had the spirit of prophesy, and the spirit of revelation, and when they taught, they taught with power and authority, even as with the power and authority of God.

John explained: "There is opposition in all things. On one hand, we are daily being created in the image of God. That image carries all the attributes of God: love, wisdom, creativity, and power. The opposition tries to prevent our becoming God-like and would rule us by substituting physical and emotional debauchery.

"When a person through conscious effort and choice determines to subdue his carnal being and gluttonous lusts, his mental aspirations! and his feelings for others, and uses the things of the world in a manner designed of God, that is fasting. This should become a pattern for his life. When it does, that person is 'fasting always'."

# FASTING FROM ALL FOOD

"I always understood that fasting meant going without any food or water," Don said. "Isn't that what Jesus did in the wilderness?"

"Yes," Lilli answered, "There are special times, when there are extremely important needs and we must draw as close to God as possible to receive the greatest blessing from him. At times like those we turn to total abstention."

John explained, "The reason for this is that the channels through which Satan reaches us are physical, such as desire for food, pride, such as political or social power, and earthly glory, such as praise from people. These are the three ways which Satan used to tempt Jesus. We must learn to control and reject them as Jesus did. Through total fasting, not only food and drink, but also our pride and emotions, we cut off the channels through which Satan tempts us and we can approach God in purity."

"What was the special occasion for Jesus in the wilderness?" Art asked.

"If you recall that in Matt.28:17 Jesus said *'All Power is given unto me in heaven and in earth.* Resisting Satan's greatest temptations was the final test Jesus faced before being granted these powers," John said. "When Jesus returned from fasting in the wilderness he had proven that he was totally God's and Satan had no power over him. This was the moment he was granted all power in heaven and in earth.

"The only possibility left for Satan to win was to try to dissuade Jesus from dying for us on the cross and, fortunately for us, Jesus triumphed over Satan again."

# CHAPTER 31

## STEWARDSHIP

The members of the study group were taking their places around the dining room table as John passed out the papers for the evening's study.

Jan looked at Lilli, and said, "I certainly learned a lot from our discussion about fasting Saturday. I had always thought it was just a matter of going without food for a time, but I didn't know why."

Lilli replied, "Fasting is an important part of our spiritual lives. It is one of the ways we control the physical half of ourselves, so we don't serve ourselves instead of God."

"You mean there are other ways?"

"Yes, in fact we will look at this tonight"

Art laughed, "Fran, I think it is time for your question."

Fran made a fist and hit Art on the shoulder. "Okay, you are so clever, you ask what we are studying tonight."

"Before that fight gets too heated, I'll tell you," John laughed, "We will be studying stewardship tonight."

"Stewardship," Sandy exclaimed, "Nobody but accountants can find that subject interesting. Everytime I've been in a stewardship class its been a repetition of obey the financial law, pay your tithing, give special offerings, etc. etc."

"Let's wait and see, Sandy," Bob suggested, "I thought several other subjects were going to be boring, but when we got into them and learned what they really were I found them fascinating and I suspect this will be the same."

"Thanks for the vote of confidence," John nodded to Bob then continued "I think you will find stewardship interesting also. It is much more than lists of figures and scriptural laws. It encompasses everything we have studied.

"Let's go back to our first play in the study of creation. You remember that because of the problem of man's agency he was to be placed in the laboratory of life. This is an excellent place to consider the paradigm of the simulator, because stewardship clearly demonstrates our skills, and our willingness in following the directions of God. If we are functioning within the simulator, and our movements are being monitored, we clearly reveal our attitude toward the things of the world. Are we using them in the manner designed of God, or do we greedily hoard them and keep them from others?

"When viewed from this paradigm it is easy to see that not only material things are a part of our stewardship but also our relationships with others, and especially our use of time."

"Wow, it sure does," Sandy declared. "When we think of daily life as an on-going affair we lose track of time, as though it is endless. But when we think of ourselves being on a test, or training, run in a simulator, all these things become important, and the time for us to complete our run becomes critical."

Art sat up straight and momentarily waved both hands in the air. "I can just see myself. At precisely the moment I think I have the simulator under control and running smoothly, the power shuts off and my run is over. The hatch opens and I step out and meet the Lord. He says, "Let's see how you did," as he tears off the computer printout that records everything.

"I'll want to go hide somewhere, because I know I wasted a lot of time and I was more concerned with running my life to my own advantage than I was with following God's directions, or in being concerned about anyone else."

"This certainly makes you think." Sandy said. I wonder how the Rich Young Ruler felt when he stepped out and met Jesus. He would be able to see then how great a blessing of eternal life Jesus had offered him here, and he turned it down to hang onto his money."

"Maybe, if you could put yourself in his position, you wouldn't be so critical in your judgment of that young man," Lilli commented.

"How can I do that?" Sandy asked, "I've never been rich."

"Then suppose for a moment that the state lottery this week is thirty-five million dollars, and you have a ticket. Of course like most other people you have prayed to the Lord that this will be a winning ticket, and you have promised what you will do for him if he can make it so. By the time five numbers have been drawn, and you have all of them, you are jumping up and down and breathlessly waiting for the last number. When it comes, it is your number. At first you can't believe it, you are too stunned to think clearly for a moment. Then you begin thinking of all you can do with the millions of dollars you have won. Then just before you have mentally spent all of it you remember your promises to the Lord and you drop to your knees and say 'thank you Lord, thank you so much for making this happen.' At that moment the voice of the Lord comes clearly to you. He says, 'tear up the ticket.' In disbelief you say to him, but, but, but, Lord, think of all that money and the good things I can do for you.' His voice comes back, 'Tear up the ticket.'"

"Does that help you see the situation the young man faced," Lilli added.

"Oh man!" Don groaned, "Does it ever."

John broke the pall of serious thought that quieted the group by asking, "Sandy, would you begin reading for us?"

## STEWARDSHIP

Stewardship tests our use of agency in all areas of our lives. It also reveals the stage of life we are in, and it shows how well we have responded to the second great commandment. It even goes beyond that. It tests our faith and our submission to God.

"How can paying tithing do all of that?" Fran asked.

"I can assure you," Lilli told Fran, "Stewardship is much more than tithing"

"Hold on," Bob joked, "Here we go again."

John joined in the joke and said, "I think it is a trip you will enjoy—and beyond what I told you, stewardship encompasses our total character. There are scriptures you should know.

D.C. 28:9 'All things unto me are spiritual. And not at any time have I given unto you a law which was temporal, neither any man ....neither Adam your father, whom I created; behold I gave unto him that he should be an agent unto himself; and I gave unto him commandment, but no temporal commandment gave I unto him; for my commandments are spiritual; they are not temporal, neither carnal or sensual.'

"So you see, when we speak of the Law of Carnal Commandments or the Laws of Temporalities as they are often called, we are not using correct terminology, because these laws have a great spiritual significance. Any person attempting to achieve the Celestial Kingdom should know how Stewardship impacts his spiritual being."

"Do you mean that the way I manage my money has spiritual implications?" Bob asked.

"Isn't money one of the most tempting things in life, an area which causes us most trouble? And isn't money at the center of nearly everything in our lives? Here are a few more scriptures to consider before we get into the heart of our study." John handed out papers with a list of Scriptures:

> D.C. 42:8c In as much as ye impart of your substance unto the poor, ye will do it unto me.

> D.C. 72:1c It is required of the Lord at the hand of every steward, to render an account of his stewardship both in time and eternity

> Jacob 2:22-Think of your brethren like unto yourselves, and be familiar with all, and free with your substance, that they may be rich like unto you, but before ye seek for riches seek ye the kingdom of God. And after ye have obtained a hope in Christ, ye shall obtain riches, if ye seek them; and ye will seek them, for the intent to do good; to clothe the naked, and to feed the hungry, and to liberate the captive, and administer relief to the sick, and the afflicted.
> And now my brethren, I have spoken unto you concerning your pride; and those of you which have afflicted your neighbor, and persecuted him, because ye were proud in your hearts, of the things which God hath given you, ...Do ye not suppose that such things are abominable unto him who created all flesh? And the one being is as precious in his sight as the other...

"This sounds like we are going back to our study of the second commandment" Don suggested as he studied the list of scriptures.

"Exactly," John answered, "You see, no part of God's great plan stands alone nor do we as individuals stand alone;

nearly everything we do has an effect upon others. These things are all integral interwoven parts of the fabric."

Sandy, "Would you continue reading the text for us?"

## STEWARDSHIP AN EXTENSION OF FASTING

The warfare between our physical and spiritual beings exists in all areas of our lives, especially in our use of money and material things. There is continual conflict within us between choosing either to use our wealth to boost our esteem and for pleasure, or on the opposite side, to use it to help others.

John interrupted, "At this point my thought goes back to the paradigm of the simulator. Suppose God has richly blessed you with material things, but you treat with scorn a person in desperate need who comes to you for help. Then, when your time has ended, you discover you were only in a simulator being trained and tested. How will you feel? Remember, of course, that even if we reject the idea of the simulator, the end result will be the same. We will still come before the Lord for judgment, and we will 'know as we are known.' Nothing will be hidden."

## THREE LEVELS OF RESPONSE

The Law of Temporalities, sometimes called "the Law of Carnal Commandments," outlines tithing and our stewardship over possessions we have obtained. This law states the dynamics of what we must do with our property to be right with God. We will not go into the details of these rules in this study, because our intent is to interpret God's superb design for our stewardship.

"This sounds a lot like our discussion at the restaurant Saturday about fasting," Don commented.

"Of course, because stewardship is an extension of fasting. Controlled use of everything we have is basic for the highest spiritual blessings. These blessings are more than an accumulation of material wealth. When following the rules of fasting as applied to food, we receive the benefit of healthy, energetic bodies. When the rules are applied to stewardship, society as well the individual is blessed." John responded.

"This sounds like everything in our lives becomes a stewardship," Bob observed, "even how we use our social standing and political power, or, for that matter, how we think about our ability to help others."

"It makes you think about your accountability, doesn't it," Jan added.

## THE SAFE ZONE

A balance can be achieved by keeping our physical person subject to the direction of our spiritual being which functions under obedience to the directions of God. This is the level in which we fulfill what God desires of us and become acceptable to him. This is the one in which we use the things of the world in a manner designed by the Lord, and live our lives in tune with the Infinite. On this level we manage our stewardships in ways that are acceptable to God. We pay our tithes, we make oblation offerings to help the needy, and we use the remainder in conservative ways which never suggest we conceive ourselves to be more loved by God than others. When we have done this we have proven our compliance with God's laws for stewardship. Nothing more, or less, is required. This is a safe level entirely within the law.

# FUNCTIONING ABOVE THE LAW

We may exceed the safe level of compliance with the law. We can progress to where we need no law, because our longing heart is so compassionately concerned for other people and our desire is to be acceptable to God so we reach beyond the demands of the law. we rise above the allure of material things and our greed. When our spirit is touched by the Eternal, our hearts are torn for the misery we see among God's destitute people whose plaintive cry goes unheeded by a mercenary world. Therefore we are concerned with those things which bring relief and a better life to all people rather than the things which bring only pleasure to ourselves. Our liberal response, either through money or service, to alleviate the suffering of people is rooted in compliance with the second great commandment. But it is not a perfunctory response to the commandment, instead we are compelled by our compassion and stirred by the spirit within us so we spontaneously open our hearts with concern for other people and the world upon which we live.

Jan was looking back at the paper with scriptures listed on it "That scripture from Jacob about God who created all flesh, and one being as precious to him as another really touches me. It says so much about the love of God and also about our failure when we put ourselves above other people. It makes me want to reach out and love everyone."

"Yes," Lilli agreed "There is no love like his and when we sense how great it is, ours is always enlarged. I look forward to the kingdom of God when all people will come under the shelter of his love and there will be no more division and hatred and anger. It will be wonderful."

# FUNCTIONING BELOW THE LAW

Multitudes of people, still in the infant stage, in which they think only of their own desires, never meet the minimum requirements of the laws of stewardship. They become their own law and refuse to have consideration for others and in fact, they intensify the pain and poverty when they take from others.

# MAN'S PRACTICE IS NOT GOD'S PLAN

Apparently few individuals understand God's plan for our stewardship and use of earth's wealth. Certainly it is totally different than that which is in use by any nation today. God would have no dollars to be hoarded by a few while others starve. In his plan the earth will provide an abundance for every individual upon it, and all will be rich in material things and there will be no poor.

"Let me interrupt just a moment." Bob said. "What is the premise for the statement that all will be rich?"

Lilli was eager to respond to this. "The person who has everything he needs for a full happy life is as rich as a person who has a huge accumulation of goods beyond his need. For example, if you have a dish of wholesome food which satisfies your hunger, and you know more will be available for each meal, you are as rich as the person who has ten dishes of food. Nine are a surplus which he cannot eat; they are only a responsibility to be cared for and preserved. Having more than is needed does not make him richer. Does that make sense?"

"I understand," Bob replied.

John continued: "The status of class created by money will be erased along with the plague of pride with which money infects people. The population of earth will live on the interest which the earth produces yearly, leaving the principle to replenish itself."

"Isn't that wonderful?" Sandy marveled at the thought of how God's world was prepared to continually reproduce.

"This sounds like an eccentric's proclamation for a new world order." John added. "That's because so many people are hoarding wealth and others have made it their life's ambition to obtain it. They cannot conceive any other way. And today few people would be brave enough to suggest such changes, but the time will come when the money systems will fail and the coming of Zion will bring God's system. When that happens society will be so transformed we do not have space here to describe it even if we had sufficient imagination to envision it."

"Until that great event takes place, we are saddled with a system designed by man in which greed motivates men to grasp beyond their needs and appropriate another's share." Lilli pointed out. "Because of this we reap a harvest of hatred, distrust and war. It is characteristic of God to make us dependent upon each other binding us together. For example he did not give one person all the spiritual gifts and leave others with nothing to contribute; we need each other to receive the benefit of all gifts. The system designed by God will pull all people together, whereas the system designed by men alienates people."

"Fran, would you start reading at that second paragraph?" John asked.

# PERSPECTIVES OF STEWARDSHIP

Putting stewardship into perspective we acknowledge we never actually own any material thing. We came into life without anything except our bodies and we will leave without even that. There is no possible way we can enrich ourselves by hoarding those things God put on deposit here for the comfort of all. Any thought of ownership is condemned to be fleeting.

We confuse ourselves and distort God's simple plans by complicating the original meanings. We have changed the meaning of being rich and blessed to mean someone who has a great accumulation of temporal things. A society in which all individuals have everything needed for a comfortable happy life is rich. Since everyone has his needs fulfilled there is no motivation for envy, or theft, or fear of one person taking advantage over another. It results in peace of mind (No locks required except for safety). No police to guard against criminals, no attorneys to litigate property ownership, more leisure time and educational opportunities for everyone, and finally higher respect for all people in a caring and concerned environment. This society will be blessed by better health resulting from peace of mind.

The Lord tells us In D.C. 6:3 "Keep my commandments and seek to bring forth and establish the cause of Zion. Seek not for riches but for wisdom; and, behold, the mysteries of God shall be unfolded unto you, and then shall you be made rich. Behold he that hath eternal life is rich."

Because of the distortion of being rich and blessed we often do not recognize our rich condition. Society has come to hold in high esteem the person who demonstrates skill in acquiring money or material goods and to consider this person to be very wise and intelligent. Because of this, many people have squandered their lifetime in pursuit of money with no greater motivation than to get the adoration of other people. Ironically, this view has caused individuals to be held up in respectable esteem who have gotten their riches through wanton, selfish greed and disregard for others.

Man's distorted concept of riches has led to a form of stewardship that has completely reversed the intent of God. Being rich by world standards draws an immediate line between people deliberately creating separations. The world considers a rich person to be one who has accumulated goods far in excess of his needs. This creates power because he can purchase the goods and services of others. The result is envy by those who do not have great possessions, and crime by those who attempt to take from others. There is a burden of costs imposed upon everyone in this kind of society. This is in the form of all the legal expenses of trying to contain crime; police, attorneys, prisons, insurance, medical costs related to stress, slums in the cities, undereducated people with lives made hopeless, and violence are a few of the penalties.

It has been estimated that if all people had all things in common and all contributed to the general welfare that we could live on a higher average standard of living at a cost of only fourteen percent of what we are now paying. This means that of every one hundred days we are now working to provide for ourselves, eighty six of them could be used for other pursuits.

It is only because God holds our gift of agency sacred that mankind has been permitted to proceed on this course for a time. God has resources deposited in the earth sufficient for all people of all nations to live on the interest accrued annually without withdrawing any of the principle. His instructions for us to satisfy our needs and just wants and love our neighbor enough to leave his share for him has been so severely violated that neighbor cheats neighbor, and nation rises against nation. Not only have the greedy reaped the fruits of the interest and withheld them from their desperate and needy neighbors, they have despoiled the principle and destroyed much of its earning and replenishing power.

In man's every-person-for-himself plan of stewardship, possession of things become a scale of values. The value of a person, his position in society, security, comfort, and desirability as a marriage partner are all largely determined by where he is on the money scale. We are so caught up in this system that it is difficult to be objective in considering the value of material things relative to the Kingdom of God, and God's plan has been so thoroughly replaced on earth that few even know of its existence and fewer still have the courage to believe it can work. For most of us the concept of God's plan seems startlingly new and few will undertake the risks that seem to be involved in face of the deeply established plan men live by.

The Rich Young Ruler who came to Jesus asking what he must do to inherit eternal life faced a dilemma when Jesus said, "Go sell all you have and give it to the poor." He was asking the young man to do more than give up his money and material possessions. He was telling him to give up the powerful social position he held and to give up the respect of his family and friends, and his secure future. He would have to exchange his career and the comforts it promised for the lot of a vagabond.

Jesus offered him peace beyond that which money can buy, but it was also beyond his comprehension.

We too stand before Jesus with the same question on our lips, "What must we do to inherit Eternal Life?" and Jesus answers "seek ye first to bring forth the Kingdom of God and all these things shall be added unto you." Our response to this determines the degree to which our spiritual control is extended in stewardship. This response needs to be tempered by an understanding that God does not need our money. All instruction in the scriptures concerning the use of temporalities and sharing and care of the underprivileged or poor is for our good.

It is imperative that we accept two things: 1. we cannot ever own the material things of the earth, 2. God's instructions or commandments concerning the use of material things are so we can get the best use from them for all people. God is asking that we fully as possible use his creation in the manner for which he created them. When mankind does this every person is assured a rich full life and the earth is cared for.

This leaves us two ways to go in following God. The first is a meeting and balancing of the material and spiritual. This is the result of following the financial law. When people do this, they prosper. Funding for needed projects is provided and people are cared for. In doing this we fulfill what God requires of us: we are right with God.

Compare the nine Nephites who wanted to serve throughout their mortal lives, then join Jesus in his kingdom. This was a good service acceptable to Jesus. However there were three other Nephites disciples who saw their ministry in a different way. To them the souls of men and women were so precious and their compassion so great they could not think of stopping their efforts to reach out to as many as they could bring to Christ as long as the earth should stand. This meant going beyond the life span of man in order to continue to reach out. In their hearts they wanted no time limit on their work. Jesus recognized their desire which was far past the requirements of their call to ministry. They went beyond the law of service first by fulfilling the law, then exceeding it. To these three Jesus said, "More blessed are ye...and for this cause Ye shall have a fullness of joy and ye shall sit down in the kingdom of my father."

## EXTENDED MINISTRY OF THE THREE NEPHITES

"I wonder why no one ever sees the three nephites," Jan mused. "I'd certainly like to meet them sometime."

"Perhaps you will, for that matter, perhaps you have." Lilli answered as she reached for her book. "Here in III Nephi 13:38-40 it says, 'I was about to write the names of those who were never to taste of death; but the Lord forbade me...for they are hid from the world. But behold I have seen them, and they have ministered unto me; and ...they will be seen among the Gentiles and the Gentiles knoweth them not....They are as ministering angels of God, and if they shall pray unto the Father in the name of Jesus, they can shew themselves unto whatsoever man it seemeth them good...' So who knows, Jan perhaps you will meet them."

"I think I would know them." Jan said, then added, "at least I hope I would."

"Would you take over reading, Art?" John asked.

There are those also who have so far exceeded the demands of the stewardship laws that they have fulfilled them and gone beyond. They have seen the suffering and misery and grim conditions of God's peoples and their hearts have longed so much to aid them that they could not rest with the thought of using only a tithe of their material things; they gave all they had and sought more to relieve mankind's suffering. Material things to them meant only having the vital means to feed the starving and administer relief to the suffering. People like Eartha White the black woman of Jacksonville, Florida who went from poverty to become a millionaire only to use it all to help the downtrodden. She walked the streets of Jacksonville at all hours and in all kinds of weather to help people in need. She traveled from the streets to the banks, and to the office of the President of The United States in her efforts to raise money in behalf of others.

Doctor Tom Dooley who was left in Asia by the Navy as the only medical doctor in that area of the world to minister to the suffering of people there chose to remain and become one of them and finally die with them rather than return to the comfort of a respectable practice in the United States.

Mother Teresa who won the Nobel Peace Prize in 1980 is another of thousands of individuals who have gone beyond where the law of temporalities has meaning because of their concern for people.

In our study of "Works" we concluded that the works by which we shall finally be judged are those which we allow God to do within us. The work God does in us is the work of molding us into his likeness. It is apparent then that as his work progresses we will begin to see from his eyes and see the need of his people and have his kind of concern for them. Because of this we respond by doing for them what he would have done for them. In this we are cooperating with God to bring to pass the kingdom of God.

"Let me point to a comparison between fasting and stewardship." John began. "In fasting we use wholesome foods as needed to maintain health and vigor, avoiding eating in excess of our needs. We control gluttonous appetites. Our stewardship is an extension of fasting in that we use the material things of the world for a comfortable living, but avoid their use for our own aggrandizement. There is ample evidence the desirable features of Zionic stewardship were tailored by God to provide abundant, peaceful conditions of life. Man has never matched the rich pure living experience of God's superb concept."

See Appendix C for the reprint of "For God's Sake Don't Tithe" published 1974. Demonstrates some stewardship principles.

# CHAPTER 32

## ANCIENT HISTORY INSCRIBED ON SHEETS OF BRASS AND GOLD

"Say, this is the right place to meet on a day like this," Art exclaimed as the group took their places around Don's and Sandy's patio table. "These nice days make it hard to go in early."

"Meeting outside like this reminds me of our experience at Big Dipper," John mentioned as he distributed papers around the table.

"We should go there again, soon," Fran said, then scanning the paper John gave her, added, "I'm not asking what we will study tonight because it says 'Ancient History,' but where do the sheets of gold and brass fit in?"

"Well, let's see; if you lived thousands of years ago, and had to write something important enough, you wanted it to last forever, what would you write it on?" Lilli asked. "They didn't have the quality paper or plastics we have today or many of the other materials, and it needed to be written with an ink that would not fade."

"Gold." Fran nodded.

"Gold would undoubtedly be their best choice, but even in those days it would be costly, and if they had much to write, it would be a big job," Bob remarked. "They could have used clay tablets like the Babylonians did."

"That is true," John agreed, "but this history was of a people who had to be able to transport their records. Can you imagine carrying eight hundred clay tablets about?"

"Gold it is." Bob laughed.

"Okay, let's see who these people were. Jan would you begin reading for us?"

# PILGRIMAGES TO THE AMERICAS

"I don't believe in God, because God didn't know about America until Columbus told him about it."

These words by Robert Ingersoll, the famous agnostic of the 1800s, make a powerful argument, if true. If there is a God who is the creator of the earth, he certainly should have known about the Americas. If he didn't know of this land, there would be good reason to question the validity of belief in God the creator. Mr. Ingersoll's statement was, however, based upon a false premise. Certainly there is no reference in the Bible to a land America. This land was not named America until early in the sixteenth century, long after the works in the Bible were written. But this does not suggest that God did not know about these lands, only that Mr. Ingersoll did not understand his Bible. The Americas are plainly spoken about; however, since the land had not been named, it was described in other ways by the people to whom God revealed it and those he brought to it.

We will look first at Biblical references to this land, then we will investigate ancient records inscribed on sheets of gold and brass by people God led around the world.

Jan continued reading:

# BIBLICAL REFERENCES TO THE AMERICAS

Genesis 11:5-6 The Lord said, Behold, the people are the same, and they all have the same language; and this tower (of Babel) they begin to build?....So I, the Lord, will scatter them abroad from thence, upon all the face of the land, and unto every quarter of the earth....And from thence did the Lord scatter them abroad upon the face thereof.

One group that was separated from the tower was led by Shem who was the father of Arphaxad whose son was Sahah; who was the father of Eber, the father of Peleg. From Peleg, the line descended to Reu, to Serug, to Nahor, to Terah, to Abram (His name was later changed by God to Abraham), to Isaac to Jacob (whose name was changed to Israel) who was the father of the twelve tribes of Israel. This genealogy is known to us because the lineage fathered by Shem kept the record which became the Bible.

But God led other groups away "unto every quarter of the earth." The records of those groups are not contained in the Bible because they went different directions and were lost to those who became the Israelites, who kept the Bible.

One group was led to what is now known as the Americas. They kept a record inscribed on gold sheets which were soft enough to be engraved, but durable enough to survive through the years. The writers of the Bible never knew of these people whom God led over the sea after they were separated at the tower, so thy could not have told of them in the Bible. They were unknown until the record which they kept was obtained centuries later. They were not, however, unknown to God.

An abridgment of their history has been known for over one hundred and fifty years.

The people of this group are called "Jaredites" because the group's leader's name was Jared. They had with them a record described in Ether 1:2-5 . The book of Ether was an abridgment of the eight hundred year history of the Jaredites and the nation they built. It was inscribed on twenty four sheets of thin gold by Ether, their last prophet. This was later abridged by another prophet who left us an abridged version of the histories of the early groups God brought across the seas prior to Columbus.

The last prophet wrote:

I take mine account from the twenty four plates which is called the Book of Ether. And as I suppose that the first part of this record, which speaks concerning the creation of the world, and also of Adam, and an account from that time even to the great tower, and whatsoever things transpired among the children of men until that time is had among the Jews, Therefore I do not write those things which transpired from the days of Adam, until that time; but they are had upon the plates; and whoso findeth them, the same will have power that he may get the full account.

The records the Jaredites took with them are apparently those mentioned in Gen 6:5-7 which says:

And then began these men (Adam, Seth, and Enos) to call upon the name of the Lord and the Lord blessed them; and a book of remembrance was kept in the which was recorded in the language of Adam, for it was given unto as many as called upon God, to write by the Spirit of inspiration; and by them their children were taught to read and write having a language which was pure and undefiled.

In addition to that record the Jaredites kept a record of their own history. This record comes to us as the Book of Ether.

# THE EARTH IS DIVIDED

The story of the earth's creation tells us that in the beginning the land of the earth was all in one place surrounded by the sea, but later God divided the land.

> Gen 1:12-13 I, God, said, Let the waters under the heaven be gathered together unto one place; and it was so. And I God, said, Let there be dry land; and it was so. And I, God, called the dry land earth; and the gathering together of the waters called I the sea.

The earth was divided shortly after the great flood and the Tower of Babel.

> Gen 10:16 tells us "Peleg was a mighty man,...in his days was the earth divided."

The Americas were separated and isolated from the rest of the land and it was being prepared as "a land choice above all other lands." So even though it was not known as America, to the writers of the Bible, but it was known to God.

The Jaredites began as a very righteous and holy people whom God led from the Tower of Babel into this choice quarter of the world. However, after they were blessed by living in a land choice above all other lands for several generations, their history turns to a story of insurrection, intrigue, and war. They forgot the God who had blessed them so richly, and turned they their swords upon each other and fought until they destroyed their nation down to one last man who was discovered, apparently insane, by a later group that God brought to this continent to replace those he had previously planted here.

"That's an interesting story," Bob said, "And I don't question that the Jaredites were brought to this country, but it really does not seem to give conclusive evidence that Ingersol was wrong."

"There's more," Lilli added.

"Yes, We have more information about the next group that was led to the Americas," John affirmed, "Because they came from the people of the Bible. Actually, they were descendants of Joseph of Egypt and King David, In fact, there is more than we will have time to discuss tonight—shall we let Sandy take over reading and give Jan a rest?"

# THE URIM AND THUMMIM

Following the exodus of the Hebrew people from Egypt, their priests came into possession of a strange instrument called the Urim and Thummim. Directions for making it were given to Moses by God on Mt. Horeb at the time he was given the directions for making the tabernacle and all of its furniture, including the Ark of the Covenant. It could not be used except by the priests or others especially endowed with a gift from God.

"What in the world was the Urim and Thummim?" Don questioned, "I never heard of such a thing."

"The literal translation of these two words is 'lights and perfection' or 'the shining and the perfect.' According to St. Jerome they mean 'Doctrine and Judgment'," John explained.

"They were two onyx stones set in gold bows similar to our eye glasses but they didn't set on the nose or hold to the ears of the person using them. They were mounted on a breastplate which the high priest wore when inquiring of the Lord, or translating languages. The priest, apparently, looked upon them rather than through them."

"They must have worked something like a TV program descrambler." Art suggested.

"I don't know how they worked" John continued, "but the directions for making them were given to Moses by God. This information is found in the twenty eighth chapter of Exodus."

"What was their purpose?" Don wondered.

"If you recall in the old testament, the leaders of the Israelites would ask the high priest to inquire the will of the Lord before entering upon a major event, such as a battle, and the high priest would pray to God for his guidance.

"Either a vision of the event according to God's will would be displayed through the stones, or a message would be written across them."

"A good example," Lilli injected, "came after King Saul had been rejected by God. He desperately wanted guidance from God about a pending battle with the Philistines, but according to I Samuel 28:6

> The Lord answered him not, neither by dreams, nor the Urim
> and Thummim, or prophets.

When God rejected him he was cut off from all revelation."

"About the same time, David, previously anointed to be the successor to Saul as king, but not yet crowned, needed guidance. He called for the Urim and Thummim and received direction from God," John pointed out. "That story is in I Samuel 30:7-8"

"How does this fit into the story of people coming to America?" Bob asked.

# URIM AND THUMMIM MISSING

"In 600 B.C. a group of immigrants were led by God from Jerusalem to this country," John said, They brought brass plates which contained the five books of Moses, which gave an account of the creation of the world, and of Adam and Eve. They also had the record of the Jews from the beginning down to the reign of Zedekiah, the King of Judah at that time. And they had the laws of Moses, and the words of the prophets down to part of the words of Jeremiah. Since the early record of creation was in 'the language of Adam' which the Lord had confounded at Babel it seems reasonable to believe they brought the interpreters with them."

"This is further born out by two historical incidents" Lilli told the group, as she turned the pages of her bible. "In 586 B.C., just fourteen years after that group was led out of Jerusalem, Jerusalem was destroyed by the Babylonians. Most of the people were taken to Babylon, and Jerusalem was destroyed. King Zedekiah was forced to watch his family killed and then he was blinded. Fifty years later, King Cyrus allowed the Jews who wished to return and rebuild Jerusalem. Among those who returned were four men who claimed priesthood, but their names were not found in the records, so they searched for the Urim and Thummim to inquire of God, but it was not to be found. This story in Nehemiah 7:61-62 is the last mention of the use of the Urim and Thummim in the Bible. The next mention of them comes in their use by King Mosiah in the Americas. Over here they were called "Interpreters".

"Lilli, this isn't something you got from Agatha Christie is it?" Jan Joked.

"No, it's all in the scriptures," Lilli laughed. "But it has all the intrigue and fascination of her stories. There was a successful raid on the Jewish national archives, murder, travel through the wilderness, and a battle with the sea, and more. It adds a lot to it just knowing this is not fiction; they were real people in real situations. If you like Agatha Christie you would enjoy this."

# SCRIPTURAL REFERENCES TO THE AMERICAS

Fran begins reading:

On his deathbed, Israel, the father of the twelve tribes called his sons to him for his patriarchal blessings upon them. In the blessing given to his son Joseph, he said,

'Joseph is a fruitful bough by a well; whose branches run over the wall (the sea) Gen 49:22.

This was a continuation of the blessing of Moses upon the twelve. When Moses blessed Joseph (Deut 33:1-13-17) he had said:

...His glory is like the firstling of his bullock and his horns are like the horns of unicorns; with them he shall push the people together to the ends of the earth; and they are the ten thousands of Ephriam and the thousand of Manasseh. (Ephraim and Manasseh were sons of Joseph of the twelve tribes of Israel.)

Isaiah also foresaw the descendants of Joseph going over the sea.

Is. 16:8...They wandered through the wilderness; her branches are stretched out, they are gone over the sea... Jeremiah also spoke of them, Jer. 48:32 Oh vine of Sibmah (Sibmah was a rich grape growing area near Jerusalem where descendants of Joseph lived) I will weep for thee with the weeping of Jazor; thy plants are gone over the sea... Ps. 80:8 & 11 Thou hast brought a vine out of Egypt (Joseph of Egypt) Thou hast cast out the heathen (the Jaredites) and planted it ...She sent out her boughs unto the sea, and her branches unto the river.

# A VISION OF THEIR DESTINATION

Where did they land after going over the sea? Isaiah, the prophet, stood in Jerusalem and pointed across Ethiopia (Africa) and said

> To the land shadowing with wings which is beyond the
> rivers of Ethiopia..." (Is. 18:1)

Looking across Africa from Jerusalem, there is no place for them to land except the Americas. And if you were to superimpose the body of a bird across the narrow area of Panama it is apparent that the two continents look like a huge rough shadow of wings of a great bird. Although Isaiah could not call the land "America" he described its shape and location very aptly.

# THE NEPHITES

In the first year of the reign of Zedekiah there were "many" prophets in Jerusalem. The best known was Jeremiah. Another was a man named Lehi who was a descendant of Joseph through the lineage of Manasseh. Lehi prophesied the destruction of Jerusalem unless the people repented and turned to God. Rather than repent, they threatened Lehi's life. Totally rejected, Lehi turned to God and was told to take his family and go into the wilderness. Later they were joined by another family and were led across the continent, a trip taking eight years. Then they built a ship which carried them over the sea to the Americas.

During their travels dissension and bickering had kept turmoil in the group. The two oldest sons of Lehi, Laman and Lemuel, resented leaving the luxury of their home in Jerusalem, and did not believe God had led them away. The youngest son, Nephi, was totally dedicated to God and supportive of his father. A fourth brother, Sam, slightly older than Nephi, also sided with their father. Through divine intervention, Nephi became the leader of the group. After Lehi died in their new land, they separated into two nations, the Lamanites, and the Nephites.

Nephi had made thin plates of gold and kept the Nephite records on them. These were later handed down from one leader to another until the nation left God and fell from his grace, and was ultimately destroyed.

# MULOK

A third party of immigrants came from Jerusalem. While Nebuchadnezzar's army was conquering the city, King Zedekiah's attendants spirited his infant son, Mulok, away to save his life. That group came around the world in the opposite direction from the Lehi group. Eventually they met in their new land and joined with the Nephites. Both Isaiah and Exekial had foreseen this event. Is. 65:8-9 foretold "An inheritor shall be saved out of Judah."

King Zedekiah, as all the kings from the time of David, was a descendent of Judah. All of Zedekiah's family were killed by the Babylonian soldiers except Mulok who had been secretly whisked away.

> Ezekial 17:22-23 Thus saith the Lord God; I will also take of the highest branch of the high cedar (the king) and will set it; I will crop off from the top of his young twigs a tender one (the baby son Mulok) and will plant it upon a high mountain...(a great nation).

# THE RECORDS

"This is fascinating," Bob exclaimed. "Did you say the records of these people have been available for a hundred and fifty years? I would like to read them."

"Bob, do you remember that, with our first study, you said you were going to red-line any scripture references, you questioned so we could look at it later?" John asked.

"Sure, that was for Book of Mormon references, but I didn't redline any because they all made so much sense and were supported by Biblical scriptures."

"Okay," John continued, "that book is the record of all three of the migrations we have spoken of. It is not the complete detailed record because there was over a thousand years of history written. Mormon was next to the last person charged with keeping the records. He went through them and made an abridgment of them. The abridgment alone is nearly eight hundred pages of what we know as the Book of Mormon. Then he buried the original records, which must have been a large library, and charged his son, Moroni, with keeping the abridgment. During the last great battles which destroyed the Nephite nation, Moroni added the final words of their history. He then took the abridgment and the interpreters, and placed them in a stone box which he buried in the earth in what is now New York state. These were brought out by divine intervention in 1827.

"Moroni, now the Angel Moroni, has been charged with protecting the records. He was sent by God to a young man, Joseph Smith, an uneducated farm boy of only fourteen, and began preparing him to receive and translate the record and to present it to the world.

"The library, which is believed to be hidden in a hill in Central America, will remain hidden until a time chosen by God. However, the fulfillment of prophecy suggests that the time for it to be brought forth is very near; it could happen any day. Many archaeologists and Book of Mormon scholars are uncovering the ruins of the great civilization in that part of the world and new findings are being made everyday."

"That is a book I'm going to have to read." Jan determined.

## PAUL AND TED APPEAR

The evening shadows were turning into twilight, so Don turned on the patio lights. Returning to his chair, he said, "This has been a fascinating narration until now, but I have heard some real strange things about Joseph Smith."

"I am not at all surprised," John said. "When the angel first appeared to Joseph Smith, the first thing he told him was that God had a work for him to do, and his name would be had for good and evil among all nations, kindred and tongues. Since then there have been a lot of terribly revolting stories manufactured about him."

"In fact," Lilli added, "as far back as 1830 his enemies dragged him from court to court making allegations against him, but the allegations all proved to be vicious lies, and he was always exonerated."

"Maybe we can help on that question," a voice spoke from the shadows.

Everyone looked up and saw two figures coming along the sidewalk around the corner of the House.

"It's Paul," Fran exclaimed.

"And Ted," Jan said. "What a great surprise this is."

"Where did you come from?" Sandy asked as Art and Bob extended their hands to welcome the newcomers.

Lilli took the hand of Ted who was nearest her. "It's surely nice to see you. We have thought of you so many times since you left us at Big Dipper Lake."

"Did you finish your hike through Oregon and California?" Don asked.

"No," Ted answered, "We decided it would be well for us to return to the land of Lehi's descendants. So we chose to fly down to the Yucatan Peninsula. We landed at Merida. From there we motored to Chichen Itza and the other little towns in the area where some of the great Nephite nation used to be."

"We have spent most of our time mingling with the people and learning their culture. It has been a pleasant time." Paul added. "We felt like we belonged there. We hiked the back trails and met the country people. We will be going back."

"What brought you back here? This is a long trip from the Yucatan," Bob said.

"We had some business we needed to take care of." Ted replied. "It is good to be with you again. When we came up it sounded like you were discussing the same subject you were on when we first met. Do you mind if we join you again?"

"We would be delighted," John answered. "In fact, we would like very much to hear of your expedition to Chichen Itza. I've always wanted to make that trip myself."

"I'm sorry if I seem to be moving in on your class," Paul said as he pulled a tattered and well-worn leather-bound Bible from his handbag, "But there are a couple of scriptures you might want to look at before we tell of our experiences down south."

"The class is yours," John said. "It will be a good relief for them from listening to me."

"I agree with that," Lilli nodded.

"If I heard you right, you were discussing the coming forth of the Book of Mormon, and Joseph Smith's name being had for both good and evil."

"My, you must have excellent ears," Lilli said.

"I might suggest that instead of being overly concerned about what prejudiced people said about him, you look at what the prophets tell about him?"

"You mean the Bible tells about him?" Bob sat up keenly interested.

Ted nodded as Paul flipped the pages and said, "Let's turn to the twenty ninth chapter of Isaiah to begin"

John and Lilli passed a smile between them as the group turned to the passage in their Bibles.

## ISAIAH 29

"Vs 1 Woe to Ariel, to Ariel, the city where David dwelt," Paul read.

"Ariel is one of the many names that the city of Jerusalem has been known by through the years," Ted pointed out. Verses 2-3 point out that despite the fact the Jews were making sacrifices in the temple, it was only a superficial ceremony. They were not repentant or following God. They refused to listen to the prophets and they persecuted them, so God was going to bring armies to destroy the city."

> Vs 4, And she shall be brought down, and shall speak out of the ground, and her speech shall be low out of the dust; and her voice shall be as of one that hath a familiar spirit; out of the ground, and her speech shall whisper out of the dust.

Ted interpreted, "The prophet was looking to the time when the record of the people would come forth from the dust of the ground, which of course is where the book was hidden. It would have a familiar spirit because it was a record of the God of Israel and his dealings with people such as they were familiar with in the Bible. Also it had the teachings of Jesus when he came to them after his crucifixion."

> Vs. 9-10 Behold, all ye that do iniquity, stay yourselves, and wonder; for ye shall cry out, and cry; yea, ye shall be drunken, but not with wine; ye shall stagger, but not with strong

drink...The Lord hath poured out upon you the spirit of deep sleep. For ye have closed your eyes and ye have rejected the prophets, and Your rulers; and the seers hath he covered because of your iniquities.

"Isaiah is seeing the period we call the dark ages." Ted explained. "He sees that because of the sins of the people and their rejection of the prophets they were in spiritual darkness. (Even today there are people who say revelation is done away with and God no longer speaks to men.) It is because they reject the word that comes from the Lord. And the result is they are confused as though they were drunk." Then Ted added, "Go on to the next verse, Paul."

Vs 11-14 It shall come to pass, that the Lord God shall bring forth unto you the words of a book; and they shall be the words of them which have slumbered.

"This is exactly what happened. The Lord God sent the angel Moroni to reveal the book to young Joseph and assist him in bringing it forth. By the power of God, it was translated through the Urim and Thummim. It was of course the record of those who slumbered in death.

"They were sealed in two ways. First they were in a language unknown to Joseph which could only be translated with the interpreters, and second, a part of the record which the Jaredites had that contained a record of God's dealings with men back to the time of Adam was sealed by a gold band around it. and Joseph was not permitted to read it."

Paul continued:

Vs 15, The book shall be sealed by the power of God, and the revelation which was sealed shall be kept in the book until the own due time of the Lord, that they may come forth; for behold; they reveal all things from the foundation of the world unto the end thereof.

"I would certainly like to read that book," Jan interrupted.

"We are looking forward to when the Lord will allow it to be read. When that time comes, and I expect it will be soon, the whole world will know it." Paul answered. "Listen to the next words:"

> Vs 16: And the day cometh, that the words of the book which were sealed shall be read upon the housetops; and they shall be read by the power of Christ; and all things shall be revealed unto the children of men which ever have been among the children of men, and which ever will be, even unto the end of the earth.

"Before Paul reads the next lines, let me tell you some history of what took place when the gold plates of the record was brought forth. The record was shown to Joseph by Moroni, and he was instructed to retrieve it from the ground but to guard it and allow no one to see it. Later the Angel Moroni allowed three men to see the records and to handle them. A short time after this Joseph was allowed to show them to eight other people. All of them became witnesses to the book.

"Isaiah lived about twenty five hundred years before, this event, but listen to what he tells us."

> Vs 17- At that day when the book shall be delivered unto the man of whom I have spoken, the book shall be hid from the eyes of the world, that the eyes of none shall behold it, save it be that three witnesses shall behold it by the power of God, besides him to whom the book shall be delivered; and they

shall testify to the truth of the book and the things therein. And there is none other which shall view it, save it be a few according to the will of God, to bear testimony of his word unto the children of men; for the Lord God hath said, that the words of the faithful should speak as it were from the dead. Wherefore, the Lord God will proceed to bring forth the words of the book; and in the mouth of as many witnesses as seemeth him good will he establish his word; and woe be unto him that rejecteth the word of God.

"You know," Art said "Isaiah must have seen that happening in a vision or something. There is no way he could have been more precise in his prophecy than that."

"Yes, but there is more," Paul stated. "Listen."

Vs 20-22 Behold it shall come to pass the Lord God shall say unto him to whom he shall deliver the book, Take these words which are not sealed and deliver them to another that he may show them unto the learned saying, read this, I pray thee. And the learned shall say, bring hither the book and I will read them; and now because of the glory of the world, and to get gain will they say this, and not for the glory of God. And the man shall say I cannot bring the book for it is sealed. Then shall the learned say I cannot read it.

"This prophesy was fulfilled literally," Ted said. "Joseph Smith made a copy of some of the characters from the gold plates. He gave them to a man named Martin Harris who took them to New York City to a professor of languages at the university. The Professor asked to have the book they came from, but Martin Harris told him he could not bring them because the book was sealed. The professor told him 'I cannot read a sealed book'."

Vs 23-24 Touch not the things which are sealed, for I will
bring them forth in mine own due time; for I will show unto
the children of men that I am able to do mine own work.
Wherefore when thou hast read the words which I have
commanded thee...Then shalt thou seal up the book again,
and hide it up unto men, that I may preserve the words which
thou hast not read until I shall see fit in mine own wisdom to
reveal all things unto the children of men.

"Joseph did just that. He completed the work of translating the Book of Mormon, then Moroni called for the plates and they were turned back to him to keep until the time for the sealed part to be opened." Ted said

"There is much more in this chapter relating to this because the entire chapter is dedicated to this great event. In chapter 11:12 Isaiah called the presentation to the world of this book an ensign which the Lord would set up for the nations as a signal for the beginning of the latter day events which will culminate with the end of the world. The rest of the chapter has been fulfilled just as literally as the part we have discussed," Paul stated. "For example, there was a time set by God when this book has to have been brought forth. Look at verse 29.

Behold saith the Lord of hosts, I will show unto the children
of men, that it is not yet a very little while, (following the
coming of the book from the ground) and Lebanon shall be
turned into a fruitful field; and the fruitful field shall be
esteemed as a forest..."

"Well, today Lebanon has been turned into a fruitful field. It is a forest of fruit trees. So it is too late for any other book to come forth in fulfillment of these prophecies."

"You certainly have a thorough knowledge of these things." Don told them, then asked, "Is there more?"

385

"Yes, there is much more," Paul said, "but we will only read one more passage to you tonight. Ted will read from the thirty-seventh chapter of Ezekiel."

## EZEKIEL CHAPTER THIRTY SEVEN

"This chapter has to do with the seemingly impossible return of all of Israel to their promised land. Of course what seems impossible to man is accomplished by God. We will only use verse 15, however. It is easily understood if you know that the sticks spoken of are books, or scrolls. scrolls were rolled on sticks, so they were often called sticks in the slang of that day."
Art begins reading at Vs 15:

> The word of the Lord came again unto me saying, Moreover, thou son of man, take thee one stick, and write upon it , For Judah and for the children of Israel his companions; (This would be the Bible because it was written by those of Judah at Jerusalem.) then take another stick and write upon it, for Joseph, the stick of Ephraim. (The descendants of Joseph were those who came to the Americas and kept the record which is now the Book of Mormon) and for all the house of Israel his companions; and join them one to another into one stick; and they shall be one in thine hand.

"It is very obvious these two books were meant to be used together and support each other," Paul said. "The book itself proclaims its purpose. It says that it is to be another witness that Jesus is the Christ. It was 'to shew unto the remnant of the house of Israel (The Lamanites which are the American Indians) what great things the Lord hath done for their fathers; that they may know the covenants of the Lord, that they are not cast off forever; and also to the convincing of the Jew and Gentile that Jesus is the Christ, the Eternal God, manifesting himself unto all nations.'"

Ted continued, "The Lord added his words to this. He said:

> Know ye not that the testimony of two nations is a witness
> unto you that I am God! that I remember one nation like unto
> another? Wherefore I speak the same words unto one nation
> like unto another. And when the two nations shall run
> together, the testimony of the two nations shall run together
> also (II Nephi 12:59-61 )

"The world's people have become close enough together that these two records have run together, but we need to remember that the record of the Nephites was written for the Nephites. God, who is just, would not bring a large nation of his people to this side of the world and leave them in darkness. He sent his word with them, he inspired leaders to write, and he sent prophets among them to assure that nation of the same message that he had given to those in their native land. Finally he sent his crucified son to his 'other sheep'."

"The many legends of the people we visited this summer bear out the facts of the stories that have come to us through the Book of Mormon," Paul said.

"What legends?" Jan was eager to hear.

## INDIAN LEGENDS LIKE BIBLICAL STORIES

"The greatest of them is the legend of a bearded white God who came and taught them, then left promising to return some day. This is interesting, because the Indians are neither white or bearded, but nearly every tribe, even in very widely dispersed areas seems to have a legend about him, although he is called different names by different tribes," Paul answered.

Paul reached into his pack and withdrew a notebook. Here is a list of some of the names he has been given by different tribes:

To the AZTECS he is———————QUETZALCOATL
"     MAYAS       "      KULKULCAN
"     INCAS        "      WIRACOCHA

The legends say of him:
> The creator God
> God of Peace
> Born of a virgin
> Crucified on a cross
> Descended on a cloud
> Promised to return

"In fact," Ted interrupted, "this belief was so prevalent that when Cortez arrived to conquer them he had no opposition because they bowed down to him believing he was the white-bearded god who had promised to return.

"They believed God his father had begotten him, not by connection with a woman, but God had sent his ambassador to the virgin of Tula and breathed his life into his son. They also believe The Father created the world, and later sent his son to reform it."

"That's right," Paul continued "they believed a new star appeared at Quetzalcoatl's birth. And they have other legends that sound like they came right out of the Bible."

"For instance," Ted said, as he took the notebook from Paul and turned the page. "There was a book written about them by Lord Kingsborough called *THE ANTIQUITIES OF MEXICO*. In Vol. 6, page 409, he says: '...They in ancient times had been in possession of a book which was handed down successively from father to son, in the person of the eldest who was dedicated to the safe custody of it and to instruct others in its doctrines'. On the same page Kingsborough continues: 'It is so singular a fact that the Indians of Mexico and Peru should have believed with Christians in many doctrines which are held to be peculiarly and exclusively Christian and to constitute a line of demarcation between Christianity and all other religions, that it appears a convincing proof that Christianity must have, in early ages, been established in America'.

"There are also legends apparently about the Jaredites whose leader they call Votan. According to Bancroft in the book *NATIVE RACES* Vol. pages 27-28, he says: 'Votan...is said to have been a descendant of Noah and to have assisted at the building of the Tower of Babel. After the confusion of tongues he led a portion of the dispersed people to America.' This is an interesting note we found in *MYTHS OF MEXICO AND PERU*, page 305, by Lewis Spence: '...by means of his word (Nisca) the creator, a spirit powerful and opulent, made all things. We are provided with the formula of his words by the Peruvian prayer still extant: 'Let Earth and Heaven be,' 'Let Man be,' 'Let woman be,' 'Let there be day,' 'Let there be night,' 'Let the light shine'."

"It is no wonder that Isaiah said the book that came out of the ground would speak with a familiar spirit." Jan observed. "Those legends sound like they came from the Bible."

"They were led by the same God," John commented.

Ted continued turning pages in the notebook, "We found what seems to be references to the family of Lehi. Brinton wrote in *MYTHS OF THE NEW WORLD*, page 101, 'Hardly a nation on the continent but seems to have had some vague tradition of an origin from four brothers; to have at some time been led by four brothers, or princes'.

"In Baldwin's *ANCIENT AMERICA*, page 264, we found this information," Ted continued, "'He (Montsinor) gives the Peruvian nation a beginning which is, at least, not incredible. It originated, he says, by a people led by four brothers, who settled in the valley of Cusco, and developed civilization there in a very human way. The youngest of these brothers assumed supreme authority and became the first of a long line of sovereigns."

"We even discovered many similarities between some of the Indian dialects and the Hebrew language," Paul added. "Here are a few from the Chiapenecs just for an example."

| English word | Chiapenecs word | Hebrew word |
|---|---|---|
| son | Been | Ben |
| Daughter | Batz | Bath |
| Father | Abagh | Abba |
| King | Molo | Maloc |
| Adam | Abagh | Abah |
| God | Elab | Elab |
| To Give | Votan | Votan |

"This is amazing," Bob declared. "There seems no question whatever that these people had Jewish roots."

"And that would mean that the American Indians and those aboriginal people of Mexico, Peru, and other countries down there are Israelites," Don exclaimed.

"Descendants of Joseph through the lineage of Mannasseh," Paul responded. "But more important is the fact that this is the testimony by another nation that Jesus is the Christ, the son of God, and those things promised to come to pass can faithfully be depended upon."

"I'm surely anxious for that library of records that Mormon hid to be found." Jan said.

"Yes, and I can hardly wait for those sealed plates with the history which goes back to the foundation of the earth, and prophecies to the end of time, to be opened," Fran added.

# DOCTRINE AND COVENANTS

"You have really opened my eyes about the Book of Mormon. I had heard a lot about it but I actually did not know what it was. I had no idea there was so much information to support it." Bob said.

Art had been reflecting on past studies and asked a question which had bothered him. "Now that we have resolved the question about that book, what exactly is this book of *DOCTRINE AND COVENANTS* which we have quoted so freely?"

"This is a good time to cover that question also," John responded. "God had called Joseph Smith to a special work just as he had called Abraham, Moses and others. He sent angels to instruct him, and he gave him temporary use of the Urim and Thummim and he called Joseph to the woods where he was given a vision of the Father and the son.

"The coming of the Book of Mormon was the ensign which was to signal the beginning of the restoration work. Isaiah, Daniel, John the revelator, Nephi, other prophets, and finally Jesus, all told of the restoration gospel. This came about quietly; however, it was a major event in God's plan. In all major events, God has called for some man whom he has worked through, like Abraham, Moses, Daniel, Joseph, John the Baptist, David, and others. In nearly every case he chose very young men. This time he chose a fourteen-year-old boy named Joseph Smith. He worked with him for several years to prepare him for the work of bringing the Book of Mormon to the world and bearing the persecution which God knew would accompany the task."

## THE TIME FOR THE RESTORATION

"The time for this restoration had come and God was again speaking to the world through Joseph, who by now was his prophet. The book of *DOCTRINE AND COVENANTS* is a book of many of those revelations given through the young prophet. They are directed at giving new light concerning the will and purposes of God. They also speak out to restore truths which had been changed through the years, and they led in directing the way of the restoration. Finally, the book presents a new testimony of the divinity of Jesus Christ as the son of God.

"Those who have followed God's work from Adam, through the apostasy of the Dark Ages can readily identify the work through Joseph and the restoration as a major turning point in the historical affairs of men. Beginning with the restoration in the early 1800s, the world has changed more dramatically, and more rapidly than at any previous time. Many of the things God told us through this young man have been dramatically fulfilled, and others are in the process."

"That sounds to me like that could be a whole new study in itself," Bob said.

"You are right," Lilli stated, "That is the beginning of a new book built upon the restoration and the Book of Mormon scriptures supporting Biblical scriptures, *DOCTRINE AND COVENANTS*, and the inspired version of the Holy scriptures."

"Wait a minute," Fran said, "What is the Inspired Version?"

# THE INSPIRED VERSION

"The Inspired Version is a rendering of the Bible which has had many of the omissions replaced and distortions erased, so the original message and meanings have been restored," John explained.

"I don't understand," Bob said. "You said Joseph Smith was a young uneducated country boy. How could he have restored the Bible like that?"

"That is just the point," John continued. "Joseph Smith could never have done it. But remember, he still had the Urim and Thummim when he began this work, and by then he had become a major prophet, so God did it through him. That is very evident just in reading Genesis."

Paul had picked up his backpack and he and Ted were moving toward the sidewalk. "It is getting late for all of us and we are going to have to go. It has been a pleasure being with you."

"Oh no," Jan said. "We hoped you would be with us for a few days anyway. You are welcome to stay with us."

Ted and Paul exchanged smiles and Paul spoke, "The business we came here to take care of seems to be completed and we have urgent work calling us elsewhere. It has been a definite pleasure being with you." They moved around the corner of the building

Art called to Don who was standing nearest to the sidewalk, "Catch them and tell them I can drop them off at their motel, or the airport, or wherever they wish."

Don hurried around the house after Ted and Paul.

"They certainly appear and disappear abruptly, don't they?" Sandy commented.

"I wish they could stay, they have shared so much with us," Fran agreed.

Don returned, "I couldn't find them. I don't know where they disappeared to so fast. They were just gone."

"I wonder who they really are," Jan said with a thoughtful look in her eyes.

John and Lilli exchanged smiles. Lilli commented, "Yes, I wonder."

# APPENDIX A

# A LETTER TO A CHURCH SCHOOL TEACHER
## by John Henderson

Dear Sister Sue,

Your letter indicated to me that you feel obligated to teach a class in church school since there is no one else to take the job. You also seem to have a degree of resentment which I surmise would make the job drudgery. Your statement that you are frustrated in helping the students to learn their lessons says to me that you are a dedicated person trying to serve your branch—in a totally miserable situation for you. If these are your true feelings, it is doubtful that you are accomplishing much of real value. It is also evident you are cheating yourself of one of the greater pleasures and satisfactions of accomplishment.

I believe you can easily change the entire unhappy situation if you will examine your attitude and make a few "repairs" on it. Wouldn't it be nice to be looking forward all week to your class on Sunday, impatient to get to it because you have so much to share with your students? A little serious thought should bring about this transformation.

Consider your teaching a ministry which you are fortunate to have the privilege to give. Forget about trying to teach a chapter from a book, don't worry about trying to cover certain prescribed instructions or doctrine. Don't attempt to pour a chapter-a-week into the minds of disinterested kids. Put away the thought that you were "appointed" or "obligated" to teach a class. For the moment stand outside yourself and look back. See your situation as it really is.

In the realistic view you see yourself before God who, speaking to you by name, says, "Sue, my child, I have given to you certain special talents, and your understanding has been opened so you can see a degree of the eternal kingdom. I have chosen you for a special task which is important to me."

Then turning you around, he rests one hand on your shoulder and points with the other. "See the little children I created," God says, "I love each one and have a special place reserved in my kingdom for each. But, look...see how many have lost the way. They don't know of my kingdom and have nothing of value to build a life on. Their lives will be miserable without a worthwhile objective.

"See those who have fallen into Satan's grasp and the agony they suffer; some are on drugs, some sick because of sin, some bound for a life in prison, others living in doubt and fear. Throughout their lives they will seldom know real freedom and happiness.

"It tears my heart to see their inability to come to the place prepared for them. I cannot go out and bring them in, because I cannot take away their agency. I sent my Son to break Satan's bonds and open the door for them, but now, someone must point the way so they will come. Someone must give them the desire to find me. I have chosen you to take the light to them. Go out and call my children. Give them love. Teach them that I created them and loved each one from the beginning and want them to come to me.

"During your life if you can love just one and bring that one to me, your cup of joy will overflow. If you can reach two and save them from Satan, your joy will be beyond comprehension. If you reach ten, your happiness will be ten times ten. Go to them now. I will work with you and inspire your efforts. You will be loved by me and my children.

"So you see, Sue, as a teacher, when you serve God's children as a vessel of his love and bring his own back to him, the satisfaction you receive is such that words cannot explain. You must have the experience to understand it. When you become concerned for God's own, who are lost, and give them direction your church school classes will be a delight instead of drudgery. Your concerns for God's little ones will help you to find the means to illuminate the road to eternal life for them. From one Sunday to the next you will find yourself analyzing each student's problems and needs. You ask yourself, "How can I best teach Mary to have faith in prayer? What is in Johnny's way of being able to accept others? Why is Janice so unhappy? How can I illustrate to Tommy how much God loves him?"

You will be using bits and parts of our natural world as examples. You will use old curriculum, history, newspaper articles, automotive books, and a host of other sources to get the message through to each child. You will no longer be concerned with "trying to teach a Sunday school lesson to a kid"; you will be molding a life.

Because the time in class is so short, your concerns for those lives entrusted to you will cause you to reach for additional ways of drawing the children to you and to God. Even years after they have gone from your class your concern will follow. Your work won't be measured in chapters covered but in the beautiful characters you have helped to shape. Your prayer will change from, "Why should I teach them?" to "Lord help me reach them."

Don't waste one moment on resentment and self-pity. If your own child were lost in a jungle full of dangers you could not be restrained from going out to save that child. God's children are wandering in a dangerous jungle, and he is sending you. How great shall be your happiness as you come out of that jungle with one of his children in your arms.

Best wishes for a happy, fruitful life in teaching.

John

# APPENDIX B.

# A TESTIMONY OF ETERNAL LIFE BY JUDITH HAWLEY
### Reprinted with permission of the author

When my husband, Max, died, I was given an experience that showed me that life on this earth is not the end of living, but only a part of our eternal lives.

Max had been bedfast for seven years and had spent the last five years in a nursing home. Diabetes had claimed his eyesight and one of his legs. For the last few months of his life, Max lost his ability to speak due to the hardening of the arteries in his brain. He was forty-three years old when his earthly body was laid to rest.

We had always prayed that Max and I might share his death alone. Knowing of its coming long before it occurred, we planned that it might be a peaceful time. We were blessed in our desire. We were alone in his hospital room when his body functions ceased to do their work. As they did, I saw his spirit leave his body through the top of his head.

The nurse immediately came in and asked me to leave so they could make the body more presentable. I felt something pulling me back to that room, so I did not go away from the door.

When they allowed me to return, I found the room filled with the most peaceful, soothing, golden light. I did not even look at Max's body, for he was standing in spirit in the middle of the room. I went to a chair and sat down. I had waited for so long to ask him a very important question and now I could ask it. He had been blind before our marriage and had never seen me. I asked him quite hesitantly if he was disappointed in me, for this was the first time he had ever seen me.

He did not talk to me in words, but through thought transference. He conveyed to me that he was not disappointed. We talked on for at least half an hour—he in thoughts and I often finding myself not speaking, but conveying words through thoughts, also. He was so at peace.

He was dressed in a white gown like I had seen angels wear. He had a perfect body and the most beautiful sky-blue seeing eyes I have ever seen. Then I noticed two angels in the room. I had seen his guardian angels in a vision, so I was not startled by these beings.

Then Max did something I had missed for all those years of his confinement. He came around the bed, put his arms around me and gave me a big strong hug. He then turned and with the two angels went out through the wall which seemed to open for them. He looked back once and then turned, looked ahead and walked out of my life.

At that moment, just as he passed out of my view, the Holy Comforter descended upon me in such abundance. He wrapped me in a warm mantle of love. I did not mourn. This comforting spirit was with me for three weeks. I did not cry, nor feel any sadness. I felt completely loved and comforted.

But the amazing thing I want to share with you is that when Max's spirit left his body, there was no point at which there was any pause from life to death to life. He simply never stopped living. He went from life to life in one continuous movement. Thus eternal life is eternal with no pausing or ending. Max died physically, but he did not stop living.

Praise Jesus Christ for eternal life.

*...and if you keep my commandments and endure to the end, you shall have eternal life; which is the greatest of all the gifts of God.* D.C.12:3b

# APPENDIX C

## FOR GOD'S SAKE DON'T TITHE
### by John Henderson

Our old pastor Arnold was at it again, "...you must obey the financial law..." A flick of my elbow jabbed my wife, and I whispered, "They oughta' repeal that law." Her tight lips and icy stare said "Shut up," so I sank a little deeper in the pew and studied the light patterns on the ceiling while the old fellow's message of financial doom sailed over my head. However I did catch a few of Malachi's words, "...you have robbed me..." and I almost laughed aloud as I envisioned members of the congregation astraddle cloudy steeds-bandannas covering their faces-breezing though the sky to surround God's gold-laden stage-coach. I was just beginning to fill in the details...like Sister Joy adjusting her bandanna for the most coquettish effect and old Sister Alice holding a pistol by two trembling fingers...when Malachi again broke through my daydream: "How have you robbed me? By tithes and offerings..." I thought, That's not robbery, that's embezzlement. By the time I had conjured a picture of staid Brother Joe altering the books and creaming the profits to sneak a few extra bucks into his pocket, the pastor had covered all the commandments, threats, pleadings, and laws from Genesis to Moroni, and I looked at the clock. I was getting hungry but I was sure there had to be one more step-as sure as I was that he would talk ten minutes overtime. Right on schedule Arnold pulled out the church statistics which proved we had dropped down another notch from eighty-ninth place for the quarter. "We could come up considerably if some of the other 99 percent of the congregation would just file a statement...even if they didn't pay much," he closed.

I pumped his hand at the door saying, "Fine sermon, you really had the facts, good advice," and went on out thinking, At least it won't give me indigestion because I didn't swallow much of it.

A few weeks later on my Sunday-to-go-to-church-with-the-wife I tried to find enough work on the car to keep me home, but Lilli was insistent, so I went. There was a guest speaker that day—a really important one. He was a general church appointee and a bishop besides. When he read the scripture, which is the custom after the offering, I thought we were in for it again because it was the same scripture old Arnold always used to launch his financial law lectures. But this fellow was a different sort—real smooth. In fact, he didn't make a single threat. He didn't even tell us what our rating in the church was. He just started telling us stories like the one about Jim and Mary back in his hometown. Jim was sick and out of work. Mary was expecting their fourth baby and didn't have any money for the hospital. Despite their problems they got to thinking about the tithes they had never paid, so they sold their only car and sent the money in to the church to pay up. It sounded stupid to me, but the Bishop said that today Jim is in good health and has his own business which employs twenty-three people. He gives money to the church by the bucketful, but he earns just that much more. Mary's sixth was born at the hospital where she had one of the nicest rooms.

After three or four stories like that I got to thinking that if this bishop was telling the truth-and he did seem honest-I wouldn't have to be much of a businessman to see what a good investment this could be. I wouldn't mind giving the church a few bucks if I would wind up like Jim. Maybe I should check into it. So after lunch I tried to nonchalantly slip Lilli's books from her bedside table to my office. She caught me, though, and asked what in the world I was doing with them. Not about to tell her what I had in mind, I said, "I just want to check on a couple of things that guy said this morning," and went on.

Well, I started checking and pretty soon I thought I had it all figured out. It seemed that in at least one way we have God over a barrel—and that's in tithing. Apparently it's important to him for us to make this contribution to him. There were scriptures such as Malachi 3:8-10 in which he seemed very upset if not outright indignant because people were not tithing: "Will a man rob God? Yet ye have robbed me. But ye say wherein have we robbed thee? In tithes and offerings...Bring ye all the tithes into the storehouse..." In other scriptures we are commanded to tithe continually: "Thou shalt surely tithe all the increase of thy seed, that the field bringeth forth year by year:" (Dueteronomy 14:22) and "...after that, those who have thus been tithed, shall pay one tenth of all their interest annually; and this shall be a standing law unto them forever." (DOCTRINE AND COVENANTS 106)

I knew, as anyone who has been in a leadership position knows, that a command is a command when it is obeyed, but it is merely a plea when followers refuse to obey. So I assumed God was pleading with us to give to him. If this was true I could exercise a degree of power over God by keeping him in a begging position. Now I had leverage to bargain with him: "You give me a blessing and I'll pay you some tithes." Maybe this is how Jim got his business.

In a day when we face an unjust income tax over which we have no control, it is almost a pleasure to equate tithing with income tax and refuse to pay it. I know a lot of people who have never paid tithes and apparently get away with it, so why should I?

There was one disquieting factor however, in light of God's power to provide for himself, "Why should he need my money?" When the rich young ruler came to Jesus to ask the way of eternal life (Matthew 19) Jesus certainly could have requested a tithe or at least a good fee; instead he told the young man to give it all to the poor. He surely didn't covet the young man's wealth; in fact, he didn't seem at all interested in it. He just wanted him to get rid of all that money, yet here he was asking for a tithe. Another example that bothered me was the time in Capernaum (Matthew 17:23-26) when Jesus was challenged about the payment of tribute. He didn't agree to pay, nor did he disagree. He simply told Peter to go to the sea and catch a fish. In the mouth of the first fish would be enough money to pay the tribute for both of them. With this kind of power he could have a lot of money, so I didn't see any reason why he would need mine. When he fed the five thousand he clearly demonstrated he didn't need the money to buy food. Finally, God flatly stated that if he ever did need anything he wouldn't ask man for it. (Psalm 59:9-12)

This bothered me because if God didn't need anything and had no use for my money and wouldn't take any help from me, how could I bargain with him? I had lost all of my leverage and was right back where I had started except that now I seriously wanted to find out how it worked. To me it all seemed to pivot around one point: obviously God neither needed nor wanted my money, so if he doesn't need it, why does he insist I pay it?

While I was searching I discovered something in passing which interested me. It was a comment about the keys to the mysteries of the kingdom of heaven. I thought, "I'd sure like to get my hands on those; I'd open things up and have a look." However, I was now ready to mark tithing off as something else in religion that did not seem to make sense. I let the pages of the Bible slip through my fingers as a way of saying, "I give up." They stopped at a place just under the leather cover at a conversation between God and Moses. It was quite a story, and near the end of it God said, "My work and my glory is to bring to pass the immortality and eternal life of man." I read it again and thought, "Well, that's the most important thing I've read all day."

What God is saying is that everything he has done and is doing is for our sakes. Then I thought, it must be that everything he commands us to do is also for our benefit. Apparently he gives us commandments as direction for what we have to do to have a better life. If this is true I don't need leverage to bargain with him; I need to learn to cooperate with him in bringing to pass my own immortality and eternal life. It was becoming obvious that God had been on my side all the time, so my struggles were self-defeating. Then I thought that maybe I could use this idea like a key to figure out the tithing business. I considered some of the promises which I had been studying in which God seemed to be saying, "If you will do this, I will thus." I went back to the scriptures and reread them, keeping in mind that the commands and directions were always given to benefit man. The key worked. I didn't have to bargain with God. He was telling me how to get anything I wanted which was good for me.

I was getting excited and decided: "God is a contractor. Let's look at the contract. This kind of business is a little more in my line." I began to hunt up the promises God had put into this contract he offered us. I found in Genesis (9:22-23) the Everlasting Covenant: "When thy posterity shall embrace the truth, and look upward, then shall Zion look downward...and the general assembly of the church of the first-born shall come down out of heaven, and shall possess the earth." This amazed me because I had always understood that the church people were going to have to go to Independence, Missouri, and build the city of Zion, and it was going to take a lot more work than just embracing the truth and looking up to God for the rest. Then going back to

Malachi 3:10 I found this promise: "Bring ye all the tithes into the storehouse, that there may be meat in mine house, and prove me now herewith , saith the Lord of hosts, if I will not open you the windows of heaven, and pour you out a blessing, that there shall not be room enough to receive it." That is a contract if I ever read one! The party of the first part, God, requests certain action of the party of the second part, Man. If the party of the second part responds as requested, then the party of the first part will pay with a great blessing. I could put a date on it and take a contract like that to court. When God says "Prove me now herewith" it is dated.

These seemed like pretty important promises to put into a contract—especially for God who doesn't have to contract at all. Of course a contract has two sides, so I started looking for the fine print to find out what I had to do. On my scout's honor, I found that it boiled down to this: I had only to follow his directions and prove myself worthy of his trust. The first part didn't seem too difficult, because when I studied his directions I found they were all things for my own good anyway. I had to be in favor of anything that would make life more tolerable here now and offer such fantastic fringe benefits at the retirement end. The second part—that of proving myself worthy and dedicated, was another matter. I thought of making an oath of reliability, but that seemed pretty weak; besides I had done that once when I was baptized and hadn't lived up to it very well. Sacrificing burnt offerings was out; that had been done away with long ago. I considered something like a Father's Day present for God, but I couldn't think of anything I could give that wasn't already his by right of creation.

I certainly was in a quandry, and after worrying about it a few weeks I went back to the scriptures to study the fine print to see if I could find a loophole. There wasn't any, but I did find one item which at first seemed to be the answer. In Genesis 7:40 I found that God had given to me one thing for my own: "...and in the Garden of Eden I gave unto man his agency; and unto thy brethren have I said, and also gave commandment, that they should love one another; and that they should choose me their Father." This gift—agency—is my will to do as I choose. "Okay, God," I said, "I give back to you my will. I'm all yours again." That wasn't too hard to say; in fact, because it was so easy I knew I had to have some sort of tangible proof. How could I possibly show I was serious? How could I ever demonstrate that there were no other gods in my life? I finally concluded I could prove it only by going back to the first half of my part in the contract and being obedient, living life as God directed. In studying how I could begin living as God directed, I found that the directions to tithe popped up again. This time, though, I grasped them thinking how wonderful that here at last was a way I could prove I was serious about this business of a contract with God. Now I could show that God was more important to me than material things.

The desire to pay my tithes became the most imperative thing in my life, but how was I ever going to tell Lilli I wanted to take money from our bank account to settle an account with God? Finally, after several sleepless nights, I faced her directly and said, "Sweetheart, I want to have our pastor come over and help figure out what we owe in tithing...and I want to pay it." I'm sure I'll never understand a woman's thinking. At first she seemed in shock, then she began to hug and kiss me and cry all over my shoulder. Then she ran off for a towel mumbling something about, "I've been praying and praying..."

It made me choke a little when I made out the check. I had a good job, and we had bought a lot of nice things and even saved some money. I was proud of the position I had in the company. There were plenty of guys beneath me who were just itching to get a crack at my job, but I had always kept their respect because we had a nice home and I drove a big car and did other things I knew they couldn't afford to do. It hurt when I had to account for all of this, of course, but when our check was in the mail and on its way we were two happy people. It seemed we were released from an oppressive prison we hadn't even known we'd been in. Now we were in the fresh air and daylight. I had never experienced such an elated feeling. I was a worker with God; I was right with him for the first time in my life and involved in his work as an active partner. I remember frivolously thinking "Okay, God, I'm living up to my part of the contract. What are you going to do?"

It didn't take long to find out. The next morning my boss called me into his office. "John," he said. "Our company has been forced into a very strict economic posture, and we have had to reevaluate our expenditure position. We must take steps to assure our financial stability. In doing so we have been forced to conclude we can no longer afford an executive of your caliber. I am sure a man like you will have no problem finding a position with another company." I was stunned. This simply could not be happening. I was much too important to the business. I had helped make it what it was. Why, just last week I was being praised for the slick way I put a deal over on a subcontractor we hired.

I started formulating my response very carefully. When I finished with this ex-boss he was going to know he had met a tiger. After I finished telling him off his secretary would have to pour a drink down him and help him to his car. I guess he knew what was coming because he suddenly got very busy with the telephone. Then, just as I was ready to cut loose, a silly question popped into my head. "This' is a blessing?" Now I was mad at God too; he was cheating on our contract! But in a split second I had repeated the phrase with new emphasis: "This is a blessing!" With this thought all my anger seemed to go away. With a big smile I said, "Thank you Mr. Elsor. Thank you very much." As I left his office chuckling about how quickly and unexpectedly God had responded, I noticed that Mr. Elsor lowered the telephone very slowly into his coffee cup, spilling the contents all over his desk.

I never would have dreamed I could derive so much pleasure from getting fired and cleaning out my desk. I kept catching myself humming "The Old Old Path" and "How Great Thou Art."

The next few weeks were exciting ones. Lilli and I discussed the events enthusiastically. We knew that if God was concerned enough to move me out of the wrong spot so dramatically he could easily open the right door, and it was an adventure trying to determine what the next opening might be. We looked forward to each day as *the day* in which God's plan would be unfolded for us. Whenever the telephone rang an expectant look passed between us. Each trip to the post office box had a new meaning; perhaps it would come by mail.

I was always alert for just the right position and almost immediately thought I had been led into it since the new opportunity came by seemingly miraculous means. It promised better working conditions, better hours, and a far higher salary that my previous job. We thanked God for opening the windows of heaven and pouring out this blessing. My new salary was such that we spent freely from our savings, even though I had not received my first paycheck. In two months our savings were depleted and I demanded my salary, but my boss said, "Sorry John, our creditors have not paid us. We are insolvent. The bank is foreclosing our machinery loans and we are filing bankruptcy." So there wasn't any check. I can't explain how I felt. I was certain God had put me into this position, so I wasn't mad or worried. I didn't even bother to attempt to bring suit. Lilli agreed God was directing this for our good, and somehow it had to be a blessing despite our lack of understanding.

When the big house was sold and most of the money went to the mortgage, we weren't as upset as we would have been a year earlier; it just was not that important anymore. As other possessions which we had once prized were disposed of one by one it actually seemed as if our burdens were being lightened. Lilli summed it up one day: "I seem to be repenting today of what I aspired to last year."

We were concerned though, when friends offered sympathy. They thought we were extremely brave, and they were unable to understand when we said we were not at all worried because we knew that in his wisdom God was blessing us. Our own failure to understand how this was a blessing was offset by the assurance that we were in God's care and only good would come to us. We did not feel brave because we felt no need for bravery; rather we felt as if we were on a wonderful adventure to areas unknown to us but we were confident we had a Leader who knew the way. We simply could not bring ourselves to worry. I was even amazed at myself in the way I was so unconcerned when we were buying groceries on our credit card and our bills were a month overdue. We simply turned that over to God to take care of: after all, we had a contract.

The most difficult part of the experience was the day I finally had to go to our bank to ask for a sixty-day extension on our loans. I had freely asked for loans in the past just by pointing to my position and salary. The money was easily obtained, and I was proud to be considered a preferred client. Now I was mortified to have to sit in the same chair I was previously proud to be seen in. I knew of no way I could make the loan officer understand that somehow God had placed me in this position, and although I was out of a job with no plan for obtaining a position I was satisfied that God would take care of this temporary problem with finances. I just asked for the extension and made a weak promise to have things worked out. When the loan officer imposed the highest interest rate I had ever accepted, I knew I had fallen from the preferred client status.

Day after day of the extension went by. Lilli and I carefully examined every letter we received. Each phone call continued to be answered with expectation. I continued to search for employment, but employers who had previously tried to recruit me turned me down for reasons so unbelievably silly that I was prompted to misquote Romans 8:31-"If God be against us, who can be for us?" Finally the due date on extension came, and Lilli asked, "What are your plans?"

"I think I can get away with letting this slide for ten days if I avoid the bank, but then if the way has not opened up I'll have to do some more talking."

Nine days passed and we still had no apparent response to our prayers. Somehow we managed to go to bed that night still confident that God was with us. As the sun rose on the tenth day, Lilli propped her head on her elbow and asked, "You know what day this is?"

"Yes."

"What do you think?"

"I think God must want us bankrupt."

"If you had known what was going to happen would you have paid the tithes?"

"If I had it to do over, I would do the same."

"How do you feel about the future?"

"I feel that if God wants us on welfare it will be a blessing to us."

"Honey, I love you."

On the way to the bank we went first to the post office as usual. There were a few ads, a couple of repeat bills, and a letter from a company I had worked for several years earlier. I tossed these onto the seat and drove the three blocks to the bank. When I parked, Lilli handed me the contents of the envelope from my long-past employer and without a word she took my handkerchief and wiped her eyes. In my hand I held a check. We didn't know if it was the result of an error of several years standing or a new one, but since it was in the amount we had to have at the moment, we felt the check must have been written by God! The most critical day of the next month brought a tax refund we had no idea we had coming. That kind of a check from the IRS had to be a miracle, especially since it was also the needed amount. So it went for nearly a year. I continued to seek employment, but every door on which I knocked remained solidly shut. During this period we were entirely dependent on God. We found ourselves helpless to provide for ourselves, yet we were never in actual need.

Lilli began to remember how much she had enjoyed serving people as a registered nurse and wanted to work again, but she had allowed her nursing license to lapse a number of years earlier and was required to complete a comprehensive refresher course before she could return to her profession. She registered at a school twenty-five miles from home not knowing where the money for books, tuition, transportation, and uniforms would come from. Within three days we received a letter from an organization we had never heard of. The letter explained that it was unusual policy to give assistance in this kind of case, but the officials had heard of her need and if she would come in they would provide whatever funds she would need for her retraining.

While Lilli's life was being directed to active service, I began to slowly see a pattern in what was happening to us, and in the picture that emerged, I saw myself in the image of the Rich Young Ruler. I considered my arrogance of position, my pride in what I had owned, my tainted ethics...and I was ashamed and humiliated by the image that came through. I saw that God was doing for me what the young man who went to Jesus did not have the strength to do for himself.

The past few months have been happy ones for us. We have drawn nearer to each other; after twenty-seven years we are honeymooners again. Lilli has resumed her nursing career and loves her work. She knows that each day in some way she serves God. I'm back at work in a position at least as good as the one I lost but with the promise of a better future. The direction of our entire lives has been completely realigned. We are no longer occupied with the status concerns which used to consume so much of our time and money. We have found there is far greater pleasure and lasting satisfaction in lives of service.

I have learned by experience what Alma meant (Alma 16:136) when he spoke of those who were blessed although they had to be compelled to become humble. God had to force us to see how utterly dependent we are on him and to reveal to us how unworthy our motivation had been. Once we could see ourselves as we really were from his viewpoint our shame was such that it tore away our pretenses and hypocrisy. Then God could begin rebuilding our lives on a clean new foundation of firm faith and honest humility.

Through this rebuilding we have been able to grasp a most precious element which had always escaped us—the ability to have sincere love and appreciation for other people. Old grudges and animosities have given way to concern and understanding and compassion. As bitterness was uprooted and discarded a warm inflow of tenderness and insights has multi-plied the joy of living and enriched our relationships with people. The world is more beautiful than ever before, and our sensitivity for people has so enlarged that the future seems a series of daily adventures with God to which we look forward. We know there is a presence with us with which we communicate freely. Most of all we are happy and we couldn't ask for more than that.

I don't know what will happen to you when you tithe, because the blessings are tailor-made to each individual's needs. I can only suggest that for God's sake don't tithe, but for your own sake don't miss the opportunity!

**************************************************************

Published in Saints Herald April 1974